Walking Mannequins

Walking Mannequins

HOW RACE AND GENDER INEQUALITIES
SHAPE RETAIL CLOTHING WORK

Joya Misra and Kyla Walters

UNIVERSITY OF CALIFORNIA PRESS

University of California Press
Oakland, California

© 2022 Joya Misra and Kyla Walters

Library of Congress Cataloging-in-Publication Data

Names: Misra, Joya, 1967– author. | Walters, Kyla, 1987– author.
Title: Walking mannequins : how race and gender inequalities shape
    retail clothing work / Joya Misra and Kyla Walters.
Description: Oakland, California : University of California Press,
    [2022] | Includes bibliographical references and index.
Identifiers: LCCN 2021033435 (print) | LCCN 2021033436 (ebook) |
    ISBN 9780520384644 (cloth) | ISBN 9780520384651 (paperback) |
    ISBN 9780520384668 (epub)
Subjects: LCSH: Retail trade—United States—Employees. | Retail
    trade—Social aspects—United States. | Equality.
Classification: LCC HD8039.M4 U65 2022 (print) |
    LCC HD8039.M4 (ebook) | DDC 331.7/38114—dc23
LC record available at https://lccn.loc.gov/2021033435
LC ebook record available at https://lccn.loc.gov/2021033436

Manufactured in the United States of America

31 30 29 28 27 26 25 24 23 22
10 9 8 7 6 5 4 3 2 1

For retail workers everywhere, and with gratitude
to the Movement for Black Lives

Contents

Acknowledgments

Many people supported this book's creation. While we cannot hope to thank everyone involved by name, we appreciate you all. The project started as an analysis of workers and customers visiting fancy new malls in Doha, Qatar, which were springing up like mushrooms amid a growing, global city that also had traditional and "new" *souks*. A sudden return home, due to health issues, and the loss of fieldnotes and transcribed interviews in transit, meant that the project came to a halt. Academics fear these moments of losing data and access, but they can be transformational.

One of the key insights from the work in Doha seemed surprisingly similar back in the United States. In Doha, employers literally advertised for workers based on their nationality, gender, and age. Yet in the United States, walking through the malls, it was soon apparent that although advertisements were open, the workers in stores were surprisingly uniform. Our partnership solidified when we co-taught a course on consumption and inequality. We owe a debt of gratitude to the students in that course, who provided us with thoughtful insights on their experiences shopping and working in malls, and who carried out shopper observations in a range of stores, which allowed us to identify where to focus our attention. Based on this work, we knew we wanted to look at stores aimed at teens and people in their early twenties that focus on promoting themselves as not just clothing stores but lifestyle brands.

Soon afterward we began collecting data in earnest. Our shopper observations allowed us to develop a more systematic understanding of how the work was organized, and more importantly, who was doing the work. The websites of the stores we targeted tended to emphasize their interest in building a diverse workforce, yet the workers all seemed white or racially ambiguous. This deepened our interest in thinking about how race is embedded in aesthetic labor, how it is both hypervisible and invisible in the organization of the work. While we were able to interview many workers and some frontline managers, corporate managers were unwilling to respond to requests for information and interviews.

Our colleagues were enormously supportive of this project. We had the good luck to be embedded in an area with many superb scholars of race, gender, and labor, both faculty and doctoral students, who were willing to give feedback on early drafts and listen to us talk endlessly about our research. Among the most helpful and patient were our Connecticut River Valley colleagues: Irene Boeckmann, Steven Boutcher, Enobong Hannah Branch, Michelle Budig, Debadatta Chakraborty, Dan Clawson, Mary Ann Clawson, Celeste Curington, Jennifer Curtin, Derek Doughty, Naomi Gerstel, Venus Green, Sanjiv Gupta, Clare Hammonds, Tom Juravich, Miliann Kang, Jasmine Kerrissey, Veda Kim, Agustin Lao-Montes, C. N. Le, Jennifer Lundquist, Ragini Saira Malhotra, Sancha Medwinter, Eunmi Mun, Yalçın Özkan, Anthony Paik, Z. Fareen Parvez, Cassaundra Rodriguez, Wenona Rymond-Richmond, Laurel Smith-Doerr, Marc Steinberg, Eiko Strader, Donald Tomaskovic-Devey, Eve Weinbaum, Nancy Whittier, Melissa Wooten, and Jon Wynn. A talk at the University of New Hampshire, made particularly fun and exciting by Cliff Brown, Rebecca Glauber, and Catherine Moran, involved another friendly, insightful set of interlocutors. We also appreciate the support of James Joseph Joseph Dean, Melinda Milligan, and Debora A. Paterniti.

We also had opportunities to give talks at conferences, most notably at Eastern Sociological Society and American Sociological Association meetings, as well as a 2016 preconference on precarious labor. At meetings, we often overlapped with and received incisive feedback from colleagues.

We wish to thank Augustus Anderson, Stefan Beljean, Paul Carruth, Yasemin Besen-Cassino, David Brady, Julia Beckhusen, Francisco "Chico" Raul Cornejo, Cedric de Leon, Marlese Durr, Giovanna Fullin, Kjerstin Gruys, Peter Ikeler, Patrick Inglis, Jerry Jacobs, Arne Kalleberg, Joseph Klett, Marcel Knudson, Linda Laughlin, Robin Leidner, Kevin Lin, Laurie Ann Michaels, Michele Lee Maroto, Jennifer Nelson, Eileen Otis, David Pettinicchio, Dana Prewitt, Robert J. S. Ross, Brian Serafini, Carrie Shandra, Chris Tilly, Steven Vallas, Kelcie Vercel, Phoenix Chi Wang, Christine Williams, and Zheng Zhao. From this group, Yasemin Besen-Cassino, Peter Ikeler, and Eileen Otis deserve special mention for their consistent engagement with our work. You made our work better.

The book itself was the true slog. Figuring out how to organize the enormous amount of data we had collected took more time and effort than we had imagined possible. Here, our friends truly supported us, allowing us to talk incessantly about the findings and how they fit together, including Michael Ash, Zeke and Rafi Ash, Enobong (Anna) Branch, Kristen Barber, Tristan Bridges, Matthew Charity, Dan Clawson, Celeste Curington, Derek Doughty, Krista Harper, Miliann Kang, Marina Karides, Ivy Ken, Jennifer Lundquist, Ragini Saira Malhotra, David Mednicoff, Juyeon Park, Deirdre Royster, Sudha Setty, Mohan and Mira Setty-Charity, Wendy Simonds, Laurel Smith-Doerr, Donald Tomaskovic-Devey, and Adia Harvey Wingfield. We are also deeply grateful to members of writing groups, including Amel Ahmed, Sonia Atalay, Debbie Felton, Ximena Gómez, Holly Hanson, Serin Houston, Beth Jakob, Miliann Kang, Amy Lonetree, Cathy Luna, Kristen Luschen, Melissa Mueller, Teresa Nguyen, Kimberlee Pérez, Lise Sanders, Caroline Yang, and Youngmin Yi. Many folks also read chapters or drafts of the manuscript, including Kristen Barber, Kjerstin Gruys, Miliann Kang, Eileen Otis, Adia Harvey Wingfield, and the anonymous reviewers from the University of California Press, who graciously commented on the entire manuscript and improved it enormously.

Special thanks to Naomi Schneider, Summer Farah, Julie Van Pelt, Jon Dertien, and the diligent folks at UC Press. We are enormously grateful to the excellent Letta Page and Sharon Langworthy, who played a key role in making the manuscript readable. Much gratitude to Zeke Ash and Shelby Casimir for their thorough reading of the entire manuscript to help us make the text one that undergraduate students could read—and would enjoy. Thanks also to the Labor Action and Research Network for supporting this project.

Our respective families and support networks who never left our side—David Mednicoff, Amina and Rabi Mednicoff-Misra, Therese Misra, Sima Misra, Maya Misra, Tara Misra, and their families, Derek Doughty, Adalai Jay Doughty, Glenn Doughty, Nikki Doughty, Jody Auletta, Niles Walters, Jim Walters, Kim Walters, Lana Ciociolo-Hinkell, Sherron Carson, and Angela Carter—we love and thank you. Amina and Rabi were particularly patient despite the excruciating experience of having their mother ask workers lots of questions whenever they were shopping in teen stores.

We recognize that this book would not be possible without our interview participants, who willingly expressed their excitement, anger, sadness, and disgust to us, allowing us to understand retail work from their perspective. While we use pseudonyms throughout the book and avoid any stories that might make them identifiable, we never stopped thinking about their stories and seeing their faces as we wrote. We are so grateful for your support for this project and hope we have done justice to all you shared.

PART I Introduction

Introduction

> If they could put you in the store as a mannequin, they
> would; I'm pretty sure they would.
>
> —Kathleen (Black, a boutique)

> They're very dressed like mannequins, so we're manne-
> quins, and we are very much aware of that.
>
> —Angela (white, Old Navy)

> [We'd] just be like walking mannequins.
>
> —Gabe (white, American Eagle)

> I'm like a walking mannequin.
>
> —Rachel (multiracial, American Eagle)

> If you're wearing something that looks like one of the man-
> nequins, then you're good.
>
> —Tia (Black, Forever 21)

At teen-oriented clothing stores like Abercrombie & Fitch and Forever 21, workers do more than fold jeans and work the cash register; their work parallels the mannequins on display. These workers need to have the right "look" to model the merchandise, and managers ask these employees to wear the store's latest styles and embody its brand through their hairstyles,

3

cosmetics, and body size. None of this is lost on retail clothing workers, who recognize their role as models. Indeed, at some stores, the workers' title actually is "model" rather than "sales associate," allowing managers to hire based on appearance. As we conducted interviews with these workers, we were surprised by how many repeatedly told us their jobs involved becoming "walking mannequins."

These workers, especially those visible on the sales floor, are mostly young, white, and light-skinned people of color, considered eye-catching but replaceable by their managers. As they arrange, watch, and sell merchandise, representing the store and its brand, we see the unfolding of a labor paradox quintessential to capitalist systems. On the one hand, clothing retailers value workers' looks and expect them to embody the store brand. On the other, corporate managers devalue these workers through labor practices that combine cost cutting and intense surveillance. Rather than hiring workers with customer service skills, they focus on workers' youthful looks, enforcing beauty norms that generally valorize whiteness. As models who mirror the display mannequins, workers are supposed to fit standard sizes sold by the store, have attractive faces and bodies that reflect and promote the store's "look," and be both passive and malleable. Yet human workers clearly differ from plastic mannequins; they require wages, respond to dehumanizing labor practices (by compliance, resistance, or a combination of both strategies), attempt to find meaning and social connection, and endeavor to ensure their dignity in their workplaces.

As employers deploy workers' beauty, imbued with racial, gender, class, and sexual meanings, to signal the store's "look" and attract consumers, retail workers struggle with their employers' emphasis on appearance. They vacillate between appreciating the validation of their beauty and criticizing their employers' superficial ideals. They sense that their loyalty is undervalued, particularly in terms of pay, scheduling, and work hours. They identify multiple challenges to purchasing their own "uniforms" from their employers and maintaining the narrow aesthetic—so key to their employment—that prizes white, middle-class, and binary gender norms of attractiveness. To some extent, these workers expect surveillance of and control over their bodies because clothing retail is part of the beauty industry. But they also experience it as onerous and morally suspect. The emphasis on looks and what we refer to as *racialized beauty hierarchies*

Figure 1. Model worker as mannequin. SOURCE: iStock.com/PeopleImages.

stands at odds with common individualist ideals of rewarding workers based on job performance, illuminating how companies construct "merit" based on social categories rather than specific skills or qualifications. Ideas about race, gender, and social hierarchies are embedded in the very organization of retail clothing, as prominently displayed as the outfits on the workers helping customers on the shop floor and on the mannequins in the store windows.

This retail organization shortchanges both workers and customers. Corporate-determined sales goals and constant surveillance of store "metrics," also known as data, by corporate managers lead to scripted forms of interaction and high-pressure sales tactics. Workers draw attention to how these practices, attempts to appeal to a small segment of the retail market, undermine customer service and may ultimately repel shoppers. Fashion retail employees also vehemently criticize the high-pressure sales pitches for branded credit cards with high finance charges that they are exhorted to push onto unsuspecting consumers. These workers, most of whom are between eighteen and twenty-three years old, frequently find themselves facing moral quandaries at work, even as they are underpaid and undervalued.

How can retail employers require so much while offering so little in return? Although retail workers may identify with the brand and value

.ts status and the employee discount, discounts alone do not fully explain these jobs' persistence.[1] We focus on teenage and twenty-something clothing retail workers to understand how employers—store-level managers and more senior corporate managers—organize the labor process and regulate how workers must look and act to evoke the brand that they represent. Drawing on interviews with fifty-five current and recent clothing retail workers who vary by race and gender, we point out that working conditions lead to constant turnover, as workers recognize the mismatch between their employers' stated values (prioritizing "cool" and "hot" status above effort and customer service) and the limited rewards for doing a good job and maintaining the look prized by managers. We analyze how workers, customers, corporate managers, and store managers interact in these workplaces, consistently calling attention to how race and gender shape these interactions.

Brand-oriented clothing retail work is organized to emphasize workers' bodies while undermining their humanity. How do workers experience racial, gender, and class inequalities in retail clothing stores, which the focus on *aesthetic labor* exacerbates? Originally conceptualized by sociologists Chris Warhurst, Dennis Nickson, and their colleagues as the "embodied capacities and attributes possessed by workers" at hiring, aesthetic labor has been further specified to include "a worker's deportment, style, accent, voice, and attractiveness."[2] Workers' bodies are not abstractions; they reflect racial, gender, sexual, and class identities, ideologies, and material realities. We analyze the organization of labor dynamics within retail clothing and how this labor process reinforces and even justifies inequalities.

RETAIL LABOR, SURVEILLANCE, AND THE ORGANIZATION OF WORK

This book speaks to several important ongoing conversations about work and labor. Researchers studying work in the twenty-first century emphasize the polarization between good and bad jobs.[3] Retail exemplifies the latter: workers receive low pay and status, varying and limited hours of work, and minimal benefits, and they respond with high turnover. Yet retail is the largest industry in the United States and a key driver of the world economy.[4] Clothing and accessory stores are among the largest retail employers; although they pay their nearly one million US workers less than employees in other retail sectors.[5] Thus, studying retail clothing work provides a lens through which to understand how corporations organize low-wage work at the nexus of beauty and consumption.[6] Focusing on this case allows us to examine how retailers organize low-wage work to compete within a branded market, including how managers treat their workers, how workers respond, and what these interactions reveal about workplace inequality. We thus address some unanswered questions about how these jobs are changing in the twenty-first century, with a new focus on technology and surveillance, and how racial and gender inequalities are reinforced in these increasingly diverse workplaces.

We build on the service work literature to show how relationships between customers, workers, and multiple levels of managers play out given new forms of data collection and surveillance. We did not originally expect to focus on surveillance and related technology, but these themes cropped up regularly in our interviews, leading us to consider how each is changing twenty-first-century workplaces in significant ways. In previous decades, corporate managers tracked stores through weekly or monthly sales data, phone calls, and visits; today, software systems allow near-constant communication between store- and corporate-level management.[7] Corporate can peer into each store in real time, identifying how many customers come in and out, how much they buy in each transaction, and how effectively cashiers have convinced customers to apply for store credit cards or upsold them with "add-ons" at the point of sale.

Corporate managers can use these data to direct frontline managers' decisions—even though the metrics don't capture the full scope of the situation. For example, corporate counts "footfalls" of people coming into and leaving the store; children running in and out of the store as they play artificially increase footfalls but not purchases, counting against worker productivity.[8] Customer surveys, which are disproportionately filled out by unhappy customers, may differ from frontline managers' direct observations, yet play an outsized role in corporate's evaluations of workers.[9] That is to say, new technologies and greater surveillance have lowered autonomy among frontline workers and managers, centralizing decision-making in corporate managers. This range of surveillance technologies shapes how store-level managers train and supervise workers and expect them to perform their tasks, while ironically failing to improve (and often undercutting) the quality of customer service. Managerial technologies used in these workplaces produce worse jobs, higher turnover, and lower customer service: a virtual trifecta of failure in the name of market rationality.

Previous scholarship has established that in service work, there is not a simple binary relationship between worker and manager, but instead a more unstable worker-manager-customer triangle.[10] Sociologist Robin Leidner argues that this service triangle complicates the workplace, as workers and managers try to appeal to the customers to win concessions. With the introduction of new technology allowing for greater corporate surveillance, however, we theorize that this triangle has become a *service quadrangle*, with realignments of power between corporate managers (who have gained control) and frontline managers (who have lost autonomy), workers (who face increased constraints as well as new opportunities for resistance), and customers (who have gained greater voice).

Within this four-pointed arrangement exists what we theorize as *the service panopticon*. Theorist Michel Foucault posits that modern society involves ubiquitous surveillance, forming a panopticon or a structure in which people can always be observed, but do not know *when* they are being observed, which leads them to regulate their own behavior in case they are being watched.[11] Building on labor process theory, we argue that workers and frontline managers operate within a broader set of corporate control mechanisms that are distinguishing features of the twenty-first-century retail workplace. Through a range of technologies—including video cameras, computer software, motion sensors, secret shoppers, customer surveys, and corporate visits—corporate management maintains a watchful eye on each of its stores. Management exerts control by making workers constantly visible. Workers recognize that managers frequently observe them, but they also self-surveil, disciplining themselves. For example, although not every customer is a secret shopper, workers may act as if they all might be, not only to provide good customer service but also to be *witnessed* providing corporate-approved customer service.

The *service quadrangle* and the *service panopticon* are power-imbued processes. At each point in the service quadrangle, race and gender shape the interactions between workers, customers, frontline managers, and corporate managers. The service panopticon is also used to differentially surveil workers and customers, such as when Black workers are asked to follow customers suspected of shoplifting simply because they are Black. Thus, the organization of retail work in the twenty-first century entails both changes in technology and increased surveillance as well as racialized and gendered organizational processes.

Researchers increasingly recognize the significance of how class, gender, sexuality, and race intersect, especially in workplaces and service jobs.[12] Examining how companies organize retail work around these social locations provides insights into the specific mechanisms of brand-oriented service work that maintain inequalities. We draw on clothing retail workers' experiences of these jobs to argue that the labor process involves multiple levels of management to enforce labor-savings strategies and develops workplaces that alienate many workers of color who do not "fit" the store brand.

Organizational scholar Joan Acker emphasizes that organizational practices tend to reinforce social inequalities, which are "baked into" the structure of workplaces.[13] Workplace practices may appear neutral, but they reflect the "ideal workers" or "appropriate labor" management has in mind.[14] Sociologists Adia Harvey Wingfield and Renée Skeete elaborate on how these processes occur at ideological, interactional, and physical levels.[15] At the ideological level, the organizational culture reflects ideas about race, class, and gender; for example, store advertisements may primarily display men and women who appear attractive according to white, middle-class norms. At the interactional level, workers may need to present and contort themselves to avoid disrupting white, middle-class workers' dominance in the workplace, such as when Black women must wear their hair in ways that mimic white-associated hairstyles.[16] At the physical level, workers may perform tasks or be spatially organized in ways that reinforce hierarchy, such as when workers in the stockroom are more often Black and Latino men and workers on the retail floor are more often white women and lighter-skinned women of color. These racial, gendered, and classed tasks may be invisible to workers and managers, even as they reinforce inequality. Racial tasks are thus "embedded in the everyday interactions, development of organizational culture, and physical construction and maintenance of worksites is the labor that minority workers do to maintain the normalization of whiteness and to obscure or hide the ways they are assumed to be different from the white mainstream," as Wingfield and Skeete argue.[17] White women compose the majority of the clothing retail workforce; their racial-gender advantages are organizationally repurposed to fit the employers' needs.

Conflicts are inherent in capitalism, as managers seek to extract capital—or value and resources that produce value—from workers.[18] Capital takes several forms that are central to the retail workplaces we study. Each form stems from social relationships and arrangements. Thus, these forms of capital should be understood as social constructs, not as naturally occurring phenomena. First, *economic capital* refers to financial resources, namely in the form of money, such as wages. Second, *symbolic capital* encompasses the meaning that individuals, groups, organizations, and institutions attribute to more abstract social entities, such as beauty, that have material consequences.[19] Third, *cultural capital* refers to different types of socially meaningful status markers, such as consumer tastes, leisure activities, fashion sense, speech, and so on.[20] Fourth, *social capital* reflects relationships and networks that can affect a worker's opportunities, such as friends who recruit one another on behalf of their manager. All four types of capital remain interlocked within the retail sector, subject to negotiation and evaluation within the labor process.

In retail, management is multilayered and made up of at least two distinct groups: corporate and store (or "frontline"). Each group tries to minimize company losses and maximize revenue (forms of economic capital), but they perform these jobs differently given their relative positions in the service quadrangle and the embedded panopticon, as well as their differing relationships with workers. Race and gender further influence these dynamics, such as when white managers develop closer relationships (social capital) with white workers and then give them more shifts, leaving workers of color with even fewer hours, or when women of color recount the most unpleasant customer interactions but recall fewer instances of support from coworkers in dealing with unruly customers. Both corporate and frontline managers judge workers based on their perceived beauty (symbolic capital), trying to create a certain status associated with the brand (cultural capital). Even as these companies publicly project racially and gender-progressive identities, their practices reinforce societal inequalities.

Surveillance operates in complex ways.[21] We argue that the clothing retail sector creates a matrix of multidirectional controls to cultivate the company's value both monetarily and symbolically. Workers watch customers to prevent theft while following corporate rules for how to dress. Customers surveil workers' performance through shopper surveys or "secret shoppers." Frontline managers style workers' bodies before a shift and inspect their bags to ensure that they haven't stolen merchandise after they clock out. Corporate managers monitor frontline managers, workers' bodies, and sales-related metrics in each store. Across these interplays, retail work routines appear neutral, but they tend to perpetuate racialized and gendered scripts for workers, customers, and both sets of managers. The service panopticon creates such extreme circumstances that some workers quit their jobs. Others regularly resist certain desired practices (like scripted interactions and upselling shoppers). Gendered and racialized surveillance within the retail workplace is both a tool of domination and a catalyst for resistance.[22]

Managers aim to routinize work so that they can assert control over the timing, staffing, and quality of work. At the same time, they deskill that work, decreasing worker power to determine wages, hours, and working conditions. Labor scholar Harry Braverman asserts that routinization robs workers of their autonomy and ability to derive a deeper sense of satisfaction from their labor.[23] Routinized interactive service work may further alienate workers by restricting their emotions, making them feel increasingly inauthentic.[24] Coining the concept "emotional labor," sociologist Arlie Hochschild analyzes how employers expect workers to manage their emotions as they interact with customers, produce an emotional state in customers, and allow employers to control their feelings. Just as companies sell clothing sewn by factory workers, they sell feelings performed by retail workers. This interactive work, assumed to be low skill, requires substantial skill if it is to be done well.[25] Such work reinforces certain racialized and gendered ideals; indeed, white men are most vehement in their objections to doing emotional labor, perhaps because they are less accustomed to "acting" in these ways.

Routinization in interactive service work has other potential dangers for laborers. Robin Leidner argues that "rigid routines strictly enforced can actually prevent workers from doing an adequate job, harming both customer satisfaction and employee morale."[26] As managers script workers to do ineffective things, workers feel increasingly alienated. We heard many stories of workers frustrated by following stiff scripts that impede connecting with customers. In her ethnographic study of fast-food workers, for instance, Leidner theorizes how workers may come to make sense of, resist, and even use routinization, actively negotiating rather than passively accepting managers' attempts to control their work.[27] Workers consistently endeavor to reshape their workplaces and find dignity in their jobs. They also attempt to find or create solidarity with coworkers, and sometimes succeed.[28] However, these opportunities for solidarity differ among workers; for example, workers of color develop fewer relationships when they work in stores primarily staffed by white workers.

Since the work products of emotional and aesthetic labor are less recognized, contestations between managers and workers can be somewhat murky. Labor scholars Cameron Macdonald and Carmen Sirianni argue that conflicts between managers and workers are less clear when they focus on the self-presentation of the worker, as opposed to, for example, how many widgets they make an hour.[29] Class, racial, and gender inequalities similarly "hide in plain sight," as workers, for example, are asked to adopt white middle-class, cisgender styles, with no recognition of how these expectations disadvantage minoritized workers. We explore how twenty-first-century retail clothing workers negotiate, resist, and experience work, attentive to how race and gender shape these processes.

Another aim of this book is to understand the specific labor practices that stem from the ever-expanding branded service economy.[30] In an economy predicated on unnecessary consumption, businesses are compelled to constantly create the impetus to buy more. Brands play this role, producing value simply by virtue of their signifiers and encouraging customers to buy things they do not need.[31] Workers are key to convincing customers to buy for the sake of remaining in style; they use their bodies to model new fashions and their emotional labor to encourage consumption, making the consumption and production of the service deeply interconnected.[32]

Scholars know relatively little about how now-ubiquitous branding shapes labor conditions and work experiences. Companies attempt to best competitors through a carefully curated set of appealing cues intended to create and reinforce a market niche: to set them apart in a recognizable way meant to entice consumers. These styles often also reflect white middle-class ideals. Workers' bodies become corporate canvases on which to communicate the store's signature style. In one notable example, the airline industry in the United States pushed such branded labor practices and aesthetic standards among flight attendants in the 1960s. Appearance-focused labor practices remain commonplace throughout the service industry.[33]

Treating workers as "models" is particularly prominent in the beauty and fashion industries. And with good reason: they sell products and services meant, ostensibly, to boost consumers' attractiveness, sex appeal, and self-image. From fast-fashion and cosmetics retail to hair and nail salons, employers expect entry-level service workers to embody the company aesthetic.[34] How do workers respond to these beauty demands, alongside the more traditional labor-cost-cutting strategies in these jobs?

AESTHETIC LABOR

Burgeoning research on aesthetic labor seeks to answer these questions. At the heart of the twenty-first-century service economy is how branding shapes corporate labor practices, often exacerbating the worst of conditions within the workplace and broader society.[35] Extending the literature on emotional labor, aesthetic labor scholars consider how workers do not merely perform tasks but are expected to look, act, sound, and even smell in highly specific brand-oriented ways.[36] Workers help produce this branding through modeling the merchandise, as "the lines between consumption and work are blurred for both employees and consumers."[37] Interactive service workers' bodies factor into the labor that they do; retail managers may require their sales associates to dress and style themselves in particular ways.[38] In practice, aesthetic labor means that managers expect workers to handle mundane sales-related tasks, like cashiering and folding tank tops, while also *looking*, *sounding*, and *acting* like a stylish customer, representing the store's brand to shoppers through their performance.

Beauty is also conceptually attached to "soft skills," including communication, empathy, and approachability, which reflect employer preferences for a certain social performance. In the United States, these performances are often associated with the white middle or upper class. As a result, when hiring and scheduling workers who fit the store's brand, employers often discriminate against those from "other" class and racial groups.[39] While employer expectations regarding emotional labor and appearance are not confined to frontline retail work (for example, principals expect teachers to do emotional labor and dress in certain ways), these performances are the central services that clothing retail workers endeavor to produce. As an "emerging subsector" of the service economy, aesthetic labor has four key components: (1) it occurs within customer-worker interactions, (2) workers and frontline and corporate managers control workers' bodies in these interactions, (3) this labor is meant to evoke positive customer perceptions of the company, and (4) it forms part of the wage agreement.[40]

The twin imperatives of emotional labor and aesthetic labor involve workers performing specific feelings and embodying beauty expectations of hair, makeup, nails, and body size, among other corporeal domains. Labor scholar Steven Lopez cogently explains the connection between these two forms of labor:

> Aesthetic labor is thus broader than emotional labor. It is not simply the ability to emote or display emotions that is at issue. Rather, it refers to the manner in which workers draw on cultural dispositions in order to create service interactions with a recognizable—and often even branded—style.[41]

Workers not only have to be attractive and "stylish" according to beauty norms, but must also evoke the *right* style to reflect and sell the store's brand.[42] These style expectations further reflect classed, racialized, and gendered ideals. Yet while researchers have theorized how aesthetic labor reinforces gender and class, few have explicitly theorized its racialized dimensions.[43]

Brands communicate and appeal to classed notions of style, or "distinction" in the language of sociologist Pierre Bourdieu.[44] Employers believe that if workers perform aesthetic labor appropriately—expressing a particular habitus (mannerisms and tastes that reflect class upbringing or cultural capital)—the store will attract and retain particular customers.[45] As "brand representatives," retail employers expect workers to both "personify" and "embody" the brand.[46] Store brands aim to mirror customers' cultural capital, including specific consumer tastes that signal class, race, gender, and age.[47] In doing so, stores align store taste with customer taste, while deploying power in ways that Bourdieu refers to as *symbolic violence*: imposing some tastes over others to reproduce inequality and calcify existing hierarchies.[48]

As is implied by its tendency to conform to culturally specific beauty standards, aesthetic labor also reflects gendered and racialized notions of class.[49] Employers cultivate aesthetic labor among their retail clothing workers to match the racial, class, and gender components of the brand's target customers.[50] Sociologist Beverly Skeggs argues that "bodies are the physical sites where relations of class, gender, race, sexuality, and age come together."[51] Much existing research on aesthetic labor emphasizes the gendered expectations of this work, particularly for white women, the majority of this labor force. The retail workforce, however, is becoming increasingly racially diversified, employing more women of color. Our research, which includes a racially diverse group of both women and men, allows us to address unanswered questions about the intersection of race, gender, and class in how looks-oriented labor shapes retail workplace inequalities.

Sexuality, of course, constitutes aesthetic labor, too. Gender scholar Kristen Barber demonstrates that "management mobilizes employees' heterosexual identities and heterogendered appearances to enhance both their corporate brands and their clients' social status."[52] Exploring how retailers strategically use workers' sexuality is important in delineating the dynamics of aesthetic labor.[53] We find that across race, men rarely comment on the discomfort of being "marketed" as a brand object. Women, however, vocalize more developed critiques of their appearance-based work. Appearance policies are not neutral but reify racialized, classed, gendered, and sexualized beauty hierarchies. Taking each seriously, this book addresses a blind spot in the extant research on aesthetic labor and beauty.

STUDYING RETAIL WORKERS

Beginning in the 1980s and ramping up in the 1990s, corporations in the global commercial clothing industry crafted a "fast-fashion" model of production and consumption.[54] Business scholars refer to this cyclical phenomenon as emphasizing "flexibility" across the supply chain to maneuver the "high levels of 'chaos'" that characterize the ephemeral fancies of lifestyle products, including apparel and footwear.[55] Given the limited accuracy of style forecasts and high levels of market volatility, clothing retailers rely on "quick response and just-in-time deliveries" from textile suppliers to introduce new "merchandise every six to eight weeks, or even more frequently."[56]

Clothing retailers targeting teens and twenty-somethings have embraced fast-fashion production techniques.[57] Rarely will stores like H&M and Forever 21 go more than a month or two without significantly altering their current merchandise offerings. This speed in changing up goods is only possible because commercial clothing companies also exploit the workers making the clothing as part of a global supply chain.[58] Information about customer trends and preferences is vital to corporate attempts to maximize responsiveness to market sensitivity; this point helps explain the profit orientation toward "point-of sale data[, which] is analysed daily" to inform decisions about merchandise replenishment across points of the supply chain.[59] Technology capturing sales is thus as vital to the fast-fashion mode of production as it is to the management function of controlling worker performance.

We focus on clothing retail because this industry exists at the nexus of race, class, and gender inequalities, low-wage work, and consumption. Our analysis unpacks various narratives about how workers with different identities experience and describe their labor. Brand-based markets force workers to assume the role of walking mannequins, showcasing their bodies within a beauty appraisal system in ways that tend to reinforce hierarchies of class, race, and gender. Managers cultivate workers' embodiment of the brand, making it important to understand how workers experience employers' *body rules*.[60]

Before conducting interviews, we performed exploratory participant observations at clothing stores targeted to teenagers and young adults.

Sociologist Lynne Pettinger's "shopper observation" methodology inspired these visits, in which we sought to enrich our knowledge of these spaces from the customer's perspective.[61] Although actual time inside the shop on each trip was relatively short—between fifteen and forty-five minutes, depending on the floor space and merchandise available to browse—observations gave us a living, breathing sense of the ebb and flow of clothing retail.[62] With the help of two paid assistants, we conducted thirty-five participant observations in six different commercial clothing stores that sell to women and men in the fifteen to twenty-five year old market, including Abercrombie & Fitch, American Eagle, Hollister, Hot Topic, Pac Sun, and Urban Outfitters. We also visited stores more informally while we were interviewing, analyzing, and writing, to look for inconsistencies in our interview data.[63]

Despite the limitations of shopper observations, field visits provide useful background knowledge about the stores' context.[64] We watched how sales staff went about their various tasks, greeting customers as they entered and exited, nearly always busy folding (and refolding) stacks of jeans, T-shirts, and sweatshirts. Shopper observations also gave us first-hand insights into retail employee appearances. We quickly noticed differences across the stores in workers' hairstyles and cosmetics and the visibility of their tattoos and piercings. Stores that project "alternative" branding, like Pac Sun, Urban Outfitters, and Hot Topic, employ workers with more class-diverse gender and sexual performances, such as dramatic cosmetics, visible ink, or nontraditional piercings, though these stores are not necessarily more racially diverse. Our observations also taught us that workers across brands don outfits that at least match the general appearance of their specific store's current merchandise.

We interviewed fifty-five retail clothing workers, who mostly held jobs at clothing stores generally selling a variety of teen-oriented clothing at middle-class price points. We found that stores differ in their branding, with fairly clear differences between youth-oriented stores such as American Eagle, Pac Sun, Urban Outfitters, and Forever 21; Abercrombie-owned stores such as Abercrombie & Fitch, Hollister, and Gilly Hicks; and department stores.

These clothing companies target different niches, as our interviewees explain. For example, Forever 21 is primarily oriented toward middle-class and working-class teens and twenty-somethings; it sells an enormous array of styles at very low prices, although the quality of the merchandise reflects its price point. One of our respondents defines Forever 21's vibe as "hip and trendy," noting the many different sections of the store, such as peasant tops, leather, and urban style. Another interviewee acknowledges that the fast-fashion production aspect of the store means that the clothing tends to be of lower quality: "They fall apart after about three washes." Pac Sun reflects a Southern California aesthetic; as one participant explains, Pac Sun's style is "the surf in the sun; they're all about California lifestyle. . . more towards the skater crowds."

American Eagle is preppier, characterized by one of our respondents as an "iconic American look of denim, country-ish kind of clothing with like a city twist on it." Hollister and Abercrombie & Fitch, owned by the same company, are oriented more toward upper-middle-class teens, with higher price points; Hollister maintains a more tightly curated California style, while Abercrombie provides a more expensive preppy aesthetic. Urban Outfitters is also oriented toward the upper middle class, but it highlights a somewhat edgier "look." Merrily describing the store's hipster or alternative vibe, one respondent says the customers "spend a lot of money to look like you're not spending a lot of money."

A sizable portion (38%) of the employees we interviewed had worked at stores owned by Abercrombie & Fitch (including Hollister, Abercrombie Kids, and Gilly Hicks). At the time of our interviews, these stores had narrow and highly regulated aesthetic labor body rules and tended to present themselves as hip clubs targeted toward popular kids. One respondent refers to Abercrombie & Fitch as for "jocks and preps, definitely not goths." Several workers further pointed out how Abercrombie stores' loud music and low lighting aim to make shoppers feel like they're in an exclusive "club." At Hollister, another respondent emphasizes the "cool Cali vibe," and another differentiates it from its sister brand by saying that "Hollister's more of a beachy theme, and Abercrombie's more of a woodsy theme." One of our interviewees laughingly refers to Gilly Hicks as "a teenage store that's dark and loud and has bras and underwear and *dark and loud*, I would keep on stressing." Someone else hints at the aesthetic requirements of labor when she notes that Hollister is "selective . . . they're definitely looking for a certain kind of person with a certain kind of look."

Figure 2. Abercrombie & Fitch storefront. SOURCE: iStock.com/jetcityimage.

Figure 3. Urban Outfitters storefront. SOURCE: iStock.com/JHVEPhoto.

We also included workers who had worked some smaller, high-priced boutiques aimed at teens, as well as some stores that serve a wider audience, such as the working- and middle-class-oriented Old Navy, the middle-class-oriented Gap, the upper-middle-class-oriented J. Crew, and department stores like J.C. Penney and Macy's.[65] Those who had worked at youth-oriented stores but also at stores aimed at a wider range of ages make direct comparisons between workplaces. Workers at Macy's and J.C. Penney characterize these stores as more organized and aimed at a wider age range, with J.C. Penney being more affordable. Workers at Old Navy refer to it as affordable and aimed at providing "all your fundamentals and all your basics," as one respondent describes. Workers at T.J. Maxx and Kohls refer to those stores as providing, as one suggests, designer clothing or "upscale stuff for really cheap." Including workers at stores aimed at wider populations created a tacit comparison, allowing us to understand differences between youth clothing retail and other niches of this industry.

When we began this research, we expected to find that the class orientation of the store would drive its labor practices. We thought, for example, that stores oriented toward upper-middle-class customers might have more rigid rules for workers than those oriented toward working- or middle-class customers.[66] We also expected that customer service would be better at the stores aimed at upper-middle-class customers to ensure a loyal customer base. Instead, we found that the teen-oriented stores had much more in common with one another.

Stores oriented toward a wider age range, whether Old Navy or Macy's, tended to be more open about the workers' appearance while expecting a higher level of customer service. Teen-oriented stores were particularly stringent in their expectations for aesthetic labor but tended to rely on overly scripted (and less effective) approaches to customer service. These practices may reflect assumptions that younger customers are especially focused on appearance and more likely to shop at stores where they might aspire to look like attractive workers, rather than choosing to patronize stores with better customer service. It could also reflect assumptions that youth are a short-term customer base who will age out of shopping for a given brand; building customer loyalty is less necessary, that is, than appealing to the next crop of teens.

While class did not play out as expected, there *were* interesting differences between Abercrombie & Fitch and Hollister, on the one hand, and Urban Outfitters, Pac Sun, American Eagle, and Forever 21 on the other. The Abercrombie stores, with a higher price point, had very narrow "look" policies, and managers held workers to stricter standards and sexualized them more than in other stores. Yet Urban Outfitters, with a similarly high price point, was much more lenient in its treatment of workers, displaying appearance expectations more comparable to those observed in stores with moderate price points like Pac Sun and American Eagle.

Forty-one of our respondents identify as women and fourteen as men. Compared to the overall population of clothing retail workers, our sample is younger and more educated, in part because we targeted clothing retail workers in stores oriented toward people in their teens and twenties, but also because we advertised on college campuses.[67] We purposely selected these workers to explain how clothing stores targeting a younger clientele employ this age group to embody and represent their brands.[68] By race and gender, our sample mirrors the national composition of the clothing retail workforce.[69] Interviewees included twenty-eight white (eighteen women, ten men), eleven Black (ten women, one man), seven multiracial (six women, one man), six Asian American (five women, one man), and three Latinx employees (two women, one man).[70]

In most cases, these participants hold frontline service positions that require customer interaction. We also interviewed seven people who work primarily in the stockroom; their insights about clothing retail offer a slightly different perspective. Seven people in the sample work in some type of management role, such as full-time manager, part-time manager, assistant merchandise manager, lead sales, or shift lead. Their interviews illuminate important differences between store or "frontline" managers and corporate management. Although corporate managers did not respond to interview requests, many of the workers and frontline managers we interviewed describe their interactions with corporate, and one of the frontline managers was tracked for a promotion up the ladder into corporate management and could detail the expectations from corporate.

Nearly half of the sample was currently employed in clothing retail at the time of the interview. The remainder had held a clothing store job in the past three years (usually within the past six months). We thus capture perspectives of workers who "turned over" and may express more job dissatisfaction.[71] Throughout the book, we present each interview participant with the store where they work to provide context for their quotes. In cases where individuals worked for multiple companies, we name the store they are discussing or their most recent employer. We also mention their race when it helps contextualize our analysis.

We conducted each interview as a one-on-one dialogue.[72] The semistructured interview design created space for fluid conversation, including allowing researchers to ask follow-up questions, which often gave participants, especially those with extensive retail backgrounds, an opportunity to discuss interesting aspects of their jobs that we did not anticipate.[73] For example, people who spoke about multiple retail clothing jobs provided particularly rich accounts, as they could analyze differences in managers' expectations by workplace. We also iteratively revised our questions to address points raised by our participants. During our initial round of interviews, for instance, we did not ask questions about selling credit cards, but many participants brought up this topic and characterized it as among the "worst parts" of their jobs. In later interviews, we intentionally asked about selling credit cards if workers didn't raise the issue.[74] We stopped conducting interviews when the interviews stopped developing new insights.[75]

ORGANIZATION OF THE BOOK

The book contains three parts. Along with this introduction, the first part includes chapter 1, which discusses retail clothing work to give readers a better sense of how the work is organized and what it entails. We describe hiring and training, as well as how low wages and erratic schedules make retail jobs challenging. Labor strategies like "just-in-time" scheduling degrade the quality of work, as employees don't know how many hours they will work and thus whether they will be able to pay their bills. Rather than rewarding workers with higher wages or opportunities for promotion, managers give them more hours on the schedule. Workers also criticize employers for using discounts to encourage worker consumption and requiring workers to model store products to create a captive market.

In part 2 we theorize how the labor process unfolds within the unstable arrangement of managers, workers, and customers. This section extends labor process scholarship, with a dedicated chapter for each group with whom workers interact: frontline and corporate managers (chapter 2), coworkers (chapter 3), and customers (chapter 4). Throughout, we emphasize how race and gender shape worker experiences and power dynamics within the clothing retail workplace.

In chapter 2, "Multilevel Management and the Service Panopticon," we explain how workers view some managerial expectations—turning up for their shifts, not stealing, keeping the store neat, providing friendly service—as reasonable, but note how minimizing labor costs (little advance notification of shifts, too few workers staffing the store) undermines their collective ability to fulfill these expectations. In their accounts of navigating corporate directives, workers reveal the belief that the quality of their labor is degraded through managerial observation, such as through secret shoppers ensuring that they stay "on script," and through metrics that record, for example, their credit card sales. Workers identify key differences between corporate- and store-level managers, showing that with increased surveillance via metrics, the latter have less autonomy. We argue that rather than the service work "triangle," corporate managers, store managers, workers, and customers form a *quadrangle*: a four-sided figure with shifting alliances between each group, with greater weight given to corporate managers and customers.

In chapter 3, "Coworkers and Belonging," we turn to another point in the quadrangle, considering the relationships among workers. In solidarity and contention, coworkers are an important dimension of the retail labor process. One of the stories told about why teenage and twenty-something retail workers earn so little is that because the job is enjoyable, they spend their shifts "hanging out with friends."[76] Many white workers, in particular, describe pleasurable friendships with coworkers and even store-level managers (who can provide job perks like more hours on the schedule). Yet belongingness in the workplace varies largely by age and race. Women of color voice the most isolation from coworkers and feel offended by managers who request them to surveil Black customers suspected of shoplifting. We posit that these racialized feelings of isolation and belonging stem in part from the aesthetic labor emphasis on hiring workers who reflect the target customer, usually understood to be white. Becoming part of "the family" is thus easier for white workers.

In chapter 4, "Customer Expectations and Emotional Labor," we address the final point in the service quadrangle: worker relations with customers. As chapter 2 claims, workers resist managers primarily when they feel that managers' requests lead to worse customer service. Workers view customer expectations for helpful service, informed workers, and style pointers as reasonable, even while emphasizing that the organization of the work (working too few hours a week to keep track of changing merchandise, having too few workers per shift) undermines these goals. Still, they insist customers are not "always right," particularly regarding their efforts to get additional discounts and the way they "mess up" the store. The emotional labor that workers do in the face of rude or angry customers is a central facet of their experiences in retail. Race and gender shape work with customers in several ways that we highlight. Men, especially white men, find the expectations for emotional labor challenging. Women of color offer numerous encounters with critical and angry customers.

Part 3 analyzes aesthetic labor in these workplaces. In chapter 5, "Beautiful Bodies on the Sales Floor," we examine how managers and workers control and use their bodies to personify and perpetuate the brand. These practices include explicit body rules, including attractiveness, body size, hair, cosmetics, jewelry, and body modifications to cultivate and discipline workers as models. Managers hold both men and women to the company's appearance standards; workers discuss how managers regulate their looks and the anxiety this provokes.

Within this chapter, we also assert that managers reflect and enforce racialized, colorist ideals about white and lighter-skinned workers, particularly for women. Retail employers create what we refer to as a "tri-racial beauty hierarchy," in which white workers and white-associated phenotypical traits are favored, racially ambiguous and lighter-skinned workers of color are somewhat valued, and darker-skinned Black workers (especially women) are devalued.[77] The racialized beauty hierarchies in these stores generally reject appearances associated with Black bodies, such as natural, curly, or braided hair and darker complexions. Workers also recognize how their bodies are sexualized toward sales; women vocalize more criticisms of these processes than men, reiterating how race and gender shape the aesthetic labor process.

Chapter 6, "Modeling the Merchandise," considers the "uniform," or the ways managers expect that workers "embody the brand" by becoming consumers who buy and wear the company's clothing (sometimes with the help of employee discounts). It's not enough that workers dress in store merchandise; managers insist that they wear the latest styles (despite the expense this creates for workers) and style the clothing according to company guidelines. Men and women face slightly different attire-related body rules, yet managers and corporate policy dictate that workers maintain gendered bodies in conventional ways. Managers regulate workers by assessing and styling them, asking them to change their appearance or their clothes, or sending them home when they deviate from the rules.

We conclude by building on the insights developed throughout the book to answer this question: *How can we create better workplaces?* Many of the workers who leave retail clothing work do so both because they are poorly compensated and because their values do not align with employer practices. Companies highlight values around "diversity" in these stores, primarily to ensure that they are not sued rather than to create truly inclusive workplaces. Given narrow visions of beauty within the aesthetic labor process, we emphasize how the organization of these workplaces reinforces existing racial and gender inequalities. Finally, we consider how worker organizing could help improve these stores: providing workers with higher pay and better work conditions, supplying customers with higher-quality service, and presenting managers with more effective approaches to organizing work and providing meaningful service to customers. Although we remain skeptical that corporations will follow these suggestions, we believe brick-and-mortar stores are more likely to succeed when they are staffed by unionized workers providing high-quality service.

In the twenty-first century, low-wage retail clothing work has changed dramatically, with the increasing deployment of surveillance technologies allowing "just-in-time" production and constant monitoring of worker activities. Rather than rewarding workers with strong customer service skills, employers increasingly view workers as expendable, putting little effort into training or retention. Youth-oriented clothing retailers emphasize branding and style to appeal to popular, of-the-moment influencers and ask their workers to represent that style. Since the youth market is ephemeral—yesterday's tween is, after all, tomorrow's twenty-something—high-quality goods and services are deemed unimportant. At the same time, many aspects of these workplaces remain mired in the past: race and gender inequalities are reinforced rather than disrupted, worker precarity is increased, and the "style" work prized by clothing retailers continues to impose norms that heighten inequality. Retail clothing provides a prism through which to understand troubling twenty-first-century workplace dynamics within the service panopticon.

1 Low Wages, Little Training, and Unpredictable Hours

"IT MAKES YOU REALIZE HOW AWFUL THESE RETAIL JOBS ARE"

At age twenty, Carmen, who is Latina, already has years of retail experience. She has worked at the department store Sears; the upscale, "bohemian fashion" retailer Free People; the big box chain Kmart; and most recently the older-skewing women's apparel store Christopher & Banks.[1] But all that's in her past: "I never want to go back to it because $8 for anyone is not good enough pay." Carmen is grateful that her parents "help her out," because retail wages could not cover her needs: "It was difficult for me, but it's not as bad as it was with other people that I saw." After explaining retail's low pay and demanding work, Carmen concludes, "It makes you realize how awful these retail jobs are because they don't pay their employees enough for all the work they do."

Why did Carmen, over and over again, exert herself in low-paid, demanding retail clothing jobs? She narrates the choice as stemming from her lack of credentials and companies' eagerness to exploit a younger, uncredentialed workforce: "Every single [job], I've complained about it. And, my mom has always been like, 'Find another job.' I'm like, 'I'm a college student. I'm not qualified for anything else.' These companies take advantage of that." With low pay and benefits, little training, few opportunities for advancement, and unpredictable and too few hours, these jobs also tend to have high turnover.[2] Carmen's longest stint in retail clothing was one year at Sears; she stayed at her other three jobs less than five months each. Carmen currently has no plans to make a career in retail clothing, though she had once hoped to go into fashion design like many of the youth of color who occupy these jobs.[3] Burned out on the downside of what once looked like entry-level fashion jobs, she sighs, "I hate retail right now."

In this chapter, we examine why workers like Carmen seek out jobs in retail clothing and how they experience the working conditions and organization of their labor. As Karl Marx contends, workers can sell their labor power, but they need to be able to earn enough to reproduce themselves (through food, shelter, and the like)—so that they can continue working.[4] Capitalist employers, meanwhile, do what they can to drive down labor costs as far as possible without running out of workers willing to do the job. When we look at retail jobs, the relentless turnover hints that these employers don't concern themselves with creating the conditions that would allow their workers to reproduce their labor.

Harry Braverman extends Marx's arguments in *Labor and Monopoly Capital*, analyzing how, over the twentieth century, managers worked to deskill workers, so that workers would have less leverage over employers.[5] Managers came to determine workers' actions, rather than letting workers develop the skills conducive to doing their jobs well. Over time, owners and managers have come to effectively control every step of the labor process. These employers need not rely on the skills of individual employees but can constantly replace their workers with other low-skilled workers; retention is of little concern when a new hire is ever cheaper in terms of minimal onboarding and training costs.

As a result, twenty-first-century retail clothing employers do not aim to develop lasting relationships with skilled workers. Given the availability of appropriate candidates seeking jobs and the fact that the target worker is a teen or twenty-something assumed to be supported by parents or other household members, these companies can allow wages to stagnate and, when workers quit, can replace them easily. These fashion retailers never stop hiring entry-level employees, because a low-paid, relatively young workforce best suits their needs. These are unfulfilling, underpaid, dead-end jobs, fashioned to cut every corner.

LABOR PROCESS

Labor process research concerns how work is carried out, how it is organized, and relations between managers and workers.[6] Following Karl Marx, capitalism is a system in which employers purchase the labor power of workers who rely on wages to earn a livelihood; employers aim to gain higher profits by paying workers the lowest possible wages.[7] Braverman outlined the complexities of purchasing labor power in the twentieth-century United States:

> What he [the capitalist] buys is infinite in *potential*, but in its *realization* it is limited by the subjective state of the workers, by their previous history, by the general social conditions under which they work as well as the particular conditions of the enterprise, and by the technical setting of their labor. . . . It thus becomes essential for the capitalist that control over the labor process pass from the hands of the worker into his own. This transition presents itself in history as the *progressive alienation of the process of production* from the worker; to the capitalist, it presents itself as the problem of *management*.[8]

According to Braverman, capitalists must wrest control of the labor process from workers through management strategies that disconnect workers from the process of production.

Much labor scholarship focuses on industrial settings, analyzing workplaces through contestations between managers and workers on the factory floor. The service sector, however, features a markedly different organization of managers, workers, and customers, with customer interactions central to much of the labor process.[9] Service work, which encompasses more than 80% of US jobs and is the largest economic sector in most postindustrial peer countries, generally includes occupations outside of manufacturing, agriculture, construction, and mining.[10] As Braverman contends, in service work, "the useful effects of labor themselves *become* the commodity."[11] Service work is mostly interactive, with workers directly engaging with customers, coworkers, and supervisors. The sheer size of this sector makes it important to understand how work is organized and experienced by such interactive service workers.[12]

In service industries like education, health care, hospitality, and retail, value is produced through various, often overlapping means. Owners aim to minimize costs, especially those associated with labor, while attracting patrons and providing them with a satisfying experience. Thus, the *use value*—how valuable the item or experience is perceived to be—of service industry production is a combination of the tangible goods for sale, brand-related cues about status, and the feeling that is cultivated during interactions with or observations of frontline workers.[13] Customers pay not only for the comfort, quality, and fit of the apparel, but also how the clothing design reflects a certain cultural taste shared by others they identify with, as well as the pleasure of the shopping experience. Complexities of production within branded service industries put workers in a position in which their bodies, demeanor, and identities become commodified, inseparable from the service production process.[14]

THE ORGANIZATION OF RETAIL CLOTHING WORK

In the United States, retail clothing companies often pay very low wages, usually at or near the minimum wage.[15] However, most of our participants see unpredictable hours as the bigger challenge, as this creates wide variability in monthly earnings. Many stores are open seven days per week from about 10 a.m. until 10:00 p.m. Managers expect entry-level employees to work weekends and evenings, with little power over and little previous notice about their schedules. Store managers assign shifts of four to six hours, but occasionally also longer overnight "floor set shifts" during which workers install new sales floor displays of metal shelving, lightweight wood composite tables, mannequins, and merchandise.

Nonstandard schedules are gaining prominence in the general economy but are most prevalent in retail.[16] Among all workers in the United States, less than 20 percent work part-time, while almost 50 percent of retail employees work part-time (this number has also grown from only 28 percent of retail employees working part-time in 1961).[17] The part-time retail workforce, which is disproportionately composed of Black and Latinx workers as well as workers who prefer full-time status, generally cannot rely on employers to schedule them for a regular number of hours each week.[18] Workers' schedules vary dramatically each week—and as a result, so do their paychecks. Managers require flexibility from applicants, then enforce this expectation by posting schedules with little notice, altering schedules frequently, and sanctioning or ceasing to schedule workers who push back against the uncertainty.[19]

"Just-in-time scheduling" practices, or "scheduling to demand," links employment hours to customer behavior.[20] Retailers carefully monitor sales data in constructing the schedules and making staffing decisions week by week.[21] From corporate management's standpoint, worker availability needs to be easily adjustable to match the real-time shopper foot traffic in each store. Customer flow reflects seasonal fluctuations in consumer demand—such as rising sales in the "back-to-school" season and before winter holidays—as well as weekly and even hourly variations. Tailoring schedules to this variability, coupled with a refusal to carry full-time employees, requires that retail managers maintain a large workforce; even when demand is high, individual employees don't exceed part-time hours.[22] When demand drops, the size of the workforce means many employees will receive inadequate hours.[23] Managers also make real-time calls, requesting that unscheduled workers come in when stores are busy and telling others to clock out early or canceling shifts when business is slow. Erratic scheduling is an unpredictable and stressful economic arrangement for workers and their families.[24]

It also reveals how little value employers place on workers' labor. Indeed, most employers don't focus on experience when hiring and provide minimal training.[25] Rather than creating opportunities for employees to learn new skills, management expects workers to follow rigid scripts and handbooks, all while purchasing and modeling the store's latest merchandise.[26] The retail labor model is thus based on "zero competence, zero qualifications, zero training, and zero career."[27] So why is there always a steady stream of applicants to replace anyone who gets fed up?

FINDING JOBS AT THE SHOPPING MALL

Perhaps the answer to the preceding question is that younger workers "shop" for jobs that fit their identities.[28] Yet the teenage and traditionally college-aged workers we spoke to often apply for a variety of jobs, including ones that don't reflect their consumer identities or interests. Many workers recount applying to multiple positions in person, such as Gabe, who applied to Hollister, Aeropostale, and American Eagle, or Stacey, who applied to Bath & Body Works, American Eagle, and Marshall's. Risa notes of her job at Zara, "It was just a walk-in. I walked in and asked them if they had any spots open and got it right then." Several respondents had previous experience in food service, such as Lori from Wet Seal, who states, "My first job was Dunkin' [Donut]s and I could not stand it. . . . So, I just went around the mall and applied everywhere. They were the first people to call me." Melissa also wanted to leave her job as a short-order cook, which led to getting her job at J.C. Penney: "I really just applied anywhere."

Some of our interviewees *were* customers of the store before gaining employment there.[29] Yet it does not seem that workers primarily aim to become employed at stores they frequent as customers. When we asked whether they had shopped there before getting the job, many responded unenthusiastically. Some only strategically consumed before applying, such as Gabe, who discloses, "The only time I shopped at American Eagle before I was hired was to buy a shirt for my interview for American Eagle." More workers mentioned that they shopped at these stores when they were younger, but they found these brands' styles less appealing now. For instance, Denise says, referring to Abercrombie & Fitch, "When I was like in middle school . . . [but] no, not really. It's not really my style." Researchers do suggest that workers choose jobs based on their own identity claims, though this trend didn't appear to be the dominant path among those we interviewed.[30]

For their part, managers spoke of recruiting applicants based on their appearance, usually selecting from the store's customers (apparently Gabe's strategy to buy and wear an American Eagle shirt to his interview there was well chosen).[31] Workers discuss the importance of having the right "look" to work in teen- and twenty-something-oriented clothing retail. Stores that recruit employees usually have a narrower style and refer to sales associates as "models" or "brand representatives." Denise was approached by a store manager, who lavished her with praise: "'You have a great look; we're looking for people.'" Gwen was also explicitly recruited by Hollister based on her look: "I remember exactly. She said, 'You're pretty and tall. Do you want to work here?'" Rather than feeling connected to their employers through their consumer identities, most of our interviewees criticize these processes. Gwen states, "I don't particularly agree with hiring based on someone's appearance." Like others, particularly the women we interviewed, Gwen knows that she should feel gratified that she was judged attractive and was recruited for her job, yet she describes discomfort with gaining employment due to something as baseless as "being pretty." While workers from stores who "recruit" recognize the corporate goal of hiring workers who "fit the brand," they also criticize these hiring practices as superficial.

Workers also obtain jobs via friends, who act as gatekeepers to the youth labor market. Lance recalls, "My friend, she worked at Abercrombie, so she was like, 'I'll get you a job there,' so then I worked there." And David, who knows he was chosen for his looks, shares, "I offer my good-looking friends to [my employer]," adding, "So yeah, it works out well." Retailers thus seem to benefit from workers' social capital, using their friendship networks to recruit staffers who fit the brand's look.

Sociologist Yasemin Besen-Cassino interprets this pipeline, by which younger people get jobs where their friends work, as evidence that these workers experience their jobs as enjoyable, but our respondents acknowledge problems arising from such arrangements.[32] For example, Stella explains how she got a job at Forever 21: "One of my best friends was an accessory manager there so she kind of got me in." Later she says, "I mean I did have an interview . . . but I pretty much went in there, since she's my best friend I pretty much had the job. . . . I got lucky." Still, she reveals, "Working underneath my best friend as a manager wasn't fun," and it eventually figured into her decision to leave Forever 21. "It was honestly mostly the conflict with my manager, because she was my best friend. . . . [I]t created a rift in our friendship." Therefore, friendships may lead younger workers both into and out of retail.

Whether they applied to a variety of stores or were recruited, almost all workers completed an application, either online or in person, during the hiring process. Retail applications ask about age, gender, race, criminal history, and work availability; they also include multiple-choice questions involving different customer scenarios and basic arithmetic. However, the hiring managers that we spoke with emphasize that assessments of the applicants' availability play a particularly outsized role in hiring decisions. Julian, a manager, says of hiring workers at H&M, "I think availability is the biggest reason we would have to rule someone out." Employers often require workers to be flexible at the point of hire, prioritizing availability over any specific skillset.[33]

After receiving the applications, store managers invite applicants for interviews (depending on the store, these may be one-on-one or group interviews). These interviews are crucial, too, though they rarely focus on whether applicants have any background in sales or fashion.[34] Tara comments that the American Eagle manager doesn't seem to judge applicants' experience "because obviously . . . retail and stuff, like it's someone's first job," but whether they are "personable, because you're dealing with people all the time." During Sabrina's group interview, Urban Outfitters managers asked about the applicants' favorite television shows: "The [other] girls would always try and bring it back to like their sales experience and stuff. But I was just like, 'Well, I like the show *House*.'. . . And it just so happened that both of the managers were like obsessed with *House*." Sabrina got the job. Stacey laughs, calling her hiring interview at Old Navy "wicked informal." The hiring manager, she says, "was so friendly; she was so bubbly and . . . she was just like, 'Oh, my God. We definitely want you here. Like, you're awesome.'" Assessments of applicants' cultural tastes, demeanor, and likeability, alongside their scheduling availability, appear to be far more influential in their hiring than experience or relevant skills.

Specific social traits or "demeanors" form the "soft skills" aspects of service work, especially interactions with customers.[35] Racial discrimination becomes part of the process when employers make judgments about how "warm" and "approachable" applicants and workers seem based on racist stereotypes. For example, Kathleen, who is Black, performed as the top seller almost as soon as she began working at a New York City boutique. She relays a cringe-inducing moment when her manager attempted to compliment her performance, but instead highlighted the store's exclusionary employment history:

> [The manager] was like, "Wow, you're doing really good. . . . You want to hear a fun fact?" I'm like, "What is it?" She's like, "You're the first African American girl we ever hired." I asked them: "Why is that?" I thought that it was racist or something. She was like, "No, we just never had somebody that really had good spirit that came in that was African American."

Workers must possess the appropriate "spirit" and "look" to convincingly signal their ability to perform customer service in clothing retail jobs. These idealizations draw on wider societal values about which racial and gender groups exude desirable forms of warmth, conviviality, and beauty.[36] While Kathleen was recognized as having a "good spirit," and indeed became a top seller, her manager had excluded other Black workers from the job.

Determining "fit" may also require assessing whether potential workers understand the store brand. In job interviews, some managers expect applicants to describe the store, its clientele, and its merchandise. During her interview at Free People, Carmen, whose story opened this chapter, was asked by the managers: "'What do you think the age range is for our store?' And it was an exact number . . . like 22. I was like, 'Oh, I thought it was a range.' She was like, 'No, it's 22.'" Thus, job interviews not only test respondents' knowledge of the store but also educate potential workers about the brand and its target customer base. Managers may then use consumer experience, store knowledge, and style to help identify the applicants who "fit" the brand.

When applicants' skills are brought up, these questions too tend toward determining brand fit. During Pac Sun's interview with Joyce, the manager had her "pick out different outfits. And, she asked me about my opinions on certain displays and certain styles, [. . .] how I would approach different customers." Other interviewees responded to scenario-based questions to communicate their orientation toward customer service. Managers, our interviewees say, *occasionally* attempt to ascertain how applicants handle challenging situations and function in teams, and gauge their commitment to the job, as well as how they feel working in a "diverse" atmosphere.

Whether they were recruited by managers, submitted applications at numerous stores, or were enticed by friends and other workers, our interviewees' paths into clothing retail varied. Yet unlike other research, we did not find that they primarily valued their jobs for providing proximity to friends, a "fun" work environment, or even association with brand prestige.[37] Instead, they see these entry-level jobs as simply that: jobs.

ON-THE-JOB TRAINING

While requiring little experience, managers paradoxically provide new hires with little training. Many respondents laughed when we asked about training processes, pointing us instead to the impersonal process of corporate onboarding. Nearly all of the stores have new hires watch a sequence of corporate videos about shop-floor tasks and company expectations. Beyond that, most training involved learning by doing, often during peak store hours with customers bustling about and forming queues for the next available cashier or vacant fitting room. "A lot of times they kind of feed you to the wolves, put you in on Saturday or really busy times," Steve says of his job at Kohl's. Carl uses similar language about his start at J. Crew: "I got thrown in the deep end on a Saturday, like my first real day, so it was traumatic. . . . I pretty much knew what I was doing after that Saturday because you don't have much time to learn; you just have to figure it out." Retail employers' investment in their workforces' skill development, especially new hires, is bare-bones.[38]

This means that, while some workers describe—in detail—learning skills like precise, company-mandated folds and clothing design types, more training time focuses on "loss prevention" (also referred to as "shrinkage") or minimizing shoplifting. Glenn remembers at Abercrombie Kids: "You have to watch a video . . . [about] how to spot people stealing from the store." The scripts for dealing with shoplifters include offering to hold their items at the register and chatting them up. "[K]ill them with kindness," is how Tia summarizes Forever 21's approach to loss prevention. Liz says much the same about Hollister: "You just talk to [suspected shoplifters] profusely. And I just, I don't understand that tactic at all." What these workers may not know is that some stores have been sued for wrongly accusing patrons of shoplifting; thus workers' scripts for avoiding shrinkage now focus on talking to potential shoplifters as a soft dissuasion technique.

Workers question some of these routinized training efforts. For example, Marty claims of Target: "In dealing with conflict with customers, they really gave us nothing really except if we [were] being robbed, they would tell us, 'Give them the money.' In terms of our customer arguing with us, nothing really." Most emphasize minimalist training models that direct workers to interact using rigid scripts, mirroring findings in other studies of service work, but rarely address techniques for workers who may face racist and hostile customers.[39]

Respondents describe the most detailed training at stores that target a wider customer demographic. Joyce completed an eight-hour computer-based training session for Macy's "on everything: on how to use the register, the best way to approach customers, on detecting theft."

Figure 4. Sales associate selling clothing to a woman. SOURCE: iStock.com/RyanJLane.

Corinne compares the detailed training she got at J.C. Penney to teen-oriented stores Forever 21 and Abercrombie & Fitch, commenting: "There wasn't any like customer-oriented training for either of those stores.... I think that it's definitely because they're more of a teenage store." The age of the store's target customer base seems to impact training content. Teen-branded stores seem to invest less in formally developing a skillset, perhaps because they have both high worker and high customer turnover (recall from the introduction that both groups will age out of these brands). Stores that cater to a wider age range of customers may benefit more from the long-term customer loyalty built by skillful customer service—the kind older shoppers are more likely to expect.

On-the-job training is where most workers in this sector learn how to perform their roles. Many workers initially shadow coworkers, even other entry-level staff, who act as key sources of information. Stacey remembers at Old Navy: "I was constantly asking other associates questions when I started. You know, it's very situational-based where you can't always teach someone something; it just has to happen and they learn." Others spoke of managers engaging in random "teachable moments" to train employees. That's how it went for Cheryl at Victoria's Secret: "A couple times my manager went up to me and was like, 'What's a better way that you could have greeted that customer?' And I'm like, 'I could have asked open-ended questions instead?'"

LOW WAGES AND NO RAISES OR BENEFITS

As they gain experience, workers learn sales techniques and may expand their responsibilities beyond greeting, folding, and stocking shelves to more challenging tasks such as cashiering or creating merchandise displays. The increase in responsibility is not, however, rewarded; most retail workers will wait years before earning a noticeable raise in their meager hourly earnings. Not only that, management, ensuring that no individual worker goes beyond part-time hours (to minimize employer liability toward full-time workers), will adhere to just-in-time scheduling practices that include posting schedules with little notice, varying the hours each employee gets each week, and making in-the-moment decisions to call in unscheduled employees during busy times and send home workers whose shifts end up being "dead."[40] Our workers report being paid between $8 and $9 per hour, with some department store workers receiving more. They are almost entirely part-time or seasonal. Only managers receive full-time schedules and benefits.

Workers express dissatisfaction with their wages, even though they are relatively young and most are not fully reliant on their wages for survival.[41] Being resigned to low pay is reflected in Lillian's explanation that at Abercrombie, "It's not a job that someone would try to have if they need to pay for bills, et cetera because they will not make enough." Other workers more openly vent their frustration with the stagnant pay: "My least favorite part about it is how much they expect out of you," Charlotte states regarding Hollister. "When they don't give you anything in return, like I have made minimum wage since I started. I've been there for four years." When the workplace involves repeated disrespectful interactions with managers and customers, these complaints are compounded. As Danielle comments: "Honestly, I didn't like how I was treated when I was working at Old Navy. And, I guess I felt like I did more for the store than what I was being paid." These workers recognize that their labor is worth more than their paychecks indicate. They assign value to doing a good job and desire, even if they don't explicitly demand, fairer compensation.

Few retail clothing workers receive commissions. Generally, higher-price-point stores may provide a commission, but only after sales workers meet their daily goal. Stella, who receives a commission in this way at Macy's, appreciates the boost: "If you make a $4,000 [sale] you've pocketed $40, easily." Kathleen, who worked at a boutique, remembers, "If my weekly goal is $1,000 and I sold $1,200 worth of merchandise, then I'll get an extra $100 in my check." Although uncommon, commissions elevate otherwise low and unmoving base wages.

That "unmoving" part is important: most workers never receive a raise while maintaining employment with the same retail company. "Raises were sparse," Glenn says about Abercrombie Kids, while Angela stresses how Old Navy's increases are negligible: "It's pennies. To be real honest, I don't keep track of it." Even for employees with multiple years of experience in their position, raises keep them hovering just above minimum wage. Marty, who works at Target, confides:

> My first year I got . . . like five cents. I'm surprised I didn't quit right then and there. . . . I got five cents for the whole year like for a raise, and I thought that was awful, but everyone in my department got that. . . . I've been there for three-and-a-half years, and I'm still only making $9.16 an hour.

Not only are raises scarce, but workers receive little information about how, when, or how much of a raise they might be able to get. David suggests this is true at Abercrombie: "I believe once a year they give out raises. Um, that's the myth."

Workers indicate that how employees are chosen for wage increases feels arbitrary or related to physical attractiveness or friendships with managers, rather than based on work ethic and performance. For example, another Abercrombie staffer, Mary, criticizes the company's distribution of pay raises:

> Like we definitely had girls that would like twirl their hair and just stand there or look at themselves in the mirror or be on their phones. And, I'd be like sweating, running back and forth like doing everybody's job for them. And

like, then they would get the raise. So it's really annoying. . . . [I]t was just like
obviously the most attractive people that worked there [who get raises].

Favoritism and valuing the more passive aspects of aesthetic labor—
standing around wearing the merchandise—are more likely to lead to
monetary rewards.

Workers also suggest that stores manipulate staffing, even terminating
and rehiring the same associates to avoid giving raises. Pauline explains
that Hollister uses this practice: "That way we're never technically in the
system for when they're having their raises." Employers may prefer student workers in part because they are easier to deny raises and other benefits.[42] Retail companies contain costs by minimizing full-time labor while
maximizing part-time and temporary employment.[43]

With few exceptions, the longer our workers are employed in retail
(especially after a year), the more disenchanted they become with their
employers. Despite their hard work, they feel undervalued. A handful
of workers report more positive experiences, including a sense of being
rewarded for their commitment to the company. Brendan recalls that
raises at Pac Sun "were regular." At some point, he "got employee of the
month and they have—they have things called secret shoppers . . . [or
people] pretending to be customers and evaluating their experiences in
the store. And, I got a 100% on the customer rating and everything . . .
so I got a nice raise, too." Julian also describes a supportive workplace.
After three years of working for H&M, a Swedish clothing retailer that has
unusually good benefits and paid leave, he moved into a full-time management position. These promotions and raises make Julian feel both valued
and loyal. These exceptions—our interviewees who noted receiving raises
and workplace recognition—suggest potential improvements for the
entire sector that move beyond just discounted merchandise.

DISCOUNTS AS BENEFITS

Research commonly suggests employee discounts on merchandise are an
alluring aspect of clothing retail work and imagine workers might happily
accept lower pay in return for deeply discounted clothes.[44] Indeed, most

stores offer employee discounts, but they vary widely by amount and timing. And remember, even discounted full-price clothing may remain too expensive for most workers, given their low wages. Still, they often have the first chance to buy clearance items—a perk David appreciates at Abercrombie: "I do buy things on clearance because like in the back we have more clearance than we put out, so I get really good deals on like, stuff . . . that customers don't see."

Our interviewees largely see these discounts as the "best" part of the job, though this positive assessment must be read in context: discounts are the best part of a job in which they otherwise feel devalued.[45] Tia, when asked what she likes most about working at Forever 21, responds drily: "I guess the discount, because I guess a discount is better than nothing at all, but it was still a crappy discount." Others mention that they appreciate the discount, but don't frequently use it for their personal consumption or worry that employee discounts make them captive markets for unsold or underperforming inventory (an issue that we discuss later in the book).

Frequently, however, workers comment that they began buying more apparel at their store *after* getting the job; partially, this is due to the (costly) expectation that they model the store's merchandise while working. Bryan, who works at Abercrombie, says with an edge of bitterness, "That's our uniform, and we're supposed to buy it off of them every season." Costs can be prohibitive when employers require workers to wear full-price items. For example, Lillian, who has worked at American Eagle and Abercrombie, points out, "You barely make enough money and have most of your pay go towards the clothes that you need to buy." Trent, an assistant manager at Express, explains: "That is the biggest problem that we talk [about] amongst staff, because we don't get enough discount, especially for how much our clothes cost." Retail workers largely interpret the requirement to purchase merchandise, coupled with relatively meager discounts and low wages, as a burden (see chapter 6 for a more extensive discussion of this issue).

UNPREDICTABLE SCHEDULING

Since schedules are variable and usually posted with little notice, workers often appear anxious to maximize their hours (and therefore weekly wages). Frank notes that getting enough hours at TJ Maxx is "the main struggle." Scheduling shortages are particularly common among new employees. Stacey says that when she started at Old Navy, "I only got four hours a week, if at all. There were maybe three or four weeks out of the summer that I didn't get scheduled at all, and that bothered me a lot." Workers clearly cannot survive on low wages, let alone when they are metered out for twelve hours of work over an entire summer. Lance says that at Abercrombie Kids, the worst thing about the job is "the inconsistent hours, because I really needed the work going into college, like one week I'd get a lot, [but] the next I wouldn't."

Retailers don't pay enough for workers to, in Marxist terms, socially reproduce themselves: have enough money to pay for housing, food, and clothing.[46] Instead, retailers continue to evoke the idea that parents or other household members subsidize these workers, and those workers who need more will quit. Traditional-age college students, especially those who can rely on familial support, may be "flexible" enough to adjust to the low pay. But for the majority of workers whom we talked to, this is not feasible; workers need higher pay and more consistent hours to support themselves. And the retailers know that new workers are waiting to fill any open positions. Thus, they make no attempt to maintain their workforce.

Sporadic scheduling practices reflect strategic attempts to increase profits, whereby stores and managers set worker schedules to match consumer demand. This is the practice, mentioned in the introduction, of just-in-time scheduling.[47] Rather than maintaining a smaller staff on which each employee receives a sustainable schedule, most fashion retailers keep a large workforce, with most employees working relatively few hours. Just as labor scholar Brian Halpin finds in his study of a catering company, the workers and managers we interviewed identify the manipulation of schedules as central to keeping costs down.[48] Liz shares Hollister managers' matter-of-fact explanation of this arrangement, "They're like, 'We just have a lot of people, so you're not going to get that many hours.'" Seasonality affects scheduling, too, so that workers find themselves scheduled constantly in December, then working very few hours in mid-January.

The "on-call" system also creates discontent. In these instances, either a frontline manager calls in unscheduled workers, or workers are required to call the store to ask if they are needed before turning up for a shift. Gwen discusses the on-call system at Hollister from a manager's standpoint: "If they haven't made a lot of money that day, they'll be like, 'Don't come in.' But if they are *way* over the, what they are projected to make that day, then they'll call you in, 'cause they have the extra money and they maybe need the extra help." This approach to scheduling reflects how managers use metrics to minimize labor costs: surveillance technologies magnify corporate control of scheduling based on real-time customer traffic in stores.[49] But for workers, it means keeping schedules open and declining other work commitments, schoolwork, and social plans *just in case* they might pick up a few more coveted dollars. Patricia comments about Hollister, "I didn't like having call-ins. They're a pain. . . . I'm just waiting around, you can't make plans," and Carl relays similar grievances about Abercrombie and J. Crew: "I really hate on-call shifts so much because I feel like your day is wasted, like, oh man, am I going to have to work at 6:30 tonight?" More often than not, this approach disrupts workers' lives and means that they don't actually get hours (or earn needed wages).

Even workers who *are* "called in" dislike the system. Leah, at Hollister, remembers: "So, if I started at twelve, I would call at ten and then if they said yes, then I'd have to rush out of my house, because I live like a good ten train stops away, plus a shuttle, plus a bus. . . . Yeah, it was horrible." Abercrombie Kids, Lance complains, "would call you when you weren't supposed to be working and ask if you could work. . . . It sucked. . . . [L]ike, I don't get why they just wouldn't give me the hours in the first place." Employers gain control and flexibility through just-in-time scheduling, while workers experience uncertainty and stress.

When employers notify workers of their schedules also matters.[50] At Target, managers would "post the schedule every Thursday," Elise remarks, "so I wouldn't find out until Thursday whether or not I was scheduled for Sunday." Things were similar for our interviewees across workplaces. Pauline, for instance, emphasizes that the Hollister schedule "was said to be up on Thursday," but often "it wouldn't come up until that Saturday, and I'm just like 'okay, how was I supposed to know I was supposed to work for Sunday if I didn't get it till Saturday night?'" As researcher of the low-wage workforce Nancy Cauthen explains, "These practices create unpredictability for workers both about (1) the number of hours they'll work and get paid for, and (2) the timing of those hours."[51]

Part-time schedules, as the astute reader may have intuited, are frequently stacked, so that each worker holds two or more jobs, trying to cobble together a living wage. But that can make things even trickier, especially when their multiple jobs all use just-in-time scheduling. For Stacey, Old Navy's on-call system "ended up taking away hours from my other job that I could have been working." Before he joined H&M's management team, Julian says:

> It's really hard to have multiple jobs, and we have people that do it, but every company wants open availabilities. . . . I worked full-time at [my other job] and I could only work [at H&M] at night, like 5:30 to close. And having another retail job, I also had to work the weekends, so it's not like I have an office kind of job. . . . I had to work both jobs, so it's kind of tricky.

Frustration arises over not knowing exactly when shifts will end or working extra-long shifts.

Such scheduling issues often occur when store employees must "fold down" and reorganize all the disheveled merchandise throughout the store at the end of busy weekend days, or change the "floor sets" during overnight or very early morning shifts. "I think the longest I ever worked," Hannah says of Aeropostale, "was from, I came in [at] like nine o'clock at night, and we were doing a floor set that was supposed to go until midnight, and I left the store at six the next morning." She adds that these undeclared extensions "weren't very organized." Leah tells a similar story of working a twelve-hour Hollister shift that started at midnight for its "Black Friday" shopping event: "They were like, 'Um yeah, You guys can't sit.' So, we just all just sat on the floor because we were so tired. . . . They're like, 'On your feet.' And there wasn't even a lot of customers either, because it was midnight." These scant opportunities to work many more hours boost their incomes, yet workers wish for more humane conditions, information about shift lengths, and a change to the practice of receiving standard pay for working these nonstandard late hours. Rachel, who works at American Eagle, observes, "A lot of my friends think I make more than I actually do. Yes, especially because I do the overnight work. A lot of people think you make double-time for that. You don't."

Workers understand that their availability is crucial—being free to work at any time helps assure frontline managers that they are "faithful" and deserve to be scheduled for more hours. "It's all depending on availability, like how open they are to work," claims Steve about scheduling at Kohl's. Many feel that if they demonstrate being good, available workers, managers will reward them with additional hours; workers do appear to receive more hours if they have proven themselves. Tara, a shift lead at American Eagle, outlines the scheduling process:

> Typically, you start out with like two shifts, which is about eight hours a week. . . . And then if you're showing improvement and you like do really well, we'll bump you up to like twelve to fifteen. . . . [I]f you prove to us . . . that you want that extra shift, we'll give it to you. You have to show that you want the extra hours and you're willing to work for it.

In the clothing retail market, where there are numerous workers and too few hours to go around for most of the year, employers use schedules as a key form of compensation—giving the "best" workers the best schedules, even if they cannot substantially raise their pay.[52]

How many hours each clothing retail worker receives may also correspond to the quality of their work. Veronica explains regarding the Gap, "I really feel like it's who's most productive, actually. Who's most productive, who, you know, [has] the most sales, [sells] the most [store credit] cards, and all that." If someone is good at folding and cleaning, they are more likely to get the closing shifts, or if they are good at selling, they may get the busy weekend afternoon shifts. Lauren says about Urban Outfitters, "They are always like, 'We really like that you are efficient' . . . so I was always working closing shifts." Most workers see receiving more hours as a reward. Yet as with raises, some remain critical of how employers assign the hours, claiming that managers give "more hours" to workers they are "cool with." While James thinks he is primarily given hours at Nordstrom because he is a good worker, he demurs: "But I would say to a degree that the more the manager liked you, the better chance you had of getting more hours."

On the flip side, the distribution of hours functions as punishment for unwanted employees. Rather than firing people, many respondents recount that managers just slowly reduce workers' hours until they quit. Risa remembers about Zara, "Sometimes I wouldn't get a shift at all, per week. . . . I think that was like their way of trying to make me quit."

Omission from the weekly schedules signals that managers do not favor a worker. Jason claims about Abercrombie, "Most of [the] time not necessarily fire, not give you hours and you would just quit. They would just take you off the schedule. They wouldn't fire you directly. . . . That happened all the time." Gwen, a Hollister manager, has observed this tactic:

> People were just taken off the schedule for weeks at a time, and they would call and say, "I really need to work, do I have hours *this* week," and they'd always say, "I'm sorry, your availability doesn't match what we need." . . . So then they'd have no choice but to look for another job.

Management uses scheduling as a mechanism to both reward "good" workers and punish less liked and unneeded workers (discussed further in chapter 2). Scheduling can even be used to push workers out, thus allowing companies to avoid paying unemployment, which they would have to do if they explicitly terminated workers. These practices are not unique to the retail clothing world but reflect the reality of twenty-first-century service economy jobs: employers don't hire full-time workers (to avoid paying benefits), aim to limit paying wages to only those times when they absolutely need workers in the store, and avoid paying unemployment benefits by not firing but simply ceasing to schedule their employees.

CONCLUSION

Workers tend to experience the organization of clothing retail as challenging. The lax training, low-wage work, and erratic scheduling create many issues for workers, who feel they work hard but see their diligence go unrewarded, at least in terms of raises, scheduling, and promotions. Many will ultimately seek out other jobs, and this will not disrupt such organizational practices; low-wage, low-skilled retail workers are relatively disposable and interchangeable, a situation amplified by the conditions of their employment.[53]

Clothing retail workers also don't think the discounts they receive on store merchandise are financially beneficial or compensate for the low wages, which contrasts with assertions found in other retail studies.[54] In fact, discounts effectively *lower* wages, since workers are frequently required to purchase the clothes they wear at work. Among our participants, who generally receive and use store discounts (even characterizing them as one of the main "perks" of the jobs), we heard explicit criticism of how employers leverage discounts to coerce and manipulate workers into spending at the store.

Rather than providing workers with better pay or benefits (or even deeper discounts), store managers "reward" workers with more hours or improved schedules. At the same time, rather than firing workers they wish to "punish," employers keep them on the payroll but stop scheduling them until the workers quit in search of other employment with more viable income. This labor practice allows retailers to dispose of unwanted workers without paying unemployment benefits.

Retail employers, like other companies in the United States, aim to minimize wages to ensure higher profits. In the past, many employers recognized that they must pay enough so workers could afford shelter and food and feel loyal to their employers.[55] Today, many employers are unconcerned with maintaining a loyal labor force. They use managerial controls, including just-in-time scheduling, to ensure an endless supply of cheap, deskilled labor.[56] Expectedly, these practices may, in fact, undermine customer service and come with their own business ramifications, effects we discuss later in the book.

In sum, retail clothing employers in the twenty-first century appear to have fully embraced—even extended—an unsupportable model of worker relations. Most of their staff cannot support themselves with these jobs, which are low and unreliably paid. Because employers also see the labor required as low skilled and have a ready supply of reserve potential workers, they assert control over the labor process in ways that treat turnover as natural—a reflection of a worker's low motivation rather than an indicator that the company has a fundamental business model problem owing to poor pay and working conditions.[57] Workers in our study complicate this narrative, voicing their motivation to provide good service while calling out corporate practices that aim to disempower them and undermine productivity.

In this chapter, we focused primarily on how retail fashion work is organized, contributing to our larger argument about how employers view these workers as expendable. Some of these managerial practices reflect new surveillance technologies that enable corporate managers to drive decisions about staffing to ensure just-in-time scheduling. However, as these scheduling processes drive down labor costs, we find evidence that they also drive down customer service and loyalty. That is, what's bad for workers might also be bad for business.

PART II Managers, Coworkers,
and Customers

2 Multilevel Management and the Service Panopticon

Eighteen-year-old Liz, who is Black, spent the past summer folding denim shorts, distressed jeans, and other items bearing the Hollister seagull logo. She feels frustrated with multiple aspects of the labor process, including rarely talking to her managers. Alienating experiences in retail stem from unfulfilling and even demeaning relationships, such as infrequent and dismissive interactions with the mostly white frontline managers, who will

> kind of talk to you, but not really. . . . There's no real sense of community. . . .
> They're kind of stand-offish. . . . I'm also paranoid sometimes that people
> don't like me. It might just be me and it's all in my head, but I don't think so.
> I think they're just like, "Whatever." Everybody's doing their own thing.
> They're not all that friendly.

Liz sees her managers as neither "mean" nor "strict," but she worries that they don't like her. The need for managerial approval is built into retail's organizational structure, which assigns the tasks of hiring, training, supervising, and disciplining entry-level employees to frontline, store-level managers. Workers seek validation from these store-level managers, each other, and customers to develop a sense of belonging and worth within their retail labor experience.

Management, however, structures clothing retail workplaces to focus interactions on improving the quality of the employees' output—in Liz's case, precisely fastening security buttons onto sweaters and jeans. Many of Liz's interactions with management consist of blunt corrections to her work. For example, as she was learning how to do her job, her managers were always there to comment on what she was doing wrong: "The nice thing is that," says Liz, who lowers her voice to continue, "and [the] bad thing is that usually there's somebody there. And, they'll just look at it and be like, 'That's not right.'"

The only other guaranteed interaction occurs at the end of her shift, when a manager pokes around in her purse to prevent internal theft, as Liz recounts:

> Every single day, after your shift, you clock out and then they escort you out and they check your bag. They say, "Open up all of your stuff," and they check to see if you stole anything. Even if you're just going in there to shop . . . if you're not even working that day . . . they still have to walk you out, to check your bags and stuff.

Rather than allowing this search to annoy her, Liz accepts the treatment: "It's fine. I know I don't steal." Her managers quickly check her pockets and bag, but do not "frisk you and wand you down," leading Liz to recognize this practice as searching all employees to comply with corporate policy. She knows corporate management assigns store managers the job of constantly watching the workers, whether it's to judge how they attach security tags to the merchandise or checking to make sure they aren't stealing.

Frontline managers perform surveillance inside of the store, while corporate managers closely, and often remotely, monitor store workers and managers. Liz reasons that Hollister's store managers follow corporate rules because "they have these things like secret-shoppers, I guess. They're people from management that come and see if the employees are doing what they're supposed to do, the store looks the way it's supposed to look." If the workers break the rules, "it would be a bad reflection on the company or the managers." Liz recognizes that her managers have their own bosses and that corporate dictates general store procedures.

In this chapter, we focus on frontline and corporate managers. We consider how workers view management, given that the structure of work appears to extract so much effort from employees like Liz, despite offering few rewards. We further discuss how race and gender impact these relationships, observing that white workers develop closer ties to store managers and that women experience more pressure to be friendly to customers. In addition, we examine the tensions between managers and workers shaping the clothing retail labor process. To do so, we delve into remote surveillance technologies in these twenty-first-century retail workplaces that create constant corporate management oversight at each store location. Such technologies place frontline store managers in the supervisory position of surveilling workers (and customers), while corporate managers surveil them from afar. Corporate control strategies, including both direct (through frontline managers) and indirect (through technologies) surveillance, largely explain the strength and closeness of allegiances that form in this workplace, as well as worker defiance of corporate directives.

Michel Foucault theorizes that the organization of modern society reflects the "panopticon," or the potential for everyone to be watched as they go about their lives.[1] This ubiquitous surveillance makes people feel scrutinized to the point that they begin to impose self-discipline, rather than requiring externally imposed discipline.[2] In contemporary twenty-first-century workplaces, extensive surveillance techniques allow employers to limit labor costs through just-in-time scheduling and ensure that workers generate consistent profits. Corporate also uses these technologies to watch customers, prevent shoplifting, and encourage buying more.[3] Corporate management constantly monitors workers *and* frontline managers through a range of technologies capturing how much profit the store is generating in real time, as well as on-site visits and "secret shoppers."[4] District managers are likely to be monitored by those above them, who assess them using the same metrics with which the district managers judge frontline managers.

Even when no one is directly watching them, store managers internalize the surveillance gaze to watch themselves, ensuring that they satisfy their supervisors' expectations, as Foucault also suggests. Workers similarly come to regulate themselves, even in management's physical absence. They may normalize corporate managers' expectations, like Liz, who dismisses getting physically searched after each shift as "fine." Despite these restrictions, workers resist internalization of surveillance by asserting some control in navigating customer service approaches and corporate store policies. Because workers find themselves meeting expectations of not only managers but also customers, they sometimes defy managerial expectations.

LABOR DYNAMICS: THE SERVICE PANOPTICON

Managers and workers may appear to hold direct, opposing interests, as the latter group aims to attain better labor conditions, stability, and pay, while managers endeavor to minimize costs. Routinization, or how routine systems and technology guide work, remains central to the struggle between managers and workers in interactive service work; it is part of the deskilling of workers that makes workers relatively disposable and interchangeable.[5] According to sociologist Robin Leidner, managers may exert control through their selection and training of workers, as well as through surveillance. The routinization of interactive service work entails scripting how workers act and speak to customers.[6] Surveilling workers ensures that they stay on message and carry out their routinized tasks.

Customer presence in the service sector changes a binary relationship into what scholars argue is a worker-manager-customer triangle.[7] For example, routinization in service industries requires that the work be fairly predictable and that customers be willing to engage in the organizational routines. While routinization may alienate workers, demanding they act "unnaturally" and in deference to management, it may also give them some control in their relationships with customers. Leidner conceptualizes the service labor process as one that does not include a "stable pattern" of workers and managers with opposing interests, but instead features "a complex dynamic in which each of three groups of participants has interests that sometimes bring themselves into alliance, [and] sometimes in opposition with the other two."[8]

Managers and workers still struggle with one another; however, both managers and workers assert claims in the name of good service, making customers essential to understanding worker-manager relations.[9] Shoppers sometimes boycott stores that engage in unfair labor practices but also complain to managers about poor service on other occasions.[10] Workers aim to treat customers well but prevent them from breaking store policies. Managers rely on customer feedback to assess workers, while also deploying workers to police customer shoplifting. Even as managers use customer feedback to broaden their power, workers wield customer satisfaction as a tool to resist managers.[11] In most interactive service workplaces, this "both-and" dynamic characterizes the unstable relations between customers, managers, and workers.

Recognizing key power differentials between frontline managers and senior managers, we assert that dynamics between frontline managers, corporate managers, workers, and customers form a quadrangle, rather than a triangle as previously theorized.[12] Our conceptualization of the service labor process recognizes the important power relations between management levels. We separate these two layers of management because retail workers' accounts reveal important differences in how frontline managers (in-store supervisors) and corporate managers (district, regional, and corporate managers who occasionally visit stores) exercise control.

Frontline managers directly and visibly surveil workers, while corporate managers directly and indirectly monitor both workers and frontline managers. This process creates what we refer to as a "service panopticon," emphasizing the key role that surveillance plays in this industry. Although corporate managers aren't visibly present each day, their remote and constant surveillance of the stores sustains their influence over how these workplaces operate. Corporate management uses constant communication with frontline managers, as well as automatically reported metrics on store foot traffic, customers, and purchases. Both frontline managers and workers conform to and occasionally resist the use of these technologies, which they suggest lead to lower-quality customer service. Changes in labor practice, then, create opportunities for both worker resistance and managerial domination.[13]

RELATIONSHIPS WITH MANAGERS

Workers' interactions with store managers impact the quality of their job experience. Frontline managers, present in the store each day, shape the collegiality or isolation that employees feel in their workplace. Frontline management includes store managers, assistant managers, and managers specializing in worker supervision, product displays, or merchandise processing, as well as shift leads who have a key to the store and monitor the staff from a more lateral position. In fashion stores targeting younger clientele, store managers are often recent college graduates in their early to mid-twenties. Their youth creates common ground between them and a portion of the sales workers, allowing more casual relationships to develop. Closer ties with store managers can translate into material benefits, including better schedules with more hours and predictability. Compared to whites, workers of color characterize relationships with managers as primarily professional, or what Liz, whom we discussed at the beginning of this chapter, refers to as "stand-offish." Workers also distinguish between their relationships with frontline and more distant corporate managers.

Employees often portray frontline managers as professional in their treatment of workers. The in-store managers aim at having pleasant interactions with their staff. Julian, who is a manager at H&M, exemplifies this approach: "I try to kind of make everybody have a good day. I'm not someone who demeans or looks down on people. That's never been my style so . . . whether you're on my level, you're below me, you're above me, I treat you with the same respect." Jason argues that his Abercrombie managers "try to make you as comfortable as possible," unless the worker repeatedly makes the same mistakes, such as missing shifts, talking to coworkers, and not completing tasks; "that is when they would really crack down." When managers discipline workers, they often do so politely. Frontline managers suggest that they try to maintain a comfortable and productive workplace. Most workers describe managers taking individuals aside and requesting that they avoid future missteps—unless they consistently make errors.

Beyond such moments, some workers identify their overall relationships with managers as neutral. Many Asian, Black, and Latinx workers report this experience. Cecilia (Asian) and Bryan (Latino) recall their J.C. Penney and Abercrombie managers, respectively, as greeting them and doling out task assignments, but not engaging socially. Denise, who is Black, also says that her Abercrombie managers are "very professional," expressing that "they didn't have the kind of relationship where we'd joke about things, it wasn't really like that. . . . I don't know them on a personal level." Workers of color describe their frontline managers as businesslike, and in larger stores, as not necessarily remembering their names. Corinne (Asian) shares her experience of this estrangement at Forever 21, where the manager "never really spoke to me because there was no reason to, I guess." We hear this "professional" characterization across participants in ways that illuminate less vibrant and sociable relationships between store managers and Asian, Black, and Latinx workers. As discussed in the next chapter, workers of color also describe more distant connections with their white coworkers, especially in stores with mostly white employees.

White workers are more likely to regard their relationships with managers as "very friendly." For whites, similarities between workers and store managers can help create a pleasant, sociable environment, particularly when managers are in a similar age range. Sabrina, who is white, comments on the relaxed atmosphere at Urban Outfitters:

> It was a very casual relationship . . . you can joke around, and swear with them and talk about what you did on the weekends, and even if it's not typically something that you would talk about with your boss . . . and they would talk about their relationships . . . probably because they were so close to all of our ages too, that's part of it.

Many other white workers detail having affable relationships with their managers. For instance, Stacey says her Old Navy store managers are "awesome," noting that when her assistant manager passes her: "He'll put his hand up for a high-five just to high-five. . . . It's just encouraging in such a, not strange way, but . . . he's acknowledging you. He's giving you a high-five because you're doing your job." Regular, upbeat exchanges with managers bring some fun into the workplace and convey appreciation.

Positive and affirming experiences help root a sense of fondness toward managers and the store. Jill (white) explains that "the interactions with [Forever 21] managers were very friendly. It wasn't very superior/inferior. I mean, it was, but not—it was very comfortable. We all joked around. It was very friendly and inviting." The friendliness between managers and workers eases the feeling of management being inherently adversarial to workers. White workers often report that their managers are empathetic and generous. Carolyn, for example, says of her Hollister manager: "If anyone ever had a problem, they would not hesitate to talk to her . . .

Figure 5. Smiling manager. SOURCE: iStock.com/monkeybusinessimages.

she is very understanding." Melissa (white) beams when speaking of her J.C. Penney store manager: "I love her. She is the sweetest thing, so nice; like . . . I had a ticket to a concert and I was scheduled to work, couldn't find anyone, she got it covered for me." Generous acts establish a sense of appreciation through granting flexible allowances, which matters when workers earn relatively little and face ever-shifting schedules.

Some workers of color also share close relationships with managers. Brendan (Asian) characterizes his managers at G.H. Bass: "You're my boss and I'm going to do what you tell me to do, and that's about it," but he enjoyed spending time outside of work with his previous supervisors at Pac Sun: "It was a lot more chill. It was more friendly. I considered my managers [to be] friends. . . . They would invite us to their house parties and all that kind of stuff." Lori, who is Black, also discusses one of her Wet Seal managers as "really chill, really laid back, and she really made you want to come to work." Mary (multiracial) states that at Abercrombie "we all had the same sense of humor and we were all friends, like we would go out to eat together all the time. . . . It was definitely different than any other job I've had 'cause you don't really do that with your bosses." As for most white workers, these "chill" relationships with managers improve the job and stem from shared identities and mutual respect.

White workers' better relationships with managers can pay off, literally, generating more stable incomes by determining schedules. Managers may treat their favorite employees to more hours or preference over shifts. Glenn, who is white, reports that at Hollister, "if you click with the manager well, I'd say that's really important, too. I had a manager that we got along pretty well so they were like, 'Oh, you can be on register.'" James (white) refers to workplace politics at the upscale department store Nordstrom: "The more somebody likes you, especially if you ask for something, if you ask for a day off, you know." Closer relationships lead to better schedules and assignments. Interestingly, white men were the most likely to discuss how their close relationships with employers meant that they received longer hours and more stable schedules.

Workers of color who develop strong relationships with their managers also benefit from closeness. Jason (multiracial) highlights the importance of these relationships at Abercrombie:

> It would also matter, like who you were close with, you know? . . . If you're cool with the store manager . . . then they would always have people that they enjoy working with, that they enjoyed talking to. . . . Yeah. The managers were just as social as anyone else.

Managers do not want to work alongside employees whom they do not like; thus, strong ties with managers leads to better shifts, including for workers of color. Risa, who is Asian, recalls benefiting from favoritism at Zara: "My manager loved me. She was very flexible with my hours." Tia (Black) acknowledges the potential repercussions if Forever 21 managers don't like a worker: "In general, it was more like, I don't know, you just have to be nicer to co-managers or else they'd mess up your schedule." Many workers reiterate that managers will "mess up your schedule" if they don't like you, providing more nuance to how important scheduling is when workplaces don't have to guarantee a certain number of hours to workers.

Gender also influences relationships between frontline managers and workers. Both men and women report good or neutral relationships. However, only women report seriously problematic relationships with a manager, often referring to contemptuous behavior. For example, Tia refers to one manager who "stopped being condescending when she found out that I went to [an elite, predominantly white prep school] because she went to their academy." Tia emphasizes her equivalent background to counter her manager's racism and elitism. Cheryl (multiracial) characterizes most of her managers at Victoria's Secret as friendly, but says one was "scary," noting, "we were all intimidated by her." Women workers are more likely to describe managers with whom they did not enjoy working, and who might treat workers in condescending ways. Melissa (white) feels that tone can become irksome among some J.C. Penney managers:

> There's a different way of showing your authority. . . . I know if I was a manager, I wouldn't talk the way some do; with a tone. I feel like they should be very neutral, and you shouldn't be . . . some of them are just like kind of aggressive with their tone, that's like . . . it just puts you in a bad mood.

Pauline, who is Black, further attests to the importance of manners when remembering a new Hollister manager:

> When she came in people called her a Nazi because she like so crazy and like so like, there's a difference between following the rules and like in pounding it into people's heads. You know what I mean? Because I believe that if you want people to listen to you and respect you, you have to earn it.

For Pauline, asking workers to obey the rules is not a problem, but "pounding it into people's heads" makes the woman a lousy manager. Melissa and Pauline do not dispute that managers should hold authority but critique *how* some do that. Danielle (multiracial) also recounts her interactions with an Old Navy manager on her second day of work as inducing an immediate desire to quit:

> She would tell me I'm going too slow and she would yell at me. . . . I don't know what to say because I was new there, so I wanted to cry. I was like, "Oh, okay. Sorry." She would just yell. . . . I really wanted to quit then. I was like, "Wow, I don't want to be treated like this." Like, you should work in a place where you feel comfortable, not where you feel like it's a hostile environment.

We heard several similar accounts about management mistreatment of women staff. Workers seek respect from their managers. Men do not disclose these more unpleasant relations with managers, but women across race report such run-ins. Managers may be less likely to treat men with condescension, or men simply may be less likely to disclose such moments.

Workers experience weaker ties with corporate managers, who visit more rarely. Grace details this dynamic at TJ Maxx: "As retail teams go, our managers are very good. They really care about us, [but] corporate could do better with the way that they manage associates." Frontline managers are closer to workers in age, rank, and proximity, making alliances easier to forge; corporate managers may be older and don't get to know the workers as well. Mary portrays Abercrombie upper management as less caring: "The district managers—they're not always like great. We've only had one district manager that was like a normal human being, and the rest were like, very like, I don't know, just rude." While Mary's referring to district managers as not "normal human beings" may seem extreme, her characterization encapsulates what many other workers suggest: their corporate managers do not treat them with the respect and dignity they believe they deserve.[14]

David, however, offers a friendlier view, telling a story about establishing a pleasant relationship with the Abercrombie district manager:

> Even the district managers, they might seem like tough cookies, but . . . when I met my first district manager . . . I was like . . . "I'm David. Are you the district manager?" He's like, "Yeah." I'm like, "I haven't met you, so it's nice to finally meet you." Right away we made it a connection that other people don't have because [they are] scared to come up to the district manager. . . . I try to make it friendly. . . . "I know you're my boss, cool, but . . . you have a heart, you have a life." So, he was really nice to me right away.

Although David knows that other workers, including his frontline managers, are anxious around the district manager, he established a rapport with the senior manager. David, a straight-identifying white man, is the only worker who reports positive interactions with corporate management.

MANAGER EXPECTATIONS

Workers observe that managers expect employees to keep the store clean, provide friendly service to the customers, and not steal any merchandise. While these are reasonable expectations, workers claim that if too few

Figure 6. Folded and size-figured clothing. SOURCE: iStock.com/JaysonPhotography.

people are scheduled for the shift, it can be difficult or even impossible to produce friendly service and maintain a tidy environment. Carrying out these expectations requires scheduling an appropriate number of workers.

Keeping the store neat and presentable is a central task, though few workers enjoy the endless folding and neatening.[15] Melissa explains the objective at J.C. Penney is to "keep the store clean, and constantly clean the store." One of the challenges in this job is that customers relentlessly *unfold* clothes and destroy displays. Workers must "constantly clean" their areas of the store to keep up with this task.[16] Yet managers insist that rooms be, as Carl describes at J. Crew, "spotless at all times." Pauline notes that Hollister managers enforce clear rules about tidiness: "Because this is the main room that people come into, the rule is no more than three items unfolded. Everything else has to be perfectly lined up, size figured." She illustrates how Hollister managers actively remind workers to maintain corporate standards each shift.

Almost every worker also emphasizes the importance of providing friendly, helpful service to customers. Veronica says that Gap "customers come first," so that "if you're folding, you need to make sure you go up around the store, making sure you ask everybody, are they okay? . . . Do they need any help? Do they need to check another store for something? So, it was always customer service." Frontline managers want workers to engage with customers while completing other tasks. Corporate managers monitor these activities through "secret" or "mystery" shoppers.[17] Julian, a frontline manager at H&M, discusses how monthly mystery shoppers "score us based on if people greet them and how clean the store looks and how [the] fitting room is." Corporate managers evaluate each store on its presentation and whether workers follow the store's scripted greeting and thank you lines. For example, managers ask secret shoppers to record how many seconds passed before they were greeted and if workers welcomed them using the right script. Mystery shoppers help keep both frontline managers and workers on their toes, since *any customer* might actually be reporting to corporate. This possibility encourages frontline managers to watch workers closely and workers to follow scripts faithfully.

Women speak at length about the importance of acting friendly, warm, and outgoing while they are working. Being approachable entails asking questions and acting "like you want to be involved in their purchases," as Nora explains about American Eagle, which means engaging with customers on why they are shopping and what kinds of merchandise might meet their needs. Managers also attempt to cultivate a friendly vibe in the sales staff. Some men mention the importance of exuding warmth, such as James, who argues that at Nordstrom, "those things definitely were enforced, big time," and later notes, "You always had to have a smile on your face." However, some men are less emphatic about these requirements, like Bryan, who says, "[Abercrombie managers would] like you to be more interactive like that, but it's not like they demand it." Some women, like Melissa, draw attention to the gender expectations behind being friendly, saying about J.C. Penney: "You have to seem like a perky . . . like [a] stereotypical woman, I guess. . . . [I]f you're quiet you are automatically labeled as weird or antisocial." These accounts fit with our in-store observations. While women workers usually are friendly and interact with customers, men may simply smile, or even nod at customers without smiling. Across race, women more often identify friendliness as a strong expectation from their managers and, in our experience, more regularly enact warmth with shoppers.

In teen-oriented fashion stores, sociability is central to the job because workers not only sell clothes but also represent a brand. Denise describes this directive at Abercrombie & Fitch: "We were trained to smile and be really friendly and upbeat, I would say, mirroring that cool friend that everybody wants.... Be their friend, basically." Abercrombie stores are poorly lit, with loud music, imparting a "club vibe." For Denise, friendly workers are part of this "vibe," appearing as potential friends. Managers emphasize approachability and shared style as an important type of customer service workers provide for their brand.

A final requirement is that workers shouldn't steal merchandise or cash. Some workers share gossip about theft. The tone of these stories suggests that workers recognize a consistent corporate gaze over the store and would never themselves steal. For example, Brendan discloses a story about a Pac Sun manager: "They had caught wind that he was doing false returns and false exchanges and pocketing the money, leaving a paper trail.... They built a case and ... he's got a lot of felonies on him now. Yeah, so don't steal. Don't skim anything." Most employees have limited opportunity to steal on this scale, but managers scrutinize workers to deter smaller shoplifting incidents. Corporate management ultimately subjects both frontline managers and entry-level staff to ongoing surveillance.

Many workers point out how supervisors check their person regularly as they leave the store. In some cases, workers are only allowed to carry clear plastic bags and purses into the store to further prevent internal thievery. Liz states, regarding Hollister, "Obviously, nobody would want anybody to steal, but like considering the severity of how much they surveillance [*sic*] that, and following you all the time and just like checking your stuff, I think [not stealing] is a big expectation." Several workers regard this intimate surveillance as a necessary evil that managers must do to ensure honesty. However, this practice often requires employees to "clock out" *before* they are checked, so that workers experience wage theft by not being paid for this time, which is a part of the expectations for their continued employment.[18]

All in all, managers require workers to keep the store clean, be friendly and approachable, and not steal, and they regularly enforce these expectations. Workers find it challenging to keep the store neat and remain approachable when a shift is understaffed, which may also have gendered outcomes since women appear to experience more pressure to be friendly. The constant surveillance of workers makes these elements of the job challenging, but workers point to other managerial expectations that are even more problematic.

WORKER RESISTANCE TO SCRIPTS, UPSELLING, AND SCAMMING

Workers express substantial conflict about managerial expectations that they see as undermining customer service.[19] Many of these expectations come from corporate managers and are enforced by frontline managers, yet both frontline managers and workers express resistance to these approaches, including following simplistic scripts, upselling customers merchandise they don't want or need, and encouraging customers to apply for credit cards that might harm their finances. Workers consider long-term customer satisfaction in arguing against these practices.[20] Perhaps because they identify with the customers, these workers may also be more protective of them.[21] Workers and some frontline managers contest managerial requirements that they see as counter to customer interests, allying with customers when they believe that the store's long-term interests reside in building better relationships with their patrons. Their resistance, however, was often identified by the surveillance metrics embedded in their workplace and thus had material consequences for them.[22]

Scripted Service

Sales staff generally see friendly service as a reasonable expectation, but communicate frustration about *how* they are supposed to enact a routinized friendliness. Many employers systematize service provision by scripting interactions with customers.[23] Workers at some teen-oriented stores detail strict enforcement of corporate's specific scripts. In our interviews, workers often parroted this task to us, highlighting the dull, repetitive nature of greeting customers throughout a shift. Denise rehearses the salutation wearily: "Welcome to Abercrombie & Fitch. Half off on all our jeans today. Do you want to know about such-and-such promotion?" Gwen, a manager at Hollister, states that greeters should:

> Say one of five phrases, "Hey, what's up?" "How's it going?" "Welcome to the Pier." There's a whole script of things you can say, and then when every person leaves you have to say, "Have a good one," or "See you soon." . . . You have to say one of these five things to every single customer that comes in and every single customer that leaves.

Noting that this requirement means that the entrance room to the store is a "tense" environment, she adds, "I tried to stay out of there" to avoid the monotony as well as the frustration workers express. As part of frontline management, Gwen recognizes that rather than making them persuasive salespeople, extreme reliance on the scripts drains workers.

Greeting is key to managers' expectations of friendliness and thus an enforced routinized practice. Gabe relays, "We were expected to greet customers within one minute of them walking in [American Eagle]." Jason similarly says about Abercrombie, "Every single person that walks in that room, you have to . . . say something. . . . 'Can I help you find something?'" In addition to secret shoppers, Glenn identifies managers at Abercrombie Kids as surveilling workers' compliance with scripts: "Sometimes the managers hide behind . . . indoor plants in there. They'll go to the other side and if they don't hear you welcoming every single person, you'll get yelled at because they really want you talking to everyone." Intensive monitoring allows managers to immediately discipline workers and ensure they meet the job's routinized demands.

Yet following the scripts can feel graceless. For example, Claire regards Hollister's required greeting as discourteous to older shoppers:

> They don't want you to say "Hi, how are you." They want you to be like "Hey, how's it going," or like "what's up," to sound more low key, relaxed. . . . If there was a seventy-year-old woman that came in the store, I couldn't be like "Hi, ma'am, how are you," I had to be like, "How's it going," like relaxed. It was so weird; it was horrible. I hated it.

Claire sees following the corporate-provided scripts as undercutting the quality of customer service, recognizing that customers of different ages may have different expectations for how workers should talk to them. Grace recalls about TJ Maxx:

> At one point, one of my managers was standing next to me and stayed there just to make sure that I was saying "hi" to everybody. . . . He was like, "Make sure you say hi to this girl," and she was talking on the phone, and I was like, "Do you want me to pull her aside and say hello?" I don't know, it was just very strange for me and it just felt very forced.

The artificial nature of following the script, no matter the circumstances, makes it difficult to interact casually with customers. Even as managers monitor employees, workers seek to resist routinized scripts and provide more sociable customer service.

Pauline finds it frustrating that she must deliver Hollister's confusing script to market perfumes (titled Malaia and Jake) during the customer checkout process: "Have you met Malaia or Jake?" Lance refers to Hollister's script as "a cheesy pick-up—not pick-up, the slogan, 'Have you tried our new scent?'" While Lance corrects himself, saying the greeting was a slogan rather than a pick-up line, the forced casual tone of these scripts helps explain his slip of the tongue and illuminates the greeting's somewhat sexualized nature. Workers at stores that primarily sell underwear (such as Victoria's Secret and Gilly Hicks) also cringe at the greetings they must utter. For example, Hannah describes how at Australian-themed Gilly Hicks, workers had to refer to panties as "downundies," even when customers didn't understand this reference:

> You have to tag [greet] everyone no matter what it is, and for the longest time it was "Hi, welcome to Gilly Hicks. Please check out our cute downundies." And older men and guys would walk into the store and they'd stop and be like, "Your what?" And I'd be like, "Our cute downundies," and they're like "Um, ok. If you say so." So, so weird. But that was the prompt, so that's what you had to do.

Several workers comment that corporate's requirement to use the scripts with every customer stripped them of needed discretion; women describe finding the scripts uncomfortably sexualized and creepy.

Managers attempt to monitor routinized verbal interactions between sales associates and shoppers, at least in part because they face repercussions based on corporate-led surveillance. Even if managers are out of earshot, "secret shoppers" might identify offenders. As Lance remarks, "They never liked saying it . . . but they have to because we'll have a secret shopper come in, and if [the workers] don't say it to them, they'll tell the manager. And, that person will get shit for not saying it." These random surveillance practices, routinized greetings, and multilevel management of customer service degrade how workers experience their labor.[24] Workers occupy a delicate position of needing to embrace corporate scripts or risk being rebuked. "If someone's not greeted within ten seconds, you can get in trouble," Mary explains. "Not necessarily from your [Abercrombie] manager, but say if they're a secret shopper, they keep track of that and that's why I think your managers are on you about that." Corporate surveillance plays a key role in enforcing these expectations, even though both customers and workers often wish to circumvent these scripts and awkward interactions.[25]

Why do managers require strict obedience to scripts that clearly don't work? We suspect the answer lies in their reliance on simplistic ways to measure customer service. Corporate could ask secret shoppers to simply note if they were "pleasantly greeted," but this somewhat subjective measure might lead to variations in how different secret shoppers judge stores. Instead, they choose objectively measurable factors, such as "use of specific greeting script within fifteen seconds of entry." By systematizing the work of mystery shoppers, the employer creates the need for workers to follow a stiff script, which ironically lowers the quality of customer service.[26]

Some stores focus less on scripts. Brendan suggests that Pac Sun managers encourage employees to "switch up, spice up" their greetings, making interactions "easy stuff." Lillian voices the potential of permitting worker autonomy in welcoming customers:

> For Abercrombie, you have to say "what's up" when people come, and when people were leaving I would usually say "catch you later." . . . I felt kind of more robotic at Abercrombie, whereas at American Eagle it was kind of more freestyle . . . which I thought was better.

Giving workers more leeway in greeting customers helps them develop more organic, human connections with customers. Stores targeting a wider age range also focus less on scripts to engage the clientele. Trent, a manager at Express, points out that individualizing is crucial for providing good service: "You're not going to say the same thing you are to a forty-five-year old woman as you are to a twenty-year old college bro." One of his responsibilities is "working with the talent [the sales staff]" to help them tailor "what they are saying to be unique and individual each time . . . switching it up and actually paying attention to the customer that's walking in." Trent sees this reflective salespersonship as a skill to develop in his staff, showcasing how frontline management may better identify with workers' need to do creative, cultivated service.

Pushing Back on Sales

Another concern for workers is aggressive selling, oriented toward achieving sales goals, which some workers resist. Retail work has always prioritized selling merchandise, and most workers understand that sales goals are intended to increase company profits. Yet these goals can lead to pressuring customers into making purchases and "upselling" customers, in which workers encourage buying additional items.[27] With corporate's intensifying use of "metrics" to guide store operations, workers and frontline managers share concerns about the unintentional outcomes of these practices. Aggressive "selling" to customers might lead to short-term gains but long-term losses, if customers don't like what they bought or feel pressured by sales associates in particular stores, leading them to avoid those stores. Additionally, many workers interpret an extreme emphasis on selling credit cards (or finance charges) as unethical.

Metrics have become an increasingly important form of surveillance in retail stores, as management now analyzes more and more data to inform decisions. Although stores use different acronyms for these data, they all collect similar metrics. For example, corporate managers gather information about footfalls (the number of customers walking into the store), conversion rates (the number of transactions divided by footfalls), units per transaction (the number of separate items bought in each transaction), average sales (the average amount of money spent in each transaction), and sales per hour (the total amount spent in an hour divided by the number of workers). In addition, corporate managers collect data on sales for the same shift in the previous week, month, and year. They use that information to set goals per shift.

While retailers have long collected sales data to inform management choices, metrics are now transmitted to corporate in real time. While frontline managers used to have autonomy to make decisions, because store data are now always available to corporate managers, decisions are concentrated at the corporate level. Corporate management, however, may be missing important context surrounding the "store performance" metrics. In a sense, these metrics create a new organization of retail work. For example, metrics primarily focus on short-term data, such as how many items a customer buys in the current visit, instead of on how often a customer visits. As a result, they tend to emphasize business decisions that aim at short-term rather than long-term rewards. Corporate managers judge stores on metrics and use them to relay orders to frontline managers, who then emphasize doctrinal sales approaches. In the past corporate managers received these data more slowly and based decisions on the "big picture," but technology now allows retail companies to gather this information instantaneously to, for example, adjust staffing moment to moment.[28] As a result, management's reliance on metrics and remote surveillance is transforming the retail labor process.

As a manager, Trent describes a near-constant flow of information back and forth between his store and corporate. The latter sets the daily sales goals, as Trent explains: "We have a plan, it's given to us every single day, sent down by corporate." Frontline managers then communicate corporate expectations to workers. As Tara comments about American Eagle, "Every morning, our district manager would call and let us know what numbers we have to beat." Angela relates her impression that Old Navy corporate has an exact method to produce sales goals: "They're really scientific how they come to that goal. . . . It's like what you did last year on that day and all these kinds of factors go into that number." Although the managers may be using scientific principles to identify sales goals, they also tend to rely on data that may be problematic or that undermine customer relations and the long-term economic health of a store.

Many managers encourage workers to know the metrics and work to better them. Antonia says that at Express, "there was an overall, store-wide what we want to get, per day and per week type thing." Gabe narrates the pep talk the American Eagle managers gave workers about the goals:

> We've made X amount of dollars already today, we have this many credit cards, our UPT [units per transaction] and our average dollar sale is this, and this is what our goal is. This is how far away we are, and this is what we need from you on your shift.

Estimating that he successfully upsells customers about 25% of the time, Gabe further details his tactics: "If a guy came to the register, I would try to add on boxers. If a girl came, I'd try to say, 'Hey, tank tops are ten dollars each.' Everybody needs tank tops, right? So, I would direct the lower-priced items that were probably on promotion." Sales-related metrics become an omnipresent part of the job, with managers consistently emphasizing them. According to Tia, Forever 21 workers hear hourly updates on their walkie-talkies:

> "Oh, the units per bag or units per customer [the average number of items bought by each customer] is this." They wanted it at a 3.5 or something like that. If it wasn't there, they'd like keep going on the walkie, "Talk to people, blah, blah, blah." If they stop by your floor and you are not talking to anybody, they'll yell at you.

Frontline managers update workers while also disciplining employees when they don't meet sales goals.

To boost the units per transaction metric, managers train workers to sell items, particularly cheaper "add-on" products located near the cash registers. Charlotte says Hollister staff receive daily taglines from corporate for promos such as "two for twelve dollars" on body care items. Sherrie notes that when "ringing up" customers, Pac Sun managers expect workers to recommend purchasing "stuff people don't need," explaining:

> If there was "buy two, get one free" and they only picked out one shirt, they'd be like, "You know if you just grab two more shirts, one of them would be free." It's all about framing in retail. So, they definitely try to push that on us, and they . . . would get mad if we didn't suggest things, "Why didn't you tell them about this? You should have said this." That's one of the few things that they were strict, not strict, but cracked down on.

Some workers resist these practices, even if internally. Sherrie shares her discomfort with upselling customers, illustrating her attempt to maintain her humanity within the customer service exchange: "I don't like to think of myself as just like a selling robot in a store." While Sherrie resists these expectations, managers discipline her for her defiance.

Although workers sympathize with customers who might not want to be upsold, they know that managers are watching them, keeping track of their metrics, and will discipline them when necessary. Risa reflects on this dynamic at Zara: "That was like the thing, the main thing that they focused on was just sales, sales, sales. Like sell, sell, sell as much as you can." She further notes, "Sometimes I would feel bad because you're making people buy more than they really needed." Yet the metrics are relentless. Julian confirms that as an H&M manager, he knows how many pieces each worker sells in each transaction, as does corporate; corporate managers judge stores' sales effectiveness based on the units per transaction metric.

Workers vent about how hard they are pushed to sell, worrying that this strategy might backfire and drive customers away.[29] Patricia expresses concern that the emphasis on selling creates "overbearing" Hollister workers, suggesting that shoppers "expected the opposite of what my bosses expected." Lori discusses her focus on customer service as contrasting with her Wet Seal manager's approach: "I feel like my store manager is more about making sales where I'm more about making customers happy." As Rachel states about working at American Eagle, "I'm going to be a friend before I'm going and push my numbers up." Rachel's and Lori's statements reflect how they relate to customers, buttressing their resistance to orders to sell more. Empathizing with the customers, these workers directly identify managerial strategies focused on upselling as undercutting the positive experience of their customers.

Workers describe feeling uncomfortable about the "pushy" tactics in a variety of ways. Carmen criticizes many items at Free People as "overpriced for things that were going to break, I'm sure, within a couple months," telling a story about a $150 returned raincoat. Carmen saw the item as expensive and poor quality, but the manager convinced another customer to buy it:

> Then when [the customer] came up to get it, to ring it up, she was having doubts about it. And, I was ringing her up by myself, and she . . . was like, "I don't know. I have one that looks exactly like it." I was like, "Then maybe you, like, shouldn't get it." I basically told her not to get it, and she didn't get it.

While Carmen attempts to resist her manager quite directly in this case, she also knows that the store's aggressive selling techniques remain widespread, noting that "they really, really wanted us to sell things. They'd push it so hard on us." Frontline managers add to the pressure around sales goals, simply by remaining in earshot of workers. Danielle states that at Old Navy, "If I was working in close proximity to the managers I'd be like, 'Yeah, you should really get this because I bet it would look great on you.' Even if it doesn't." Danielle has misgivings about encouraging customers to buy clothing that does not flatter them, worrying that it might make them less likely to return to the store. Yet under the surveillance of frontline managers, she pushes sales.

Other workers similarly point out that selling customers clothes that are unbecoming leads to returns, as well as to customers having negative associations with the store. Joyce argues about Macy's:

> I think that a lot of people don't know about those sales goals . . . that can drive associates to be really, really aggressive towards customers too, trying to overly talk to them. . . . Some customers might see it as them being pushy, and it does kind of force them to be a little bit pushy because they're trying to make their goals.

She further comments: "I don't want them to have to come back and make a return, because that would just be a pain." Others emphasize their desire to avoid irate customers, as Pauline explains about Hollister: "I can't have somebody coming back and blame me. . . . 'You told me I looked good in this, but I got laughed at.'" Customers might also avoid stores that have sold them expensive clothing that is unflattering or that they rarely wear. Workers resist relentless upselling from a variety of viewpoints: stress over being pressured, dissatisfaction with the items, greater likelihood of returns. Many workers convey that high-pressure tactics are ineffective and might even discourage customers from shopping in brick-and-mortar stores.

Workers also describe their managers upselling *them*, like Patricia's manager at Hollister, who said, "'Oh my God, this looks so good on you,' but, I was like 'No.'" This experience is common among workers in teen-focused brand stores. Heather recalls:

> My [Forever 21] manager was like, "Oh you should buy this, like buy this, buy this." They would push. . . . They would try to upsell it just because they wanted to get their day's goal. They would be like $100 off and they'd be like, "Anyone need to buy anything? Anyone need to buy anything?" Literally pushing and [workers] would be like, "Oh yeah, maybe." They were literally just asking [workers] to buy something so that they could make their goal, their quota for the day.

Heather sees these practices as "very degrading," explaining that frontline management used workers as customers "because it's like they're literally putting you in there to help them, to help make them look better [to upper-level management]." While we discuss the expectations that workers buy products in more detail later in the book, it's important to note here that managers recognize workers as captive customers. This practice forges alliances between workers and customers, with whom workers readily identify and whom they want to shield from excessive selling tactics.

Meeting sales goals may lead customers to feel hassled and unhappy with purchases. Store-level employees sometimes cannot reconcile metric-driven sales goals with the actual service needs of their customers. While the service panopticon makes workers' scores on metrics immediately visible to managers, the tension within the service quadrangle leads workers to sometimes resist corporate profit strategies to more fully serve the shoppers instead. Workers' experiences as customers inform their conceptualization of "good service," aligning them with customers rather than management in these moments. Workers thus occasionally try to disrupt selling customers bad deals and products, including credit.

Credit Cards

We didn't initially ask about credit cards, but when we asked about the "worst part" of the job, many workers answered with selling credit, asserting their disdain for selling credit cards, though they generate enormous profit for their retail employers. Both rewards cards (or "loyalty cards") and store credit cards, through discounts, encourage customers to buy more frequently and spend more money.[30] These cards also allow the store to analyze their buying patterns and encourage new purchases. While rewards cards track sales, creating a "loyal" customer base of "regulars" and promoting the store's merchandise to customers, credit cards increase profits through finance charges such as interest and fees. Store loyalty and credit cards thus function as a profit-generating customer surveillance mechanism, even as workers consistently resist selling them.

Retailers increasingly profit from the finance charges on debt incurred by customers, with little additional labor cost to the company.[31] Managers emphasize that the cards are good for both the company and the customers (by providing discounts). However, managers may not always be entirely honest about the benefits of these cards. This practice troubles many workers, who know that credit card debt can be a serious problem. Gabe refers to his store's credit card as "a Visa that has the American Eagle logo at an extremely high interest rate," remarking that only "gullible" customers sign up. Workers almost always view credit cards as hurting consumers, who incur debt and risk getting lower credit scores as a result of repeated store card requests. They often recount their astonishment upon realizing that credit card sales are an important part of their jobs. Melissa, for example, talks about selling credit cards at J.C. Penney:

> Surprisingly, our main focus is credit applications. They really drive that back at home. They want as many as possible. . . . Every month we have a specific goal for the whole department and then we split that into days. And, then we have our own personal [goal], what you're contributing. So like our boss will be like "Oh Melissa, technically you've met all the credit apps you have to contribute, but do you want to make more?"

While Melissa assumed that selling clothes would be the primary focus of her job, she quickly learned that selling credit cards was a central component of the position. Other workers similarly describe credit and rewards cards as the "main thing" managers want workers to sell.

Just as in upselling merchandise, management trains workers to focus on promoting credit and rewards cards. These tactics include routinized scripts that encourage customers to join the rewards program or apply for a store credit card. Trent, an Express manager, explains: "We're required to pitch our credit card and our loyalty program to every single customer. So, that's the one thing that I make sure that my staff is always pitching in a way that it has to be said because if it's not, then we're not doing our job." While Trent is generally lax about scripts with customers, he firmly enforces financial product scripts. Corporate managers evaluate both workers and their stores based on how frequently they succeed in persuading consumers to apply for cards. Many workers directly benefit if they sell more cards than expected, with bonuses, cash, or a little gift. Stella notes about Macy's; "We get credit for people who don't even get approved for the applications." Though rejected credit requests may hurt customers' credit scores, they may simultaneously boost workers' wages.

Such incentives aim to align workers with corporate mandates rather than customer needs.

Cashiers must log into each cash register with their individual user-names. They are then prompted onscreen to pitch the company credit card. If they fail to talk the customer into applying for a store credit card, this counts against the workers' metrics, as well as the store's metrics. Many of the workers knew how many credit card applications they were supposed to pick up each shift and would grow increasingly anxious as the shift ended and they were unsuccessful. Tara describes "apps per tran" as the number of applications American Eagle workers score for every ten transactions, stating that the score should be two and one-half for credit cards and ten for rewards cards. Danielle says that Old Navy "would want you to sell at least two a day. Or on the busy days, like on Black Friday they were like, 'Everybody sell at least five to ten a day.'" Workers cannot simply refuse to sell cards and escape managerial notice, because the metrics embedded in every transaction at the cash register reveal how frequently they succeed in upselling goods as well as selling credit. Indeed, these forms of electronic surveillance are expressly created to allow managers to identify which workers are "most" or "least" effective at selling credit and which workers are disregarding intended managerial scripts.[32]

Many employees articulate misgivings about promoting these cards. Rachel feels the target audience at American Eagle is vulnerable to financial products: "People, especially my age . . . don't realize that [it will hurt their credit]. They're eighteen years old and a credit card sounds awesome." Elise also argues that Target customers too rarely understood how the cards work: "The credit cards have a 25% interest rate and people didn't always read that. They saw it as 'something else I can use to pay later and not have to pay money now.'" These young workers often had learned the hard way about how damaging credit could be and didn't want to encourage others to accumulate debt. All of the workers express disdain or ambivalence, such as Angela, who says that although she "rock[s] at [selling Old Navy] credit cards," "it's the one value of that store that I just don't align with," given her own experience with credit card debt as a young adult. Although she successfully encourages customers to open credit cards, she sees this as "the worst part of the job."

Because they recognize the potential harm of credit cards (lowering credit scores, adding interest and finance charges, increasing debt), workers feel conflicted about encouraging customers to apply for credit cards. Grace shares why she doesn't want to engage in what she sees as an outrageous practice at TJ Maxx: "If they want to buy our products that's their choice, but if we are going to charge them interest rates that's another thing. It just seriously pisses me off." At times the workers interrupt these practices, usually by avoiding work at the cash register. "I preferred not to be on register for that reason," Corinne mentions about J.C. Penney, "because I usually don't ask people [if they'd like to apply for a store credit card]. I just don't like to pressure people into getting a credit card." For these workers, high interest rates and their potential effect on credit scores make the cards more of a threat than a bargain.

Nicole explains that she was initially uncomfortable about selling Nordstrom cards: "I don't want to offer people a credit card because I know what credit cards do to people." Over time, though, she learned from a coworker how to sell debit cards, which could earn her an additional $5 for each card sold:

One of the guys there gets ten rewards [$50] a shift, which is unheard of completely. You usually get one or two, and it's because he just is an intimidating guy and if someone pulls out a debit card, he's like, "Oh, I'm going to sign you up for like our debit card. It's the same thing. You'll just get points." He just assumes and goes for it, and so that's how he does it and makes a lot of money off that.

Nicole reflects about how she learned to "overcome" her hesitance about selling cards, thinking, "'Hey, these people are going to be asked anyway by other people. I might as well just, just do the job and maybe make some money for myself.'" The cash incentive for selling financial products, as well as seeing debit cards as less problematic than credit cards, helps her justify selling cards. Faced with low wages and few consistent hours, some workers find maintaining approval from frontline managers through acquiescing to credit sales a reasonable trade-off.

Nicole's experience highlights the fluid alliances that workers may forge with customers and management. Despite Nicole's initial resistance, aligning with management's financial product sales goals provides an immediate material payoff. Frontline managers try to convince workers that selling cards benefit customers, as in Nicole's case:

> [A manager] asked me, "Do you know why we have a credit card?" I was like—it was a bad answer, but I was just like, "So you can make money on the interest?" That's why I thought [the store has] a credit card. They were like, "Well, a lot for brand awareness and to remind people if they have the card in their wallet they might come to our store."

Her manager emphasizes that credit cards operate as a brand promotion rather than as another way to profit from customers. Yet Nicole's "bad answer" that the store may want to "make money on the interest" is not completely wrong. For example, 57% of Nicole's employer's $600 million 2015 earnings came from credit card revenues.[33] Workers rightfully recognize that retailers may profit more from finance charges than from selling goods.[34]

From years of working in clothing retail, Carmen considers offering credit cards an immoral practice that generally hurts the consumer: "Honestly, credit cards are the worst thing ever. . . . It's like trying to push something that you're trying to make it seem like it's something that's so good. But in the end, it's not. It's just another way to spend money." Managers enforce expectations for credit sales, creating friction between themselves and workers who are averse to selling credit and want to protect customers. Workers highlight how credit card sales are displayed in employee break rooms, including Carmen, who says: "They had a board with the percentage everyone had each month. . . . I was always at the bottom."[35] Later she laughs, sharing her reflections about the offensive nature of this practice: "Honestly, now thinking about that board being in the break room—that's pretty messed up. You know? You go and take a break and it's right there." Managers not only pressure Carmen to sell credit but also publicize her low-level performance. The service panopticon entails management identifying workers who fail to sell credit cards, highlighting their "misdeeds." Carmen's account shows how this tactic may bolster worker resolve to resist pushing credit cards, instead of cultivating competitiveness among staff.

Grace also criticizes TJ Maxx cards: "These women come in and they're like, 'Well I've already been denied twice, oh I'll just try again.' And I'm like, 'No, don't try again because that's going to pull your credit down even further and that's bad.'" Since multiple attempts to open store credit could damage an individual's credit rating, Grace sees selling store credit as against the customers' interests. "I understand why the company wants to do it because it perpetuates the cash flow; it keeps the cash within our brand," she reasons, "So, fiscally it makes sense but morally. . . [selling credit is] *not* what's best for our customers." While finance charges may boost the company's bottom line in the short term, Grace argues that selling credit undermines the brand.

Many of the workers we interviewed make this sort of moral argument. They enter into retail employment to earn wages. But they also feel strongly that they shouldn't knowingly hurt other people, either by selling them clothing they don't want or by selling them credit that could damage their finances. Marty wonders about these implications for Target customers:

> I just hear stories of . . . getting people who are on food stamps who sign up for these credit cards, which is going to hurt their credit, and they know they're going to get denied . . . but [the managers] still like push it. And it's just like, was that ethical to do that?

Most workers we interviewed wrestle with the ethics of anyone, from the corporation to themselves, profiting from credit sales.

Overall, clothing retail workers identify most managerial expectations as reasonable. However, they see other expectations—awkward scripts, aggressively pursuing sales goals, and selling credit cards—as damaging customer service and more profoundly contradicting the nature of "service" as serving in the customers' best interests. Workers empathize with customers and feel that not meeting customers' needs will hurt the company's long-term vitality, yet they rarely blame frontline managers for these issues. Instead, and in part because corporate requires and analyzes workers' "metrics," workers regard corporate management as creating and enforcing these unreasonable demands, excusing the frontline managers, who are more involved in carrying out corporate's expectations.

CORPORATE MANAGEMENT

Corporate surveillance of workers and frontline managers affects day-to-day operations in ways most employees find troubling and counterproductive.

Corporate surveillance has created the service panopticon, which alters—even destabilizes—power relations between workers, customers, frontline managers, and corporate managers, with intensive changes stemming from increased reliance on technology in the twenty-first-century. Meanwhile, corporate continues using more traditional approaches, such as store visits and phone calls.

As in previous decades, district or regional corporate managers visit regularly. Many workers discuss preparing for these visits. Leah explains about Hollister that "everyone would spread the word. They'd be like, 'Yeah, like the head is coming. Do your work because they're going to be watching you, too.'" Workers describe the intense work preceding a corporate visit, trying to ensure that every display follows company guidelines to the letter, the store is tidy and well-stocked, and both the workers and the store look "perfect." Corporate visits lead to "scary moments," as workers, supervisors, and managers attempt to guarantee a positive review. Lori depicts the preparation for these visits at Wet Seal as extensive:

> It's like epic because the night before [they are] coming in, my God, you have to clean the store from head to toe. The store's clean but it has to be in tip-top shape. And you're stressed because your manager is stressed and they're stressing you out. And it's just—eh, I hate it when I know they're coming in, I'll be like, "Can I get the day off please?"

Preparing for these visits causes substantial stress. Julian, a manager at H&M, argues: "There's certain things that we don't do on a day-to-day level that sometimes get lost, for better or worse. . . . [W]e need to make sure we're doing this, this, this, and this by the book." Although corporate managers expect the stores to always follow guidelines, frontline managers "step up their game" and lean on sales associates to do so when they know corporate will visit.

Scheduling the most experienced employees can help ensure that everything is done properly. Store managers don't always precisely follow corporate rules, in part because of corporate directives to cut staffing. Frank says about TJ Maxx: "If they were expecting like a district manager come in, the space has to look immaculate, everyone has to have their nametags on. [You] have [to] follow the policies that you might be kind of lenient on." While the frontline managers might let certain things slide, corporate enforces standards strictly in their attempts to ensure uniformity across stores. Visits from corporate stress out the entire store staff, including frontline managers and entry-level workers. Patricia remembers that when the "really head guys would come," Hollister employees would set up the store "'til like 5 in the morning, making sure it was perfect and the managers would freak out.... They were really nervous; their backs were on the line. But they did stay late, really late." The unpredictably of hours for both workers and frontline managers demonstrates the pressures that corporate places on store-level staff. Julian explains that "our district manager is a lot more likely to come down on you hard as opposed to . . . giving you solutions."

Corporate managers judge not only the workers but also the store managers, making these site visits a contested point in the labor process at which the workers and frontline managers may find themselves more allied against corporate in their attempts to collectively cope with the pressure. However, this tension also spills over, affecting the relationships between workers and frontline managers. James recalls how perturbed his Nordstrom store manager was while hosting a regional manager visit: "Definitely more irritated . . . you know the manager, more anger for that day . . . made sure everybody [and] everything was perfect. That's their performance test, is when that regional manager comes, so definitely, definitely there's more worrying for sure." For James, the manager's stress over their pending evaluation increases worrying for the staff.

Mary discusses why these visits are so difficult at Abercrombie:

> We would have "form day" and they would do all the [body] forms [or mannequins] and our district manager, their boss, would come in, and they would have to walk through them and have her look at every single form [mannequin] while they're standing there and she would pick it apart. So, yeah it's really insane, you had a lot of responsibility and they were always stressed out.

From Mary's perspective, not only the preparations but also the actual visit are traumatic, since corporate managers voice their criticism. Other workers provide similar stories of "crazy" expectations, with corporate managers quizzing workers about their store's sales goals and shoplifting loss and otherwise critiquing them in front of their coworkers. Such activity leads some workers to prefer avoiding shifts slated before or during corporate visits.

Beyond these in-person interactions, corporate managers also use newer, remote surveillance techniques to manage their workforce. Technology itself isn't new to retail work. For example, barcodes, which are scanned to identify the product being sold and simplify checkout, are nearly universal; this technology was introduced in the 1970s.[36] Retailers also used loyalty programs to encourage customers to visit again, before technology made rewards cards common.[37] Yet recent marketing tools intrude on shoppers in new ways, tracking their purchases and even monitoring their searches, offering them personalized recommendations and offers, which risks violating information privacy.[38]

Corporate managers also engage in other forms of surveillance in the age of "big data," related to the "metrics" upon which they judge workers.[39] Approaches to electronically monitoring workers, as well as customers and their movements around stores, are "increasingly sophisticated and diverse."[40] Real-time data metrics allow corporate managers to assess the productivity of each store and individual workers, including the number of items they sell in each transaction and their effectiveness selling credit cards.[41] Managers receive detailed data about their store, such as rankings of individual workers daily, weekly, and monthly—and may pass them on to their employees.[42] Thus, corporate wields these data to reward and punish both workers and their store-level managers. As economist Simon Head asserts:

> The computer rivals the industrial assembly line itself as an agent of surveillance and control. Managers can peer into subordinates' computers with their own. . . . Graphs, statistical tables, pie charts . . . all can analyze from every conceivable angle the performance of an employee or group of employees over a period of hours, days, weeks, or years, with up-to-the-minute analysis.[43]

Technology thus diminishes frontline managers' autonomy, as corporate's reading of the metrics often leads to commands about how to schedule workers, as well as whom to schedule.[44]

Another set of metrics includes customer feedback, which measures friendliness, cleanliness, and how effectively employees encourage customers to complete surveys.[45] Corporate managers also use "secret shoppers" to generate these data in the form of extensive notes about the customer experience of each store.[46] Marty explains that over time at Target, "pushing" the surveys on shoppers has become more important, with customer feedback playing a key role in managers' appraisals: "'Did this person meet this expectation, fall below the expectation, or exceed the expectation?'... They go through every single checklist and they might have an extra note here or there, like, 'Oh, do this better.'" For Marty, customer survey data hold the most weight in his performance evaluation, above his frontline manager's in-person assessments.

Corporate also directs frontline managers' decisions about staffing and task assignments, based on the customer surveys. Grace discloses that her store managers require them to follow "ridiculous" scripts thanks to survey results, noting: "We do it, and that's that." Using customer surveys and secret shoppers, rather than relying on frontline managers' assessments, corporate management makes its own evaluations of workers. Through these forms of surveillance, corporate managers deskill—take knowledge and power away from—frontline managers. Frontline managers become akin to coaches, rather than supervisors with decision-making authority.[47]

Both frontline managers and workers align in criticizing these changes, particularly because corporate management may miss contextual factors necessary to understand the metrics. They argue the knowledge gained from metrics is incomplete and can lead to mismanagement of the stores. Disgruntled customers are more likely to complete customer surveys—and corporate may direct the frontline manager to stop scheduling a worker who has received negative feedback. Yet a frontline manager may *observe* that a particular worker provides excellent customer service. In the service quadrangle, differences arise between corporate and frontline managers, in part because of how these different sets of managers interpret the data that are constantly being generated.

Traditionally, corporate surveillance focused on monthly sales. Sales, as a metric, imperfectly captures what is happening in the store, since there may be fewer sales if there are too few workers to help customers or if lines are so long that some customers leave without making a purchase.[48] With the emergence of new technologies, however, retailers analyze traffic within the store not just monthly, weekly, or daily, but hourly, setting up electronic counters to capture footfalls over the store's threshold, as well as, in some stores, video cameras or beacons to identify not only how many people enter the store, but where they walk and pause, how long checkout lines are, and what sections of the stores are most trafficked, as well as how quickly workers move from task to task.[49] Corporate can then attempt to use these data to optimize clothing displays and worker schedules.

While most entry-level staff do not know the ins and outs of how the technology works, they are aware of how management uses these data. For example, many workers bring up the metric of "conversion rate," or the number of purchases divided by the number of customers who appear to have walked into the store. However, just as sales measures are imperfect because they don't capture what may be driving sales up or down, so is the conversion rate. For example, Cheryl laughs about the conversion rate at Victoria's Secret, saying:

> They told us to leave on the sides of the store, 'cause that doesn't affect the conversion rate. So, when we come and go, we go on the side . . . and sometimes, we'll have kids running in and out of the store, and my manager's like, "I'm about to [makes an angry face]."

Since workers entering and exiting, or children running in and out, affect the conversion rate, these measures are invalid indicators of shopper foot traffic in the store, which requires seeing *who* comes in and out, not just the number of sales compared to the number of people crossing the store's threshold.[50]

In addition to the conversion rate, corporate managers continue to track sales per labor hour (the dollar amount of sales in an hour divided by the number of workers clocked in during that hour). They use those data to direct frontline managers to "call in" workers when there are too many customers or "send home" workers when there are too few. Julian, an H&M manager, emphasizes that one interpretation of these numbers would be to always send workers home, since the fewer workers, the greater the boost to the sales per hour metric. But as he notes, if you "add [labor] hours, you have that customer service, and the pristineness of your store that will increase sales at the same rate." In other words, customers are more likely to buy more goods in a well-organized store, which frontline managers can assess more effectively than sales per hour. Sending workers home undercuts frontline managers' attempts to keep the store tidy and capture additional sales. Such contradictions in seeking short-term profits reveal the importance of frontline managers' involvement in decisions about whether to cut or increase staff.

Julian argues that at one time corporate management criticized stores with metrics that show a high sales per hour ratio, since "that would mean that your store doesn't look that good. . . . You're not helping customers enough." But with the shift to short-term sales goals, corporate now celebrates stores with very high sales-per-hour rates: "They're championing you on the conference call, they're like, 'Great job!' [But] the store must look awful if you have such a difference between hours and sales." These approaches can lead to fewer customers shopping in brick-and-mortar stores, since messy stores drive away customers. Julian argues that focusing exclusively on the metrics damages each store's long-term sales potential, as customers avoid disorganized stores with too few workers.

Frontline managers express concern about corporate managers' relying too heavily on data generated through online surveillance systems, which often miss important contextual factors. Trent, a manager at Express, explains that the district manager uses data from remote surveillance technology to give "us advice on 'you need to cut hours' or things like that," but the frontline management team in the store are the "only ones that really know what's going on." Both Julian and Trent suggest that relying on metrics to make decisions misses the insights they can offer, as on-site managers know better what's going on in their stores during each shift. These frontline managers complain that corporate reliance on metrics fails to recognize the expertise and knowledge of frontline managers, leading to poor decision-making for the company.[51]

Corporate practices create some solidarities between workers and frontline managers, which may shift power relations within the service quadrangle. Workers also see corporate choices as decontextualized from what is actually happening in each store. Stella finds it deeply frustrating to follow corporate directions without the materials they need to do so at Forever 21:

> The company would give us these detailed plans on how they want the
> rooms to look but then they wouldn't always ship us the products. So, we
> have to pull stuff out of our asses and do it with the company guidelines.
> And we had these district visits and they're: "We don't like this. We don't like
> this. We don't like this." We're like, "Okay we didn't get this stuff in." And
> they're like, "You guys should make something work."

Following floor set guidelines without the requisite merchandise seems entirely unrealistic to Stella, yet she cannot counter corporate's arguments that they should "make something work." Pauline also outlines the challenge of corporate's ignoring feasibility given the number of workers Hollister hired: "Corporate has the mindset where like, you know, it can be done. It is pretty, but do this on Black Friday [nationwide shopping event]? Um no; it's not happening." When many customers are flowing through the doors, and too few workers are on shift, there is no way to keep stores well-stocked and tidy.

Employees indicate that giving frontline managers more control would lead to better outcomes. For example, many stores require staff to work late at night, refolding and arranging clothing, while others leave those tasks for the (slower) morning shift. Both managers and frontline workers see cleaning in the morning as more sensible but do not have the power to change corporate policy. Similarly, corporate may determine shipments of clothing based on previous sales, rather than empowering frontline managers to tweak orders using customer requests, which can frustrate shoppers. Risa mentions that her Zara store was ultimately shuttered, as she and her frontline managers watched corporate make a series of bad decisions that did not reflect the consumer needs of the location.

Through in-person visits, customer surveys, secret shoppers, and surveillance via various sales-related metrics, corporate holds most of the managerial control over the stores, while frontline management enforces corporate's rules and decisions. Workers in our study often characterize corporate's directives as problematic in the long term and failing to provide the resources necessary to accomplish the company's goals in the short term. At the same time, frontline managers also highlight how corporate decision-making overlooks important contextual features that frontline managers are more likely to know.

CONCLUSION

Retail clothing work involves shifting tensions and alliances between workers and frontline and corporate management. Workers ally with customers—such as when they complain about how scripts or sales goals lead them to undermine service or how credit cards are not in the customers' interests—wielding happy customers as a tool to resist managers.[52] Managers also, at least nominally, ally with customers by relying on customer surveys and secret shoppers to ensure that the experience of shoppers is a good one; these efforts are aimed at broadening managerial power and controlling workers. As management scholar Jos Gamble argues, both approaches emphasize that providing good customer service is the key to successful retail work. In this way, our data support the "triangle of service work."[53]

However, our study demonstrates that frontline and corporate managers differently influence retail workplaces, creating a quadrangle with four points of tension. We could illustrate this quadrangular arrangement with a square or a rectangle, but we see the relationships as forming a parallelogram, with corporate managers allied with frontline managers (the top line) and situated farthest from workers. For the most part, corporate managers need to "go through" frontline managers to engage with workers, but they also receive information about workers from frontline managers and through surveillance technology. Corporate managers are also "closer" to customers (the line on the left), in the form of secret shoppers and customer surveys; customer feedback "goes through" corporate before reaching frontline managers. Workers occupy positions closest to frontline managers (the line on the right), with whom they work, while customers and workers are more strongly allied (the bottom line), though struggles also arise between these groups (see chapter 4).

Power and surveillance remain embedded in these relationships, highlighting how the service panopticon shapes the labor process in the service quadrangle. Corporate managers watch frontline managers and workers. Frontline managers watch workers and customers. Workers watch customers and frontline managers. Corporate managers even track and watch customers' buying habits, although customers may not appreciate being shadowed; US customers have pushed back against certain forms

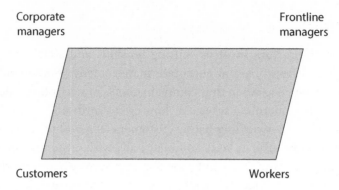

Corporate
managers

Frontline
managers

Customers

Workers

Figure 7. The service quadrangle

of electronic surveillance.[54] And customers watch workers and frontline managers, later reporting to corporate. Corporate managers who are less senior, such as district and regional managers, may also be assessed by the metrics they use in reviewing frontline managers. The service panopticon also means that workers and frontline managers discipline themselves, following corporate mandates even when they think corporate is wrong.[55] The metrics reported back to corporate mean that they are constantly surveilled; store managers and workers also assume secret shoppers are "everywhere" and follow the expected routines and scripts.[56]

These relationship dynamics are somewhat unstable, as the postindustrial economy involves changing alliances and expectations between workers, frontline managers, and corporate rule. Yet this structure can flip to indicate the power that corporate managers, and to a lesser extent customers, have in these relationships within the service panopticon.

Customers possess buying power, and corporate managers must take heed as customers make clear their wishes—whether for cheap crop tops or expensive purses. Corporate managers aren't simply allied with frontline managers but operate directly above them in the organizational hierarchy. Corporate constantly assesses them through a range of metrics aimed primarily at minimizing costs and maximizing sales, thus augmenting profits. The increasingly regular use of metrics empowers corporate managers, transforming the hierarchical relationship between corporate and frontline managers. Frontline managers and workers remain

Corporate
managers

Customers

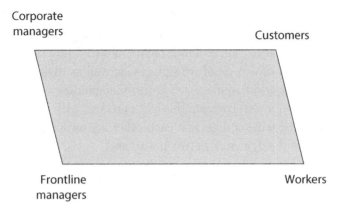

Frontline
managers

Workers

Figure 8. The service quadrangle flipped

in a clearly contested dynamic, as the latter group seeks recognition of their own value while also consistently appealing to customer interests. Workers (particularly whites), however, may form amicable ties with their store managers that provide rewards. Corporate control and surveillance help explain the relationships of the service quadrangle, as well as workers' resistance.

This chapter analyzed the relationships between workers, frontline managers, and corporate managers. Frontline managers, often not much older than their workers, can establish close relationships with workers, which can benefit favorites with better schedules and more consistent shifts. While women suggest that they experience greater pressure to be "friendly" from their managers than men do, workers of color—particularly Black women—express feeling more distanced from their managers than white workers. Workers also point to problematic management approaches, which they see as reducing the quality of customer service. They tend to blame corporate managers for these issues. This chapter further theorized how surveillance technologies employed by corporate managers play a key role in deskilling frontline managers, showing how the service panopticon exacerbates the tensions visible in the service quadrangle. As a result, corporate managers may rely on poor-quality or short-term data to make decisions that will impact the store over the long term, in ways that workers see as counterproductive.

Through the linked concepts of the service panopticon and the service quadrangle, we further illuminate the influence of corporate management and their use of various surveillance techniques to direct the day-to-day routinized operations in retail workplaces, as well as divisions between frontline and corporate managers.[57] Our understanding emphasizes the varied relationships that cocreate this labor process, with the four groups involved aligning with and against each other across specific situations. We now turn to the dynamics between workers.

3 Coworkers and Belonging

"WE ARE LIKE A FAMILY"; "IF IT WEREN'T
FOR WORK, I WOULDN'T TALK TO YOU"

David has been a sales "model" for Abercrombie & Fitch for over a year. Managers often remind David, with his short brown hair and tall, athletic physique, just how much he resembles one of the half-naked white men featured on Abercrombie's shopping bags. In fact, he was recruited to work there. A loyal shopper since middle school, he regularly gets job offers when he shops away from his usual mall. He finds himself responding, "I'm already working [at Abercrombie]." David appears to enjoy his job, gushing, "You're in your own little world. It's like a small little family that you eventually get to know them and care for them." The family connection develops over time, and often after hours:

> We spend time together like after 9:30, the store is closed and you have to talk 'cause it's quiet. So we talk, fool around. We get along well, so it is like a family, and you just bond. Whether you like it or not, I mean, you're going to bond with people you work with.

For David, it's obvious "whether you like it or not" that you will "bond with the people you work with." Those bonds and the relatively relaxed atmosphere make the job worthwhile for him. His response to the question "Why do retail clothing workers put up with low wages and unpredictable schedules?" is simple: "It's really easygoing, and I love that about the job. It's like, I don't even care that it's minimum wage because I'm having fun doing it."

As sociologist Yasemin Besen-Cassino asserts, friendships compensate for poor wages among young coffee shop workers, and David sees friendships operating similarly in retail clothing.[1] Few workers go as far as David does; indeed, the vast majority suggest that friendly relationships cannot make up for poor working conditions. However, most of those we interviewed spoke about their coworkers with affection. It seems that good coworkers can at least improve a bad job.

Contrasting perspectives, of course, illuminate racialized experiences of worker isolation rather than solidarity. Pauline, who is Black, worked at Hollister for five years. There, she says, coworker relationships lack connection and utterly fail to compensate for the low pay and other dismal conditions of the job. Where David finds some fun and camaraderie in late-night shifts, Pauline avoids after-hours work:

> There would be nights where we just left, like we did the best we could and then we'd just come in the next morning and finish it. There'd be times where I heard people would stay till two o'clock in the morning. . . . And, I just had that mindset at that point in time. I don't get paid enough to be here till two o'clock. I've been here since four in the afternoon.

Pauline emphasizes that she had little in common with her coworkers, obliquely referencing race as she says, "I live more in the city and these people lived in the suburbs." Surrounded by mostly white coworkers, Pauline recalls having only one friend at the store, an Asian woman. Indeed, few Black, Asian, and Latina workers describe a "family" feeling or "belongingness," and those who do are usually referencing other women of color. Pauline continues:

> I didn't really talk to many of [my white coworkers] because if I would just hear some of the side conversations that they talked about and I was just like, okay, I know that—((inhales)) there were just some people that I knew I wasn't going to like. If it weren't for work, I wouldn't talk to you, so let me not just talk to you now.

Disengaging from workplace ties felt like the only reasonable way to navigate the palpable tension among Hollister employees.

A frontline manager added to Pauline's discomfort. She felt constantly stereotyped, she says, relating a memorable encounter in which the manager questioned her because Pauline carried an expensive Longchamp handbag:

> The fact that you question that I own one of them, it was like one of those moments where I was like, I hope I'm giving you a dirty look right now. . . . And it was funny 'cause my friend who was there at the time, she's Asian, and then we were like joking about it afterward 'cause it was one of those things that you have to make light of it because I feel like if I let somebody see that I'm upset about it, then I let them win. So, we'd always joke about it afterward. She's like ((shriller voice)), "Oh my God! You own one of those?" I was like, "Yeah, you know, I just got off my welfare, and—they gave me one!"

Pauline later explains that while she knows the low pay at Hollister couldn't cover such an expensive purchase, "Maybe I have parents!" Pauline and her friend tried to make light of the discomforting racist and classist assumptions underlying their manager's questions. Their bond made a safe space in which they could laugh about the interaction. But Pauline also clarifies that she did not want her manager to know she was upset, to avoid being further stigmatized through controlling images about angry Black women. She understands and acknowledges that racialized feeling rules mean it's "out of line" for Black workers to display emotions like irritation and outrage.[2]

So, we see two environments, often operating in the same stores at the same time: being stereotyped makes the workplace hostile, while occupying a friendly environment with pleasant, accepting people improves job quality. Inescapably, race shapes coworker relationships. Generally, we find that whites, across gender, express more integration, and Black, Asian, and Latina women express more isolation in retail clothing jobs. These uneven connections have serious implications for feelings of alienation as well as worker solidarity and potential resistance to exploitative arrangements within the service panopticon.

In this chapter, we first consider coworker relationships broadly, as a site of potential pleasure and social challenges. We then explore how race mediates these relationships, such that white interviewees describe a sense of belonging and friendship at work, while Black, Asian, and Latinx workers tend to feel excluded and exploited. In particular, Black workers note that they feel further alienated in performing within the surveillance panopticon because managers sometimes ask them specifically to police Black customers for potential shoplifting.[3] Taken together, we see how coworker relationships, attenuated by social characteristics, impact workers' overall experiences and evaluations of job quality.

RELATIONSHIPS AT WORK AND RACIAL DIVISIONS

Workplace friendships reflect voluntary connections between coworkers. These relationships provide social and emotional support and professional development advice, and they may create more effective work environments by carving out better communication channels.[4] They can also complicate and cause tension in the workplace, when coworkers supervise friends, are seen as favoring friends, or have to remain friends because they're coworkers.[5] Also, not everyone participates in workplace friendships; contextual factors, such as proximity and perceived similarity, influence the development of friendships in the workplace.[6] Among teen-oriented stores, age is particularly critical. Younger workers are more likely to feel connected to other workers, while older workers appear disenchanted with their workplaces.

Race organizes workplaces, including the collegial friendships that may—or may not—develop.[7] In white-dominated spaces, white workers in the US context often exclude workers of color, particularly Blacks, from these relationships.[8] Racial discrimination and stereotypes may lead to greater isolation for racial minorities, which in turn influences their experience of the jobs.[9] Analyzing race among workplace relationships, then, requires theorizing power differentials and the multiple ways that whiteness operates.[10] It also means understanding racial boundaries not as natural, immutable divisions, but ones negotiated in specific local contexts. In more diverse settings, these processes may be less pronounced.[11] Belonging also reflects gender, sexuality, class, age, and other markers of difference.[12]

Race is embedded in how organizations work: their structures, their processes, and their hierarchies.[13] Racialized organizations, such as retail companies, reproduce inequality through hiring decisions and other practices that tend to reinforce existing racial hierarchies.[14] In the United

States, whiteness serves as a credential for some, disadvantaging other racial groups.[15] Racialized organizational practices further legitimate some groups' receiving more resources, such as better schedules. Sociologists Adia Harvey Wingfield and Koji Chavez argue that it is not simply a person's race, but also their position in the organizational power structure, that influences their experience of discrimination, leading us to examine racialized power dimensions of relationships within the service quadrangle.[16]

Among the stores that we analyze, racial discrimination is a point of tension. For example, Abercrombie & Fitch has a history of being associated with a "consumer celebration of whiteness, and of an elite class of whiteness at that," and the company faced a lawsuit that charged that it discriminated against Black, Asian, and Latinx people in hiring, job assignment, and compensation.[17] The complaint focused on the company's "look" policies, including sending pictures of employees to corporate, highlighting white people in store advertisements, and relegating workers of color to the stockroom, suggesting that these policies result in a white workforce on the sales floor.[18] Indeed, although the class action suit was settled, the settlement required the corporation to pay $40 million to litigants and to add diversity training, hire diversity recruiters, and diversify its marketing materials.[19] While this lawsuit may make Abercrombie seem exceptional, the accounts from the workers and customers suggest that even after the lawsuit, many clothing stores continue to operate in ways that privilege whiteness.[20] For example, Macy's also settled a complaint regarding profiling Black customers in 2005.[21] Indeed, in June 2020 workers at Anthropologie, a store owned by Urban Outfitters, alleged that Black workers have fewer opportunities and that Black customers are racially profiled.[22]

BELONGING IN RETAIL

Many workers revel in connecting with coworkers, with some referring to their store, as David does, as a "family." Others suggest that work can be another form of "hanging out" with friends.[23] The structure of the retail workplace shapes acceptance and positive social relationships among employees. Where workers interact with one another during their shifts, they're better able to establish closer relationships. Other factors, particularly the racial and age diversity of the workplace, also matter.

More than half of those we interviewed express affection for their coworkers. Cheryl, who is multiracial, says her coworkers "all say that all the time, that we're like a little 'Victoria Secret family.'" At her store, the staff chats with each other via headsets (often joking about customers unbeknownst to them) throughout their shifts: "The girls definitely make it a lot of fun. And as much as it's terrible to say, but talking on the headsets [is] hilarious." Customers can also help create worker relationships when they are particularly "difficult." At Old Navy, Angela, a white sales clerk, says about debriefing after difficult customer encounters: "That's where you bond with coworkers, it's really over customer interaction and how silly they are." And Claire, a white sales staffer at Hollister, reports that the store's dress code became a point of bonding: "It's January 1st and we're wearing flip-flops. We had to wear flip-flops throughout the entire winter. I would walk outside, and there'd be four feet of snow, and I would be in flip-flops. It was so ridiculous So we just kind of complained about that kind of stuff." The shared experiences of working in specific contexts help some retail staff form relationships.

Department store workers, who are less uniform in terms of age, race, and educational background, also discuss forming close attachments to their coworkers. This group refers to a caring, reciprocal, and "family environment." They also reference long-standing relationships with coworkers. Joyce, a white Macy's employee, speaks of her coworkers with affection:

> We're so close and we know so much about each other. Because we work so closely, that it's really personal, I guess. We share stories about what's going on at home. We ask each other and give each other advice for different things. It's really almost like a family environment in my department.

Joyce depicts workers getting to know one another, having the time to discuss their personal lives, and feeling close to one another. "Now, I work with mostly older women since I'm a full-time associate. I see them more as in a motherly role, and I think . . . they feel maternal over me too, in a way, like the way that they give me advice for boys and stuff like that." Her full-time schedule means more time at work and more time with her motherly coworkers. Steve, a white man who worked at Kohl's for the

Figure 9. Coworkers working together. SOURCE: iStock.com/monkeybusinessimages.

better part of a decade, had a similar experience: "It's kind of like a close-knit family with a lot of them who have been there for a while." When stores like these provide better working conditions, more training, and more reasonable scheduling, they have less turnover, and deeper collegial relations may result.

At the teen-oriented stores, employees are more likely to report having fun at work and deriving pleasure from their friendly connections with coworkers. Jason (multiracial) explains that at Abercrombie: "It was very friendly. People were very close. You enjoyed going to work, working there and it was like a hangout. It was fun. You know you'd go in there and just chill with your friends at work, talk about what happened at the party." Outside-of-work hangouts buttress coworker friendships. Sherrie (Latina) refers to her Pac Sun coworkers sharing her college student status and taste in music, mentioning their subtle resistance to corporate management control over the space: "We had a playlist, but whenever the manager wasn't in the store, you know, we'd plug in our own music and be like 'Yea!' You know? We had a lot in common and we also were around each so much that we kind of just grew on each other." For Jason and Sherrie, like David at the beginning of the chapter, retail jobs are enjoyable and feel like "hangouts."[24] Tia, who is Black, emphasizes that she felt an "immediate" sense of belonging at Forever 21, saying, "People liked me there." Her location employed a "predominantly ethnic" staff of "Spanish and Black" workers and managers. Sabrina (white) remembers a supportive set of interactions at Urban Outfitters:

> I really liked some of my coworkers, they were really cool and really nice. And if I was doing a good job people would always come up to me and be like, "Hey you're doing a really good job, keep up the good work." Even my coworkers, not even just my managers, would say something, which was nice.

Although toiling in a seasonal position that provides little financial compensation, Sabrina feels rewarded by kind words from "really nice" managers and coworkers. Though there is little chance that managers will reward good work with promotions or pay raises, recognition and praise can nonetheless help workers feel valued and loyal.

Many workers in youth-oriented stores see their relationships with coworkers as a positive element of their jobs, expressing a real sense of appreciation for them, as well as a feeling of belonging in these spaces. Indeed, some workers discuss socializing with their coworkers and frontline managers as their *favorite* part of the job. But how do workers fare when their coworkers are the biggest challenge?

CHALLENGES WITH COWORKERS

Relationships with coworkers aren't always so easy. For example, in teen-oriented retailers where turnover is common, workers can "age out" of coworker cohesion. The brand embodiment of the work at fast-fashion retailers also leaves some workers feeling uncomfortable among their "model" coworkers, and the structure of the work—with erratic schedules, workers divided into different rooms and tasks, and seasonal hiring—can prevent friendship formation. Workers even describe how difficult it can be having coworkers judge or discipline them when they make mistakes, leading to negative feelings about the workplace.

Among our interviewees, younger workers at the most youth-oriented stores tend to describe closer relationships with coworkers than do workers in their early twenties. Charlotte recalls a shift over several years at Hollister: as a high school senior, she made a close friend among her coworkers, but as the years passed, she became annoyed with the younger "brats" working at the store. She comments: "My coworkers are great. . . . But . . . when I go back after being in college, I don't—I can't stand them, but I met some of my best friends there." To her, it feels puzzling that simply getting older would change her experience of the job: "Everyone's like 17 and I'm 21, so it's kind of like I don't have anything in common with these people." This is essentially a turnover problem: when stores constantly hire new teenage workers who embody the store brand, longer-term employees lose their "cohorts" and begin feeling alienated. Pauline, who worked at Hollister for about five years, points out that the longer she worked for the company, the older she felt:

> The coworkers that I started with, we were all around the same age, you know, we were transitioning from high school to college. Some of them I still keep in contact with now. . . . The later ones that came in, I really didn't interact with them because there was an age difference. . . . I'm in my second and third year of college, and you're talking about what you're going to wear to prom.

Nonstop hiring, an emphasis on youthfulness and looks, and worker turnover caused by low pay and erratic schedules all lead to age-based disillusionment among those who hold onto the same retail posts for longer stints.[25]

Accounts of age-based differences frequently revolve around "drama" between workers, highlighting the tenuous nature of alliances in the service quadrangle. More experienced workers suspect younger workers may be playing out "high school" dynamics. Stella sighs and discusses "drama" as inherent among younger employees at Forever 21:

> When you have so many young people working with you it becomes like high school, so that people have these little cliques and if you're not okay with one person, no one in that little group talks to you. I was in the backroom with all of the stock . . . and one of the guys had this girlfriend who was a cashier, and she hated my guts just because I actually worked in the

backroom with her boyfriend. I never even talked to this guy either. So, she hated me. All of her friends hated me. So I was just like, "This is the worst place in the world."

Stella vocalizes no interest in engaging in turmoil with her jealous coworker, yet she also felt excluded from workplace relationships as a result of her concerns. "You still have those very cliquey mentalities whereas I was like I'm showing up to this job because I need money. I'm not here to be your friend. I just want to work this shift and get out of here." At twenty-two years old, Stella considers herself substantially older than—and substantially disconnected from—her coworkers.

Patricia describes having been warned on her first day that Hollister "is so cliquey, like the drama there is like high school and I was like 'Great.'" She seems grateful that she never actually experienced conflict, but other respondents describe tensions. Claire voices that her Hollister coworkers are all "fake and annoying," while Joyce says Pac Sun is exclusionary: "You could tell that a lot of the people were friends and had been working there. It was like there was a clique of people that I feel like, even if I tried, I wouldn't have really been able to be friends with. And it was almost more judge-y." Among our respondents, the workers at teen-focused retailers refer to a "clique" mentality among staff, pointing to the salience of age for social connection in certain workspaces. Teenagers appear to enjoy working with other teenagers. Slightly older workers, however, may have diminished enthusiasm for the "drama" they associate with teen workers.

Aesthetic labor in fast-fashion stores is another axis along which workers can connect—or be prevented from connecting. Nora shares feeling less than comfortable with other employees at American Eagle: "They just really intimidated me because they all had that American Eagle look to them." Nora feels awkward, sensing that she doesn't fit the brand's "look," and so she doesn't engage much socially on the job. Hannah compares her relationships at Aeropostale and Gilly Hicks, emphasizing the different levels of warmth and potentiality for establishing enjoyable social bonds:

At Aeropostale, all my coworkers were like super friendly and some of them go to school with me now, and like I hang out with them here . . . and like I hang out with some of them back home. . . . But at Gilly Hicks the girls were more like snooty. . . . I had a couple friends there, but other than that, like I didn't really. No one really interacted with each other because girls thought they were so like, "We're models so we don't need to—We're just better than everyone."

In her estimation, Gilly Hicks, a now-defunct lingerie store with stricter standards regarding employee appearance, drew "snooty" and less friendly employees than Aeropostale, with its broader aesthetic. While we discuss aesthetic labor in more detail in part 3, it's clear that David's experience as the ideal walking Abercrombie model differs from the experiences of Nora and Hannah.

Hierarchies, fast-paced turnover, and varying role assignments can also stand in the way of workplace belonging. Most workers comment that the way frontline managers assign them to complete tasks alone makes it difficult to connect with coworkers; in stores with multiple separated areas, managers usually place one person in each "room" of the store. Patricia declares that Gilly Hicks, with its dim lighting and blaring pop music, impedes coworker bonding simply through its setting: "It's such a loud environment, you don't really have the chance." Hannah elaborates that Gilly Hicks is "like eight separate rooms so you never really see anyone else." At Forever 21, Jill recalls, "I'd say it's isolated because we all had to do our own sections, and then we would like hop into other sections and help people if we needed to." The division of labor between sections of the store, or specific tasks, such as folding clothes, greeting customers, and cashiering, organizes the work so that minimal teamwork and ongoing coordination occurs during the store's business hours, at least for workers on the sales floor. Limited and unpredictable scheduling amplifies the alienation. Lance points out that at Hollister he received too few hours to make connections with coworkers, although his better schedule at Abercrombie Kids made the work much more fun. When workers have relatively few opportunities to get to know each other, they only see one another in passing or to assist with difficult customers.[26] They may not regularly work with the same staffers or even on the same shift from week to week.

Clothing retail has cyclical fluctuations, particularly seasonal influxes of staff, that impede coworker camaraderie. Patricia, a seasonal worker, says she never had the opportunity to grow close to other Gilly Hicks employees, while Trent notes that the arrival of winter holiday workers at

Express damages the relationships of support built among workers over the rest of the year. He reports that around the holidays, Express' staff size balloons so quickly that he doesn't recognize every sales associate. Trent recalls that "the only problem that there's ever really been [where] people don't like each other was one with our holiday worker, which we did get rid of." From Trent's perspective as a manager, the hyper-disposability of seasonal workers is anchored in their temporary position and can lead to problems. Yet many long-term. part-time staff would prefer to work full-time; investing in these workers rather than hiring seasonal part-time staff would be another solution, though it would require paying benefits to these workers.

The service panopticon also influences these processes. Coworkers, as well as managers, observe and appear to occasionally discipline each other. They judge each other's contributions to operating the store, reprimanding those who make mistakes. Since having slow workers, such as when someone is training, tends to increase already challenging workloads, coworkers can feel frustration mount. Melissa encountered a situation with a coworker at J.C. Penney who "made [her] feel very small," remembering that "whenever I did something wrong it was like a big deal. But when I started showing I was a good worker, she was much nicer to me. I almost felt like I had to prove myself to her, which I didn't feel was right." So useful to management, coworkers' internal discipline can sour peer relationships, thwarting solidarity between workers.

RACE AND ISOLATION IN THE WORKPLACE

Although many workers communicate a feeling of camaraderie in the workplace and others describe mixed dealings with coworkers, one of the most telling themes in our interviews was how race impacts coworker relations. Many retail clothing companies emphasize their interest in promoting diversity while continuing to target mostly white customers, signaled by the white or racially ambiguous faces that adorn their advertisements and walls. Although workers recognize that store websites often emphasize wanting to hire diverse workers (perhaps in response to class action lawsuits), they note that many of the workers of color are

Figure 10. Stockroom worker. SOURCE: iStock.com/kmatija.

in the stockroom, while most of the workers on the floor are white or racially ambiguous. In these spaces, especially when most of the workers are white, white staff members often characterize their relationships with coworkers as congenial. However, workers of color—particularly women of color—are more likely to describe their work relationships and environments as cold.

Racial diversity and race-based practices of inclusion and exclusion in retail workplaces shape how white, Black, Asian, Latinx, and multiracial workers experience their jobs. Since we interviewed only a few men of color, we can only offer tentative conclusions about how race and gender intersect for men in the clothing retail industry. Relatively few men speak negatively about their relationships with coworkers, though some, like Trent, a Black manager at Express, suggest their workplaces are less than ideal when it comes to racial integration. Even so, though he is cognizant of racial dynamics, Trent did not share accounts of being treated in racist ways, perhaps because of his position as manager.[27] In discussing coworker relations at J. Crew, manager Carl, who is white, unsurprisingly states that he has personally encountered no racial trouble on the job, but acknowledges that race and gender likely affect the relationship dynamics: "I'm also a white male, so it's easier for me to navigate things sometimes." Carl suggests that his workplace mirrors inequalities within US society, noting that his gender and race probably give him more power than many other workers.[28]

In contrast, Black, Latina, and Asian women offer troubling accounts. Exclusionary practices seem particularly likely to plague stores with predominantly white staff. At Free People, Carmen, who is Latina, "felt so out of place, that's what made me hate it so much. I dreaded going in for work." One of her coworkers was a particular problem, making her "feel like I was not doing a very good job." While she made "one really good friend," that coworker "left because she didn't like the work environment." Thus, Carmen reports, "I left also, because I was like, 'Well, that was my only friend.'" She didn't explicitly refer to her colleagues as racist, but Carmen's comments about dreading going to work and feeling so "out of place" are telling.

Pauline's Blackness made her feel separate from the otherwise close-knit crew at Hollister, but she insists she had little interest in being part of their crew: "They would have parties or go out to the club or whatever and all this stuff, like have Hollister bonding time. That's fine. I did not want to represent the company outside of work." Pauline's account underscores that her relatively estranged relationship with the store brand compounded her ability to feel belongingness in the workplace. While she refers to herself as a "social person," Pauline also emphasizes:

> I didn't care to hang out with these people at all outside of work because it was like if it wasn't for me working with you guys, we would not be friends. You know what I mean? And I think I told one of the girls that she was like "Oh my gosh, you're so mean," or like laughing about it. But I was just like, "I'm being honest." . . . I'm not going to lie to you because it was at the point where I was just like I'm 20 and you're 17 years old, we have very little in common besides us working together.

Pauline suggests a self-made boundary: she has no interest in spending time with the other workers because she is older, has different interests, and is less attached to the store's brand image than they are.

Our data present one positive note in this regard: in more diverse store locations, women of color are more likely to talk about having made friends among their workers. The degree of exclusion that women of color identify seems to correspond to the diversity of immediate coworkers, as well as the overall racial diversity of the staff. Lillian, who is Asian, recalls feeling "the family connection at Abercrombie," which included racially diverse coworkers, but not at American Eagle, where most of her coworkers were white. She concedes that it might have been because she was the new person among a longer-term staff at American Eagle, before adding that the Abercrombie staff was made up of a

> really good [racial] mix, and they were actually really nice, most of them were studying abroad in America so it was really interesting, meeting a lot of different people. And American Eagle was mostly art students or first-year students and quite honestly, I wasn't really a fan because [they acted like] they were kind of better than everyone, I felt they were kind of snobby and immature.

The difference in her sense of belonging at the two stores could be attributed to differences in staff personalities, but Lillian's account implies that diversity was important to making Abercrombie feel more enjoyable as a workplace.

Lori, a Black woman who sports thick, black-rimmed glasses and a nose ring, smiles while describing her unusually diverse coworkers: "Wet Seal—awesome. I love them; they're my friends. I worked there for five years [before transferring to another location], so we all have a good relationship." Kathleen was the first Black employee at her store, but she started to enjoy her job more when management hired several of her Black and Latina friends: "It was fun. I loved my coworkers. It was just a fun experience." And Frances, a multiracial worker at a somewhat diverse Abercrombie & Fitch location, states:

> It's a good feeling going in there. Not like, "Ugh, I have to go to work today, it sucks." I don't ever dread it, I'm always like, oh I'm working today, I wonder who I'm working with. . . . I feel like it has a lot to do with who I'm working with . . . they're all awesome people.

For Frances, "awesome" coworkers make her workplace pleasant. Staff diversity can improve racially marginalized employees' experiences and feelings of belongingness and thus impact the service quadrangle in ways that support worker solidarity.[29]

Black and Latina women, as we might expect, tend to report forming closer friendships with other women of color, especially in otherwise relatively exclusive and predominantly white environments. Denise, who is Black, depicts her relationships with her mostly white coworkers at Abercrombie & Fitch: "They were like cool people, but it wasn't like we were like best buddies I guess." Then, she says, "I was closer to one of the other girls, my Asian coworker, and we always had a lot of fun together. . . . Yeah, we gravitated to each other; so, I did have fun in some aspects." In stores with predominantly white staffs, Asian, Black, and Latina women may have more tenuous social ties than their white counterparts. Yet when workers are part of a more diverse staff, a sense of belongingness may be easier to develop and maintain across racial lines.

Even in relatively diverse workplaces, exclusion happens. Corinne, who is Asian, recalls that her Abercrombie coworkers mostly looked racially ambiguous, so she feels that it was a pretty diverse staff. Nonetheless, she can't think of a single friendship she made there: "Besides talking to my manager, I didn't really talk to anyone. But other than that, I wasn't really friends with them." Maybe, she muses, this was because she was younger or newer than other workers, before remarking with some relief how much friendlier she finds the environment at J.C. Penney. Like her, some Black, Asian, and Latina women point to the distinct combination of exclusion in the workplace and a decreasing interest in the white-dominant store brand as leading them to leave certain jobs.[30]

Emotional and social repercussions, as well as material consequences of exclusion, permeate the accounts of these women of color. Stella (multiracial) shares an ongoing problem at her job at Macy's, where her managers sent her Indian woman coworker home due to perceived body odor. She details the consequences of managers assessing workers of color negatively:

> You're not going to ask those people to stay longer. . . . Or you're not going to think of those people. You're not going to have them in mind when you have these open shifts and you need someone to cover you. You're going to ask someone who you like. . . . The way that they treat the girl I was telling you about . . . a lot of the managers when they talk about her, they kind of brush

her off. . . . Some of the managers, the things they say can be really, really mean, and they just make fun of her all the time, and they don't even treat her like they would a normal associate. They kind of shove her to the side.

Stella views the way managers "shove" this worker to the side, assessing her less on the quality of her work than on her perceived difference, as a sign that her managers are racist and morally bankrupt. Social exclusion has clear material impacts, regarding manager favoritism in assignments, scheduling, hours, wages, and promotions. These discriminatory racialized practices aren't formally tied to workplace policies, but they do deeply impact workers' experiences, well-being, and professional mobility.[31]

CRIMINALIZING BLACK PEOPLE

Anti-Black racism is rampant in the United States.[32] Many people, media products, and organizations stereotype all Black people as criminal, making it doubly painful for Black women workers to be assigned the task of closely monitoring customers to prevent shoplifting.[33] Within the service panopticon, customers are being watched by workers and frontline managers. These observations are not neutral, but are power imbued and racialized, with Black customers more likely to be profiled as shoplifters and Black workers more likely to be asked to follow Black customers around the store.[34] Customer surveillance reinforces anti-Black beliefs, causing Black women workers pain, discomfort, and feelings of isolation.

The most extensive training most companies provide is on shoplifting prevention, also known as "shrinkage." Worker accounts of shoplifting often invoke generalizations about racial minority groups, especially Blacks, although some, likely conforming to the official company line, do mention the importance of not making assumptions. Store managers' decisions to profile Black shoppers assume even more complex racial meaning when they ask Black employees to perform this task, as if the workers' Blackness neutralizes the racism of this practice.

For Black women, it can be deeply challenging to work in an environment and for a company that uses such blatantly racist practices. Antonia only worked at Express for a few months:

> Everybody was pretty nice, but I just felt like some people were prejudiced towards a certain group of people. Or like, for example, [a] Black person comes in that's around my age, not even women, women were okay, but especially the men. It's always like, "Um. Yeah, can you make sure you watch the person?" Like that's a good thing. That's one of the reasons why I don't really like working there because I didn't really like that. And you can obviously hear it through the walkie[-talkies] because they're communicating with everyone [on staff].

The way managers openly discriminate against Black shoppers, evident through commentary via the walkie-talkies, amplifies already challenging customer service duties. Antonia recognizes frontline managers' requests to profile young Black men as reflecting beliefs that demean Black people as untrustworthy and unwelcome.[35] This negotiation of "prejudiced" managers erodes job quality, leading Antonia to "not really like working there." Such practices create more tension in how Black workers navigate relationships with customers, while also causing rifts between workers and managers.

Pauline lowers her voice as she shares similar experiences at Hollister:

> That's the thing, a lot of people think it was Black people that shoplift all the time, but most of the time it was white men and girls. And I was just like, hm.... There were times where they'd ask me to go survey other people. ((Interviewer: Other Black people?)) Yeah, and I was just like, "Oh, OK. Because it's racist if you do it. But if I do it, it's okay." But most of the time it would be like young white girls or white guys.

Research confirms that more whites than Blacks are caught shoplifting, yet the retail surveillance gaze remains firmly fixed on Black shoppers.[36] Pauline is explicit: to her, it's obvious that store-level managers ask *her* to monitor Black customers because it will make a bad practice seem less racist. These accounts illuminate the distinct, persistent racial discrimination in clothing retail. Anti-Black surveillance practices appear consistent industrywide, as attested by reports that Anthropologie employees use a codeword to profile Black customers.[37] Workplaces can be exclusive and hostile, with racist presumptions about customers constituting one source of discomfort within a broader constellation in this brand-oriented service industry.

Anti-Black surveillance extends, of course, to Black workers, as part of the racialized service panopticon. Managers, for instance, expect all staff members to purchase and wear clothing from the current line of merchandise, yet Pauline was accused of stealing a sweater that she bought at the beginning of her shift and wore while working. She raised the incident with corporate management, but their nonresponse led Pauline to quit her job of nearly five years: "The company called [the manager] asking her about the incident, she was just like, 'Oh yeah. I don't know like maybe she probably took offense to it, but I didn't mean it like that.' Like trying to brush it under the rug." Pauline felt betrayed and diminished, remembering that the manager

> did try to apologize to me afterward, but there's very little that you could say to someone after you've accused them of something like that. . . . And I was just like so insulted because I already have to deal with that when I like go to other stores. I've had people try to follow me and stuff like that but then to have my own manager accuse me of something like that—like that's just really insulting.

Knowing that store managers direct her to racially profile shoppers in her workplace and that she is racially profiled in other stores when she goes shopping is difficult enough for Pauline.[38] Despite her relatively long tenure at this store, her manager racially profiled her *and* wrongly accused her of theft. Corporate managers did nothing to enforce her rights or discipline the store manager. This marked the end of Pauline's patience with her hostile workplace. Pauline's story demonstrates how the service panopticon extends the broader racial order and has serious consequences for Black workers and shoppers.

In general, retail clothing stores promote "diversity" without actually addressing institutional practices that perpetuate racial discrimination.[39] They don't staunchly support Black and Latinx workers facing racism. Retailers fail workers of color by not implementing and enforcing policies intended to improve racial dynamics within the workplace. Given the pervasiveness of anti-Black racism in the United States and within retail labor practices, these failures particularly affect Black workers.[40] Race is embedded in the way workplaces are organized—because they are socially constructed institutions—benefiting white and disadvantaging Black workers and consumers.[41]

The service panopticon entails constant, multimodal surveillance of the kind increasingly focused on Black and Brown communities in the United States. This panopticon is not "color blind" or racially neutral, observing all workers and customers equally. It is racialized, focusing negative attention on Black workers and customers while overlooking white criminality, as Pauline suggests. Black retail workers compose a growing minority group whose on-the-job experiences have sparked few, if any, changes in corporate policies. Meanwhile, racism persistently affects Black people's homes, workplaces, schools, places of worship, recreational activities, and mental and physical health.

In the case of unfair surveillance of Black customers, Black workers feel it's difficult to resist retailers' racist practices, even though they recognize them as racist. Just as sociologist W. E. B. Du Bois theorized Black Americans' experience of the racial chasm as living under "the Veil," Black retail workers in the twenty-first century occupy a seemingly untenable position, challenging them to maintain two selves. Black women in our study narrate the clarity of their situation that emerges over time: keep the job and perform racist acts or leave.[42] In the end, quitting the job seemed to be the most effective strategy workers could imagine. Pauline and Antonia both chose to leave their retail jobs due to the mistreatment of Black shoppers.

Such racially discriminatory customer and employee surveillance tactics create conflict-ridden—if not openly hostile—workplaces. Anti-Black corporate practices, actively implemented by store managers, establish overt and subtle obstacles for Black workers to be accepted and belong in these retail spaces, causing fractures in relations between Black workers, coworkers, and both levels of management.[43] Implementing workplace policies that name and confront racism would provide an institutional pathway to redress these wrongs and send the message to all employees—and customers—that the company unequivocally rejects racial animus. Until that is seen as a profitable approach, however, the relative disposability of the retail workforce will mean continued racial control on the job.

CONCLUSION

Coworker bonds can improve work experiences for those who forge them. Those excluded are largely deprived of positive social connections, as well as the potential to be scheduled for more hours and earn higher incomes. Age affects bonding. Although teenagers or twenty-somethings are the target market for many of these clothing stores, many customers are "tweens" and young teens (ages thirteen to fifteen). As workers move into their twenties and beyond, they tend to become disenchanted with both the brand and the work. Many resign at this point, while those who stay express difficulties connecting to younger coworkers.

Race continues to structure these workplaces and interactions between employees, even after a highly visible lawsuit and settlement paid by Abercrombie. White staff members more frequently describe their retail store coworkers as "very friendly" or "like family." In fact, because these stores often target white customers and hire mostly whites, white workers may better reflect the brand, thus feeling a greater sense of belonging in the workplace. Black, Asian, and Latina women often establish stronger bonds with other women of color. Yet in white-dominated workplaces, if a key coworker friend leaves the job, women of color may suddenly find themselves isolated again. Workers across race discuss positive and negative workplace relationships, but supportive social ties are more tenuous for Black, Asian, and Latina women. Focusing on relationships among workers allows us to show how unequal and uneven social connections in the workplace deepen racial inequality.

The service panopticon is also racialized in troubling ways, particularly regarding the racial profiling of Black customers as potential shoplifters.[44] Reflecting racial divides of the broader retail sector and US society, Black women recount frontline managers asking them to police Black customers in clothing stores.[45] Racist assumptions that Black people are untrustworthy and criminal disturbed many of the Black women we interviewed. Corporate practices reinforcing racist beliefs added to their sense of isolation on the job and their frustration with workplace practices. Notably, Black women decried these directives rather than internalizing the criminalization of Blackness, but they also didn't know how to resist the rampant profiling, other than to leave their jobs. These experiences reflect a unique and important racialized dimension of the service panopticon in which retailers treat workers' Blackness as an asset to prevent theft and bolster the brand's "diverse" appeal while it is also a liability since managers accuse Black workers of criminal acts.

The "twoness" of their status is not lost upon many of the Black women we interviewed. In white-dominant retail spaces, Black workers find themselves singled out and made to feel unwelcome—even criminal. Black workers occupy both hypervisible *and* invisible roles in such workplaces.[46] The surveillance directives from store managers to police Black shoppers place Black workers in a chilling position. Race thus shapes workers' general sense of belonging, friendship, and enjoyment of their jobs, as well as the shifting relationships that constitute the service quadrangle. Black and other workers of color occupy a particularly tenuous position amid workers, customers, store managers, and corporate management.

Technologies in the twenty-first century have changed retail workplaces, but they have not disrupted the racist and discriminatory practices of earlier centuries. Although like some other scholars, we find some workers enjoying their retail jobs due to spending time with "fun" coworkers, these workers are mostly white.[47] While Black, Asian, and Latina women make friends in diverse workplaces, they also voice the greatest difficulty in white-dominated spaces. Being asked to reinforce racist and too-often lethal stereotypes by policing Black customers—or being accused of stealing themselves—Black women particularly suffer in these racialized, white-dominant workplaces. Customer interactions are clearly subject to racialized surveillance practices. In the next chapter, we further examine customer-worker dynamics.

4 Customer Expectations and Emotional Labor

Stacey, who is white, remembers shopping at Old Navy since childhood. After graduating from high school, she sought to replace her ice creamery gig with a retail job. Old Navy seemed like a natural fit. Now working part-time at Old Navy while attending college, Stacey describes her work as emotionally involved. Each shift means constant work to read customer emotions and respond appropriately: "If I say, 'How are you doing?' And they say, 'Good,' I'm like, 'Okay, good.' But they might be really engaged, 'I'm great! How are you?' You kind of bounce off the way they're feeling too and cater to however they're feeling or whatever they need." Stacey reports prioritizing customer emotions over her own. She internalizes this dimension of the service labor process, saying, "Even if I've had a rough day, I at least try and make myself feel or seem happy . . . because it's all about the customer's experience." On difficult days, she self-imposes the imperative to "seem happy." On other days it's easier for her to simply "feel happy," reflecting the elevated emotional effort Stacey expends connecting to customers. "Happiness is contagious so if the associate is happy, even if you had a rough day, maybe that can make your day better." To her and many others, "good" customer service consists of "deep acting" to conjure cheeriness within, as well as "surface acting" to appear friendly.[1]

Clothing retail profits partially depend on informed, relatable, and persuasive frontline workers. Managers instruct Stacey to customize conversations, calling on her to identify foremost as an Old Navy consumer-expert. Rather than telling shoppers:

"Oh, this shirt just came in. It's new, it's stylish. You should get it." They want us to be like, "These jeans fit me really well. I love them for x, y, z [reasons]. And I think if you're similar in style to me, you would like this. If you're not, maybe try this kind."

Managers encourage these sorts of self-referential recommendations; they want sales workers to recommend choices and share their own positive experiences with the products on offer. Stacey talks about how her employer encourages staff to personalize service: "They definitely don't want us to just be like ((flattens voice)), 'Hi, how are you? Hi, how are you?' . . . They want us to be more lifelike and ((laughing)) I don't know. Because they want their customer to feel like they're getting an individual experience." Workers following the scripts may say to a customer, "Based on what you told me about your daughter, she might like this." When retail staff attempt to encourage sales from each shopper's sojourn into the store, Stacey notes, "It's a lot more work than I thought it would be, but it's fun."

Individualizing customers' experiences requires the provision of *emotional service*. Yet some customers are challenging, evoking emotions that the ideal staffer will tamp down. Stacey describes customers who are

the cranky type of women, who just like to be very nitpicky about certain things. Like you know, they'll have a coupon and they'll be like, "But I have this coupon!" It's like, "Well, it's not valid yet." They're like, "*Oh, my God*" freak out and get very frustrated and call managers over or the kind of people who will get very angry very easily at us as associates.

Giving a recent example, Stacey recalls a coworker who was ringing up a customer with numerous items:

The associate . . . who rang her up was doing her job. She was being as polite and nice as possible. She did not do anything wrong. And, our manager came over and he was like, "I'm really sorry that this is happening," and she's the kind of lady that's snappy and she was like, "Well, you should be." He's like, "Okay. I'm sorry. I'll give you ten percent off for having to go through this" and stuff and she just was not appreciative at all. She's like, "I'm not shopping here ever again."

It is challenging for Stacey and her colleagues to maintain their composure when customers get "very angry very fast." Their shared emotional labor reinforces worker alliances. On the other hand, the work can also be rewarding. Stacey describes a woman who was rushed and how pleasurable it was to help this customer quickly choose a shirt and sweater that would pair well.

Thus far, we have considered workers' relationships with store managers, corporate managers, and coworkers. In this chapter, we discuss the last point in the service quadrangle: workers' relationships with customers. Workers identify emotional labor as central to providing good customer service, analyzing how this often arduous task is attenuated by racial and gender dynamics.

EMOTIONAL LABOR IN SERVICE WORK

Emotional labor—controlling feelings as part of labor's value production—is essential to service work.[2] Of course, all sorts of occupations invariably include specific "feeling rules," or norms and expectations about how workers should display their feelings.[3] Workers in service industries, especially, must manage both their inner feelings and their outer expressions of emotion. Customer service workers should not frown, furrow their brows, or roll their eyes when a customer is rude or petulant; instead, they should smile and appear interested in each customer's needs, to encourage sales and repeat purchases. Positive encounters with shoppers may uplift workers, providing some satisfaction; in these moments, customer service can be described as proudly providing a nourishing "social act and a human relationship."[4] However, customer disrespect bothers and alienates workers. These interactions are among the most difficult aspects of retail jobs.

Emotional labor, or how individuals control their feelings as part of paid employment, differs from *emotion work*, or the ways that people attempt to manage feelings in their everyday lives with friends and family that are not commodified in a labor exchange.[5] Sociologist Arlie Hochschild pointed out how workers use emotional labor to affect customers' emotions; for example, flight attendants project calmness to soothe anxious flyers, while bill collectors make customers fearful of the impending consequences if they do not pay their debts.[6] Just as Stacey tries to act happy to make happiness "contagious" among her customers, the retail clothing workers in our study describe contorting themselves emotionally to assist shoppers.

Emotional labor, to be sure, is a component of most jobs. It can be a site of power struggles when employers attempt to alter workers' emotional performances—for example, reminding them to "be happy" and threatening their jobs if they falter.[7] Employees are supposed to hide negative feelings, such as annoyance, and outwardly express compassionate cheer. Hochschild refers to "surface acting," which is when a worker pretends to feel something, and "deep acting," which is when a worker tries to genuinely feel an emotional state.[8] Workers must manage inauthenticity as they try to follow the feeling rules at their companies. Some researchers even suggest that employees are more likely to "burn out" or leave jobs in which they feel inauthentic as they work.[9]

Exerting the effort to please their patrons allows staffers like Stacey to foster upbeat relationships, bring some pleasure to their jobs, and leave interactions with a "great feeling." Workers often identify with their customers, informally employing "the golden rule": they treat shoppers how *they* want to be treated while shopping. Yet workers also handle their customers' emotions, such as when customers "freak out" or become "snappy."[10] In these situations, workers disassociate themselves—often expressing frustration over customers' thoughtless transgressions, but trying to keep a pleasant affect throughout difficult interactions. Between managers' and customers' expectations, workers must carry out challenging emotional labor throughout hours of otherwise repetitive manual tasks.

To dig deeper, we first present a broad analysis of emotional labor in this sector. Then we use our respondents' experiences to generate insights about the racial and gender dynamics of emotional labor in the US clothing retail industry.[11] There are tensions in the service panopticon, as customer expectations of workers and worker expectations of customers may mismatch; customer expectations sometimes align with managerial requirements and sometimes with worker preferences. Workers can get caught up in trying to internalize and fulfill the expectations of both groups. As in previous chapters, we circle back to explain how the same job plays out differently for women of color, who are most often subject to hostility from customers.

VACILLATING EMOTIONS AT WORK

Engaging with customers can be both enormously rewarding and incredibly difficult. Retail workers need to notice and interpret their customers' moods, even as customers affect workers' moods. Melissa summarizes the impact of varying tenors of customer interactions at J.C. Penney:

> There's some people that come in that do uplift your mood. Just seeing how they're excited to get what they're getting. It gives you a great feeling when you see someone leave that's happy. When you see someone that leaves unsatisfied, it really just puts a downer on your day. Or if you experience a customer that's really rude, your mood can go from [high to low] in two seconds.

Many of the workers we interviewed describe fluctuating emotions at work. They truly enjoy assisting customers and making them happy. Unkind shoppers can be jarring. At Wet Seal, Lori says mildly, "some customers can really like nit and pick," while at TJ Maxx, Frank does not characterize customers as outright bothersome, but says that occasionally they "just kind of suck. . . . You realize, wow, that person kind of made me feel like crap. I was just trying to do my job." That workers see their jobs as influenced by customers' moods and treatment is not surprising, but it is noteworthy how much difference it makes, including for workers who reported quitting to avoid the emotional burden.

Surface acting, a practice of using culturally appropriate gestures and language to engage shoppers, is necessary for most of these retail jobs. The workers' goal is to make customers feel positive about shopping at their store and be likely to come back. Nicole must "play along," portraying a "happy, helpful, optimistic" worker at Nordstrom Rack. Kathleen, who works in a boutique, explains: "Some people are annoying, and I just try to keep calm. You still have to do your job. Even though I had a bad job, I'll just try to smile and help them out." Denise maintains that customer interactions at Abercrombie were really tough because "it wasn't really me. That's not really how I am, on a regular basis. . . . You're role-playing for the time that you're there, not with the people [workers] there, but to the customers who come in." All of these workers recognize that they act a part, projecting the persona that fits the service-oriented specifications of the job. Women, in particular, tend to see these job expectations as normal, just another item populating their checklist of duties.

The "deep acting," which requires workers not only to *act* but also to make themselves *feel* calm and good, is a bigger struggle. James illuminates his internal efforts when he has had a rough day or encountered a difficult Nordstrom patron: "There's [*sic*] days that you're not happy. You have to manage that. It's almost like an acting job, and you always have to be happy. You always have to be conversational as much as possible. You have a bad day. You have a bad customer. It doesn't matter." For James, regardless of his situation, it seems there is a requirement that he inhabit, rather than just express, an emotion suited to his workplace.

Exuding enthusiasm when workers feel neutral, if not demoralized, causes emotive dissonance.[12] When Stella is drained, she says, "it's hard to put on a nice face for the customers," while Claire points to the exhaustion of performed inauthenticity: "When I'm kind of grumpy and don't want to be there, and I'm fake smiling for six hours straight, folding the same pile of shirts, I'm like 'This is just stupid. . . .' I don't know, it was fake." Claire works at Hollister and suggests the corporate scripts contribute to this "fake" feeling: "I just felt I always had to be acting how I was supposed to be acting, and not how I would usually be acting. . . . I felt it made me really fake and pressured to act a certain way."[13] Routinized approaches feel unnatural, detracting from the potential satisfaction of talking to customers.

Some research suggests that men and women both experience burnout when inauthentic emotional labor is part of their jobs, though women hide their agitation at work more.[14] Yet we observe that the men more frequently list this dissonance among the worst parts of the job. It might be that men, particularly white men, who have less practice expressing inauthentic emotions in all areas of daily life, experience this kind of labor as more arduous than do more-practiced women.[15] Frank, who is white, recognizes the importance of putting on a "phony face" at TJ Maxx, describing a fluctuating experience of customer service work:

No one's perfect. Sometimes you wake up and you're just like, "I really don't want to go to work today," but you got to do it, so you get in there and you're just kind of existing. And sometimes it will be enthusiastic, you'll have your coffee, you come in, "All right, let's do it." Other times, you're just like, "Oh God, I just want to get through the day."

Julian (white), a manager at H&M, also elaborates on the unrealistic ideal of the retail worker as a smiling helper and how this is a fiction shared by managers, workers, and customers:

I think they expect you to be happy and smiling and everything, regardless of what's going on with your life. I think people forget that you have a life and that you have issues that you're dealing with. . . . I expect [myself and the workers] . . . to be able to separate that, but sometimes it's kind of hard. I think customers may have like a false expectation.

No matter what else is happening in his personal life, Julian feels the weight of affective expectations. Both for himself and as he manages his staff, he struggles over how much emotional labor can reasonably be expected from retail service workers.

We were especially surprised to hear Brendan's (Asian) complaints; one of the most enthusiastic and extroverted workers we interviewed, he emphasized the many positive aspects of his jobs at Pac Sun and G. H. Bass. Even so, near the end of our interview, when we asked whether he would recommend the job to a friend, he responded: "Always having to put a smile on your face and interacting with some pretty abrasive customers daily grinds your gears. So, no, I wouldn't recommend it." Despite Brendan's best efforts and seemingly sunny disposition, he too understands the emotional toll of customer service, especially when internalized ideals fit poorly with in-the-moment service provision. Retail clothing workers recognize that a key part of their job is enacting positive emotions, which they find challenging, particularly when dealing with "abrasive" customers.

CUSTOMER EXPECTATIONS

Just as managers expect employees to always be well-mannered and obliging, customers invoke their own conception of "good service." Warmly greeting patrons and politely offering assistance are central and reasonable expectations. Identifying with her customers at Forever 21, Stella explains: "When you walk into a store, you expect people to be nice, and you expect people to be willing to help you because ... even though you're only spending $15 on a shirt, you're spending your money, so you want to be treated well." Although fast-fashion retailers in teenage-niche markets invest little in service-oriented training, workers nonetheless recognize interacting well with shoppers as crucial to the job. Workers thus attempt to make customers feel appreciated for coming into the store and buying clothing.

During in-store observations, we noticed that women engage more directly with customers, both verbally and nonverbally, than men, who seem to wait for customers to ask for help.[16] On one fieldwork visit to Abercrombie, for example, it was unclear whether the stretchy, white, ruffle-hemmed items on a table display were skirts or blouses. A nearby worker was folding women's jeans. Kyla made eye contact with the nearest staffer, a Black man, and held up the item. Laughing explicitly at her ignorance, she asked him what it was. Perplexed, he approached, as she inquired over the booming pop music, "I mean, is it a skirt, or a shirt?" Shrugging, he replied, "I don't know. A skirt?" They chuckled over fashion's entertaining ambiguities, and he returned to his folding task. In this service encounter, the worker answered the question at hand but didn't volunteer further assistance. His friendly but impersonal and brief engagement typifies the interactions we saw with men working in teen-oriented clothing retail.[17]

However, men and women both convey the importance of being friendly on the job. Antonia, who works at Express, sums up: workers should "just be helpful ... that's supposed to be your job, you know?" Thus retail staff associate with customers to determine how to provide ideal service, look for meaning and sincerity in these encounters, and use personal ideas about good service to ignore or challenge managers' expectations.[18] For example, Frances argues that her role at Abercrombie is to make customers share her love of shopping: "They need to have a good time shopping. I love having a good time shopping. I'd want that for anyone else." For Frances, helping customers have a "good time" is part of her job. Our interviewees consistently explain that when they go shopping, they want to see workers who are helpful and happy, not just pressuring customers to buy as much as possible. Of course, this preference involves another mismatch: workers weigh managerial pressures to sell more to more people against "the golden rule" standard of meeting customers' interests.

Because shoppers' needs vary, helpful service varies. For most of Zara's customers, Risa recalls, good customer service "was just being around if I need you," but others "needed your help, and they knew what they wanted." Joyce describes her reading of the range of service Macy's customers want:

> There will be people that say, right off the bat, "I'm just browsing." And, you're like, "Okay," I'll just step to the side, "My name is Joyce. Let me know if you need help." The people that are unsure, they're like, "Yeah, I kind of want this. . . ." Then you can stick more with them and actually have more of a sales associate role and try to show them different promotions and stuff.

Recognizing what customers need and playing the appropriate role is key for Joyce. However, Veronica conveys that it can be "a little bit more difficult" to attend to some of these support-seeking Gap shoppers:

> Tell me what you need, and I'll get it for you. I'm willing to help you, but some people . . . they expect you to know what they want. We don't. ((Laughs)) . . . And, I'm like, "You need to give me a little bit more information. You need to describe what you're looking for."

When customers have trouble voicing what they want, workers must try to figure it out, identifying the right approach for each shopper.

Workers foreground the importance of helping shoppers make reasonable and satisfying purchases. They make meaning out of finding flattering, but not necessarily expensive, outfits, to please their customers. Brendan outlines his strategy to transform onetime Pac Sun shoppers into dedicated, repeat customers: get to know them, learn their likes and dislikes, and provide the best-suited, genuine, engaged service possible: "It felt good to help people find what they want or give them a good deal." Other workers went further, highlighting their intention to help people feel great about the way they look, whether it's a teenager looking for clothing that suits their changing body or someone choosing an outfit for a major life event like a funeral or wedding. One worker mentioned finding meaning in helping women feel good about their bodies. Rachel, who works at teen-focused American Eagle, references the effects of eating disorders on girls: "If I can go to work every day and help people see their

Figure 11. Sales clerk ready to help customers. SOURCE: iStock.com/pixelfit.

body in a better light . . . then I've done my job." We were struck by how often we heard workers express wanting to make a positive difference in the lives of their customers. In a low-paid, high-turnover job that entails a lot of stress, workers still spent a lot of time reflecting on the meaning they make from their work.

Just the customer interaction is meaningful for these workers. Carl says that, at J. Crew, which is oriented toward a wider age range and has a higher price point, good customer service "is more about making them happy and representing the product well, not just pushing sales." Angela, at the more modestly priced Old Navy, also relates to shopping on a budget: "I have people who come in, and I'm not afraid to say, 'Let's check the clearance rack first.'" Financial constraints shape the *kind* but not necessarily the *degree* of sales assistance that customers may seek. When workers can identify with budgetary limitations, they accentuate their sincere aim to help customers maneuver the sales floor without breaking the bank. "Definitely having my customers leave happy is the goal," Lori says of her time at Wet Seal, then adds, "for me at least." That qualifier—"for me"—indicates that Lori's customer service goal is sometimes at odds with her store manager's focus on higher sales.

Customers at teenage-niche clothing stores also expect cheery staff to create a fun, energetic atmosphere (the sort that managers see as an aspirational environment). Almost all of the workers in these stores emphasize acting "fun," "happy," "energetic," and "outgoing." When, as Denise observes, it is "expected that we'd be very lively and friendly," workers note it's easier if you are naturally extroverted. Tia comments that Forever 21 customers look for "cheeriness," which meant "I had to be smiling all the time." Amid the intentionally "night club" atmosphere at some stores, corporate and frontline managers expect the visible sales staff to represent customers' potential "friends" or sexual partners. Denise remembers about Abercrombie & Fitch:

> Customers really did expect us to be friendly and try to interact with them, because I don't know, it's kind of cool because there's really like music going and you kind of feel like you're in a club or some cool, I don't know, getaway, so I guess they expected us to add to that experience, like "*hey.*"

Denise's "hey" suggests a meeting between two mutually attracted people, rather than a worker and a perusing patron. Brendan, the chipper worker who nevertheless says that the emotional labor "grinds your gears," describes his workplace thus: "Honestly, at Pac Sun, it was very giddy. Like, I had a lot of fun there. It was genuinely enjoyable to interact with customers." Later, he adds: "Sometimes we'd have just like random people come in and we'd end up, like, I don't know, becoming friends on [social media], kind-of chilling afterwards. I ended up partying with some customers." Workers are therefore not only fun but also potentially flirtatious and enticing actors selling the brand's attractive lifestyle. A sexualized, relaxed peer atmosphere contributes to chances to "party" with customers while allowing workers to meet sales imperatives.

Stores that don't target teens expect a slightly different kind of cheeriness from workers. James, at department store Nordstrom, provides some adjectives to describe the ideal sales associate: "Happy, bubbly—people are going to gravitate towards you and feel a better experience." Again, James recognizes that his emotional labor to project happiness helps create positive emotions among his customers. Many workers also try to induce joy in customers through humor. Grace, who considers herself an experienced theater actress, tries to transfer those skills to her work at discount retailer TJ Maxx:

> I'm very upbeat and I talk a lot and I just kind of like say silly things and I laugh and I sing and I hum. . . . It kind of makes them happy a little bit. . . . I'll have customers who will come in and they'll start joking with me and I joke with them.

Those we interviewed derive positive emotional rewards from engaging with customers, which reinforces their alliance with customers while sometimes splintering bonds with management.

For example, service suffers when managers schedule too few workers. It's more difficult for workers to provide helpful service when customers unravel the stores' sleek orderliness, and lines for fitting rooms or at the checkout counter begin to stretch (and stretch customers' patience). When too few associates are "free" to help shoppers who need assistance, everyone is prone to frustration. Jill recalls how Forever 21's staff cuts have affected her ability to perform the emotions she, the customers, and her managers expect to see:

> [In the past] it was also a lot easier because there were more people, so I could devote a little more time to actually talking to the customers. . . . When there was less of us working and there was more clothes to put away and more things to clean up, it was more of a nuisance. People would approach me with questions I had already heard before, and I was like, "I don't have time for this." I would always be friendly and everything, but it was definitely more frustrating by the end.

Demanding shifts, especially on weekends or during sales events, are exhausting. Because of the just-in-time scheduling practices, workers might have late-night closing shifts as well as early opening shifts, adding exhaustion to the test of their sunny dispositions. They describe being less able to cope with the job's stressors, less likely to smile, and more likely to become short tempered when they are tired. Worn-out workers find it more difficult to induce positive emotions in their customers through their emotional labor. Almost every store at which our interviewees worked bans sitting, even during unplanned or extended shifts. Sales employees become more disillusioned as their working conditions worsen, making it more difficult to connect with customers and each other. Corporate labor practices like short-staffing, routinization, and scripting strip the fun from customer service in these moments, undermining its effectiveness and taking away a key nonmonetary reward of the job.

Customers also expect workers to quickly find desired items. Being well-informed requires familiarity with the store and stock. Workers note that customers almost always assume sales staff know what items are in the store, where they are located, and when new shipments will come in. Antonia shares her typical response when a question came up at Express:

> "Oh, I'm not exactly sure, but I can refer you to blah, blah, blah, or ask one of my team members to come and help me," or something like that, but you can never just say, "I don't know." I wouldn't want someone that would assist me to be like, "Um, I don't know." "Okay, so, why do you work here?"

Antonia identifies with her customers; it's reasonable to be annoyed when the staff members are uninformed. And there are some stores where workers spend time learning the products so they can answer a wider array of questions to fulfill this duty; they are just rare among fast-fashion stores.

Finding items is especially difficult in such stores. Fast-fashion marketing relies on constant change; the stores modify merchandise frequently—both in terms of what's in stock and its exact location within the store—to influence customers to return more often. Yet since workers usually are scheduled for limited hours each week, they struggle to keep up, much as their customers do. Melissa details this predicament about working at J.C. Penney, saying that shoppers

> expect me to know where everything is . . . [and] know how much it costs and if it's on sale or not. And, I'll be like, "Sorry, I only work here like four days a week, and they change things like every other day." That's definitely one thing I've learned in retail, they're constantly like moving things around and keep moving, moving. If you're not there for two days, you can come back and it could be a completely different store.

Remembering the entire inventory and its placement throughout the store, given their schedules and near-constant arrival of shipments of new merchandise and displays, is a nearly impossible task for many frontline workers. Thus, many we interviewed reference the frequency of "floor set" changes. At Forever 21, Jill describes:

> If you ask me for a shirt, there's thousands of shirts. And then a lot of people's common response is, "That's really confusing. Why aren't all the shirts in the same place?" . . . [Or] "Oh, you should organize your store differently." I have no response for that because I have no control over the organization of the store.

Providing a concrete example, Jill remembers a man who came in searching for black leggings with a specific design on them for his daughter:

> I took him to a section where we have a lot of black leggings that vary ever so slightly, and I was like, "They might be in here." And then he was like, "Well, shouldn't you know since you work here?" I was like, "Well, it's a big store and there's only a few of us, so no. I'm sorry, this is the best I can do."

A quick look at Forever 21's website in spring 2020 reveals at least two hundred kinds of leggings, one hundred of them black.[19] Jill was upset that she couldn't help her frustrated customer, particularly because her company put her in this impossible position. The company sells vast varieties of similar clothing while employing relatively few workers. To navigate organizational constraints, workers see themselves operating as mediators between management and customers. Again, this tension tends to diminish their job satisfaction.

Tia recalls doing walkthroughs at a multifloored Forever 21 before the store opened, just trying to learn where all the different styles belonged. It was an insurmountable challenge with the constant influx of new products and display locations. "Go-backs"—assorted apparel that shoppers try on but do not purchase—exacerbate this organizational problem. Tia asserts:

> If the fitting room is really busy, and you know they have a ton [of go-backs], they [customers] are just going to throw stuff in certain places that they might not belong. So, we'll be searching the whole floor for this one shirt, where it goes, and then we'll figure out that it doesn't go on this floor. It goes on another floor.

Both the floor set adjustments and the mistakes with "go-backs" create obstacles for workers in their efforts to aid shoppers who seek specific pieces:

> When customers come to me and they are just like, "Oh, where can I find this?" I am just like, . . . "Even if I tell you that it's supposed to be there. It might not even be there because someone might have put it in the wrong section. It might still be in the fitting room. We might have taken it out to make room for more things. I don't know everything that's going on [with the merchandise] in the store."

Sales staff believe they should be able to aid customers by finding specific items, but this isn't always feasible. Workers conveyed frustration over their inability to answer what to customers seem like simple questions, due to corporate labor practices.

Customers may also seek certain sizes that are not available on the floor. In such instances, customers will ask sales associates, like Ashley at Target, "'Hey, do you have any more of this in the back?'" Shoppers likely imagine a large warehouse space, just out of view, with neatly stacked shelves or maybe even an electronic inventory system. That's not reality. Many workers describe huge, disorganized piles of clothing in the back, jumbles of merchandise that the computer systems cannot track and workers cannot quickly sort.[20] Frank complains that at TJ Maxx:

> We didn't have any sort of inventory system. We couldn't search what we have, but people always have this notion that we could just search on the registers . . . and get an inventory brought up, but that didn't exist. . . . This whole concept of the backroom and the inventory and being able to look [things] up is just nonexistent in my opinion.

This problem exists because, although fast-fashion corporations have invested in a great deal of technology that allows them to surveil workers and customers, they don't appear to have invested in systems that might allow workers to quickly find specific items.

When Hollister shoppers ask Lance about what's available, some ask politely, "Can you just please check this in the back?" But others, he says, give him attitude and make "rude gestures, like 'it's not hard to do your job.'" When that happens, Lance imagines retorting, "Well, 'it's hard when

I deal with people like you.'" Corporate management's panopticon exacerbates the challenges of engaging in emotional labor. In a situation of little information about the inventory and angry customers, corporate fails to use technology in ways that actually facilitate meeting customer needs and successfully moving the available inventory. Lance and other workers come to recognize the dramatic mismatch between the power customers *think* the sales staff have and the reality of working in disorganized, fast-fashion stores.

The chaos of the physical setting can fade into the background when workers have the opportunity to talk about fashion. Providing shoppers with style pointers, especially for workers who identify as fashion aficionados, can be among the best parts of the job.[21] Lauren tells us:

> I think myself and a lot of the [Urban Outfitters] employees really do care about style, and so if a customer asks, "What do you think would be a cute outfit" or "What would look good and trendy[?]" . . . This guy I work with is obsessed about it, and loves working the fitting room and says, "That looks awesome!" and "You should match it with this."

Styling customers can be a reasonable and pleasurable part of workers' jobs or a challenge for those who don't feel up to the task. Glenn works at Abercrombie Kids: "I don't really know that much about clothes in the first place, so I'd be like, 'Oh, maybe this would look good.'" Straight men say less about styling customers in their interviews, though Jason details the importance of helping Abercrombie customers learn *how* to wear the clothes, like teaching them how to roll up sleeves or pant legs to reproduce the brand's signature style. Carl and Trent, on the other hand, are both gay men who mention how much they enjoy styling work at J. Crew and Express. It may be that Carl and Trent feel more comfortable as gay men discussing fashion; men of color, like Jason and Trent, may also be given more freedom to perform more stylish forms of masculinity.[22]

Advice about outfits can lead to sensitive conversations, leading to doing delicate emotional labor with customers. As shoppers select different items and model the outfits to solicit feedback, workers cultivate effective responses. Jason adopts a tone of casual dismissal when customers don't look great in an outfit: "'Um, nah, I think the green would be better,' [or] 'Why don't you come over here and try the ripped jeans?'" Rachel, too, tries to find ways to optimistically redirect American Eagle customers to other outfits: "I'll say, 'Let's go this direction. I think this might fit you better.'" While she thinks honesty wins her repeat business from a segment of shoppers, Rachel suspects her advice against certain looks is "probably not always appreciated." To avoid that, Charlotte uses "positive phrasing" to communicate in the Hollister dressing rooms when the news is less than desirable: "'That's a really nice shirt, but the fit is just so awkward. To be honest, it doesn't work with those jeans.'. . . Show them it's the fashion, not their body type."

Informing shoppers without criticizing their style choices or bodies means threading the needle.[23] Here again, workers consider their own experiences as they shape their notions of appropriate assistance. "I would never interject, because I feel like that's so rude," Denise comments. "But if I was asked, 'What do you think of this?'. . . I'd be 'Oh yeah, that looks great,' or 'You know what? I think this would look better.'" Kathleen, whose job is in a boutique, says, "I understand I sell clothing, but I would still tell you, 'I don't think that would fit you,' [or] 'I don't like how it looks on you.'. . . I know when somebody tells me something looks nice on me, and *I know* it doesn't."

It is telling that workers tread so carefully when giving customers advice about the clothing they are considering buying. They recognize that customers have substantially more power in the interaction, even as they think about how they would want to be treated. In other settings, such as nonprofit shops aimed at helping unemployed women find work clothes, the power dynamic may play out differently.[24] The scrutiny of customers' bodies and intrusive suggestions in these settings make clear that the women volunteering at the nonprofit have more power than the "shopper." Race, gender, and body size all become topics that "workers" discuss in rude and even offensive ways; they also may expect "shoppers" to choose the first clothes that fit them, rather than trying on multiple outfits.[25] In retail clothing stores, the dynamic is switched: it appears that workers do everything they can to remain polite and respectful, suggesting that customers in clothing shops have substantially more power in the interaction.

In so many ways, workers repeatedly show how they use their consumer identities to inform their understanding of what quality service entails. They underscore communicating a balance of honesty and consideration, knowing that buying clothes is about feeling good through fashion within spending constraints, even when that goes against retailers' profit motives. In this work, their emotional labor can be challenging, such as when they have no idea where to find a particular item or when they need to deftly redirect a customer to a better style. Yet many of our interview participants discuss approaching styling customers as a shared puzzle: a fun, somewhat challenging, and ultimately rewarding collaborative project.

KEEPING THE STORE CLEAN

Workers also have expectations about how they'll be treated in customer interactions. Topping their list of annoyances is the mess that customers make. Managers have clear expectations about how stores should be maintained, as they aim for a "pristine" look. However, they rarely staff the store enough to preserve the environment as customers browse around, undoing work as fast as it can be finished. This work is also invisible labor, in the sense that workers are meant to do it in inconspicuous ways, perpetually folding and restocking in the background so that it appears that the store cleans itself.[26]

In Abercrombie merchandise displays, Mary explains, the emphasis was on detail: "The size stickers all had to be in the same exact [position]. . . . [Y]ou had to put up your [folding] board to it to make sure [the alignment] was perfectly straight." To her chagrin, customers searching for items in their size would just mess up her efforts:

> I was folding this pile, like, so perfectly, meticulously, and she came over and she grabbed one from the other side and ripped it out, and goes, "I wanna buy this!" And I was just like, "Oh my gosh." I was like, "Okay, let me grab it for you." Working retail for a long time, you lose a lot of patience.

Keeping stores immaculate while customers search through inventory is a Sisyphean task. As Lori says about working at Justice, "You will fix that and then you'll turn around and it's a wreck. It's so aggravating." It's the same at Abercrombie, Frances says: "It looks perfect and customers come in and ruin them, basically. Just like, 'Oh it's not my size, I'm just going to

Figure 12. Messy store. SOURCE: iStock.com/Andrei Stanescu.

throw this on the floor,' and just 'Oh no, I don't want this color,' and they kind of like mess things up." And at Forever 21, Stella remembers,

> people will literally just pick up a shirt, look at it, and then just toss it. That's how . . . the store gets so, so messy. You've got these people who are coming in to buy these five dollar shirts or these ten dollar shirts, so they don't care about leaving the store in good condition.

The mess can overwhelm the staff, leading them to regard their jobs as one long, impossible tidying endeavor. Carmen has worked at multiple stores and summarizes the managerial imperatives as consistent: "'Go clean up this, go fold that,' and then customers would just immediately unfold it."

This tension between customers and workers stems from managers' attempts to minimize labor costs through just-in-time scheduling practices. Managers try to reduce the hourly sales ratio, or the amount of money brought in divided by the number of workers, by scheduling too few workers.[27] Corporate managers do not allow frontline managers to schedule the workers needed to keep the store tidy, creating a no-win contest. The service panopticon's signature feature of just-in-time scheduling creates conflicts between workers and managers and between workers and customers, as workers woefully watch customers "mess up" the store, and customers walk out of untidy stores in disgust.

Workers, in this disempowered position, commonly wish aloud that customers would request help rather than ruin the neatly folded stacks of cable-knit sweaters or multicolored tank tops. Hannah recalls watching Aeropostale shoppers: "They're going through piles and piles of clothes that you just folded. And, you're like, 'Let me help you find the size.' And they'd be like, 'No, no, no, I don't want any help.'" Others, like Bryan, are exasperated when stubborn Abercrombie customers refuse help:

> "No, I'm alright." And it's like, "I was just trying to help you guys out. . . . You're messing up like every pair of jeans." Like it just takes one customer to mess up everything on one table . . . when you could have helped them, and you're like, "Oh, I know exactly what you're looking for. It's a small, right here on top."

Workers want to help customers more for several reasons, but one is undeniably to prevent excessive refolding and reorganizing. In the sales or clearance sections, it's all but impossible. Heather recalls a memorably chaotic shift at Forever 21:

> I was in the fitting room, so I was dealing with lines of people and just having to sort through everyone . . . they'd just throw clothes. You are supposed to put your clothes back on the hangers, but . . . people are like "that's their job, they got nothing to do, they can take care of it." . . . That's just rude, that's not polite.

Workers interpret the mess as an expression of customers' disregard for their labor. It feels offensive. As Pauline notes, "Nobody wants to work in [Hollister clearance] because that's the room that's got trashed the most, in terms of people rummaging through it." Sherrie calls Pac Sun's sale section "a complete disaster," while Danielle describes an Old Navy sales event: "The clothes are just scattered all over the table; and you don't even know if the clothes belong to the store or not. They're all over the place. You have to use your organizational skills and fold them and do your best." For Danielle, the mess is so challenging that she even begins to think stray items, not from the store's inventory, may be scrambled into the piles of clothing. Jill shares:

> I remember one time I was folding shirts in the men's section [of For-
> ever 21], and I just sat there. I was almost crying because I was like, "Wow,
> I really don't want to do this right now." And it was like 10 [p.m.], and I was
> like, "This sucks," you know?

Jill was overwhelmed by the agony of having to "fold down" the store
after a busy day. Clearly these jobs elicit strong and authentic emotions
in workers, beyond the emotional labor they do for customers. Keeping
the store neat requires a level of attention impossible to manage during
busy hours; corporate presentation standards are frequently infeasible,
especially given just-in-time-scheduling, creating conflict between workers and customers.[28]

Workers cite these tensions, noting that they see shoppers as responsible for contributing to the store's disorganization while also having to
field customer complaints about that disorder. Heather illuminates this
vicious cycle at Forever 21: "The store gets more messed up and then
the customers are more angry. And it's, ahhhh . . . 'Well, if you just pick
the clothes up that you dropped, it wouldn't be as messy.'" She wistfully
recommends the store "put everything up, so no one can touch anything
and [workers could ask], 'Oh, you want that shirt? I'll climb a ladder and
get it for you. *Don't touch it.*'"

Sometimes customers will even leave trash in the stores and their
dressing rooms. Kathleen recalls "horrible" teen girls violating reasonable
norms at her boutique:

> They used to drop shit on the floor if they're eating something. Yes, they
> would leave it on the fitting room floor. . . . You can't be like, "Excuse me, you
> dropped this." . . . Because that's likely to start a problem that you definitely
> could have avoided by picking it up. . . . You can ask them, "Do you still want
> this?" If they say no, then you throw it away. I didn't have a problem with
> that, though. At first, I did, because I'm like, "I'm not a garbage lady." After
> a while, I was just used to it.

Workers may grow accustomed to cleaning up after customers, but they
never find these customer actions anything but troubling and disrespectful. The mess customers make undermines solidarity between themselves and the staff within the service quadrangle. However, this mess is a
direct result of corporate managers' power and their scheduling practices.

Increased tensions and navigating a messy store space also disincentiv-
ize shopping in brick-and-mortar stores. Thus, managerial practices of
just-in-time scheduling create a loss for customers, workers, and their
managers.[29]

CONFLICTS WITH CUSTOMERS

The canonical idea that "the customer is always right" fails to resonate
with our interviewees. Workers acknowledge that customers deserve a
certain level of deference, and that managers and customers expect staff
to treat all customer desires as reasonable.[30] Yet they also understand
that the "customer is always right" trope is used to excuse rude and angry
behavior from shoppers. Workers often deploy this mantra when we
ask about their training and what they believe managers and customers expect from them. Lori, a worker at Wet Seal, is succinct: customers
are "always right; that's the major one, they're always right." But workers also use the phrase to clarify when customers are in the wrong, as
Tara, who works at American Eagle, shows: "Everyone says customers
are always right, but a lot of the cases, they're not." Brendan, reflecting
on G. H. Bass, says: "You would sometimes have to force a smile. It'd
be, I know you're so wrong right now, but 'You're right.'" And Kathleen
echoes his words as she says, at a boutique, "the customer's always right;
100 percent right, even if he's wrong."

Their voices take on emotion as workers talk about customer treatment as an amplifier of the job's other difficulties. Some customers might
treat staffers as "less than"—or even nonexistent. Women of color provide
accounts of aggressive customers, but white workers most often describe
condescending treatment. For example, Julian's worst shoppers at H&M
"are people who treat you like you're less than a human being." Dehumanizing treatment sticks out to Heather (white), who says that, at Forever 21,
"people won't even really look you in the eye," and Grace (white), who
works at TJ Maxx, says: "Those people obviously don't care about me. And
so largely I'm invisible. . . . When you work in retail or in service, people
pretend like you don't exist because you're performing a service for them,
and they just want you to get out of their way." This sense of invisibility is

demeaning and weakens allegiances workers may feel toward customers without buttressing their allegiances to management. In other words, dehumanizing treatment is also isolating treatment within the service quadrangle.

Some suggest that customer rudeness stems from classist assumptions about retail workers. Grace recalls a customer saying to her manager, "'That college degree got you real far, didn't it?' And [my manager] was like, 'Well I never went to college[,] so . . . .'" At higher-end Nordstrom, James (white) says about shoppers:

> [S]ometimes they look down on you. If they don't know who you are, sometimes they just think, at least as I feel, like an uneducated kid who's going to work here the rest of my life. You don't know me. You don't know what I'm doing. That frustrates me the most, sometimes, personalities of people.

Class-based antagonism (often using educational credentials as a proxy) can be difficult for workers to process. While workers across racial groups declare feeling dehumanized in interactions with customers, whites express more frustration about these indignities. This difference may be because white workers are less used to dealing with microaggressions, which are sadly more common for workers of color.

Contradictions in emotional labor—a double standard in which workers must always be friendly, while customer rudeness is acceptable—feel instinctively unfair. Nicole (white) marvels at this dynamic at Nordstrom Rack: "It's crazy when people will come in and have a double standard, expect you to be friendly and nice but just be rude to you or ask something outrageous. . . . That is one of the most irritating things." Workers explain that they must consistently play the part of the unruffled service worker. Nora (white) finds herself frequently hiding her frustration as she stocks the shelves and rings up customers at Dick's Sporting Goods: "It really makes me kind of mad, but you have to put on a front like you're not mad. You have to bite your tongue a lot of the time." Such encounters are maddening but necessary, workers like Grace (TJ Maxx) confirm:

> The people who come in to piss you off, they're having a bad day and they will come in and say, "The service today was horrible." And you're like, "Oh, I'm sorry. Could you explain to me what went wrong?" And they're like, "Well this associate . . . she just could not find the shirt that I wanted." And

you're like, "Oh okay, well did she go search with you?" "Yeah, and she just didn't do a good job. You people have no idea what you're doing." And you're like, "Okay. I understand ma'am. I'm sorry you had that experience." She's never going to be happy and she is just kind of an unhappy person and is just coming to spread that around. So, if anything, that's what retail has taught me, that some people are just unhappy and you just have to not let them like ruin your day because they treat you badly.

For Grace, remaining calm is the best way to sidestep the unhappiness that customers might try to "spread around." One person cannot necessarily meet an angry customer's expectations. Lori, who is Black, further details the challenge at Wet Seal: "I don't like rude customers. . . . I mean, I get it. You have your bad day but . . . those are kind-of difficult to deal with because just like you're all chipper, and this person's *not*." Lori illuminates the juxtaposition of the "chipper" friendly persona she needs to exude as an ideal service worker and the "rude" shopper. These accounts point to the difficulty of folding emotional labor into the requirements of wage labor.

Aggressive or angry customers are most notable for being poorly behaved with those retail workers who are people of color. Some seem to be *trying* to pick a fight, as Risa (Asian) recalls at Zara:

> I actually had some woman walk in . . . [and she] started yelling at me: "I'm not having a good day, like the amount of money I spend here is disgusting, and no one's helping me." And, literally she had been greeted by three different people when she'd walked in.

Disputes involving verbal abuse may even escalate to threatening physical assault. Mary (multiracial) recounts, "One woman actually threatened to punch my [Abercrombie] manager in the face because she wouldn't give her extra bags." Bryan, who is Latino, characterizes this type of Abercrombie's shoppers: "You're going to have customers that have a bad day and flip out on you sometimes." Before starting their jobs, the workers didn't expect that customers would be this aggressive; they had many stories to tell in their interviews.

Tia (Black) recounts a Forever 21 customer who insisted she leave her assigned post: "I don't know, that old lady, she expected me to be more of like a servant. . . . She wanted me to go find the pants for her and I was just like, 'No. I can't leave my floor, honey.'" Tia continues:

It's like you can't be mad if not everything in the entire online catalog is in this one store. You know? . . . She's like, "Can you look it up on that thing?" I'm like, "Um, I unfortunately don't have access to the computer or the online catalog so if you would like [my manager] to do it."

Tia has developed strategies to address angry customers, but deploying those strategies is one of the most difficult aspects of her job. A disorganized, hierarchical workplace renders workers unable to meet customer and manager expectations at busier times. Cecilia, who is Asian, remembers a J.C. Penney customer who wouldn't take "no" for an answer, either:

When I was working alone, [she] made me try to find something for her mother. Like she needed a certain nightgown, and I would point in the direction, but she wanted me to stay with her so the register wasn't open. That's kind of weird. . . . She even pointed it out, too. She was like, "Are you the only one working?" I was like, "Yea, kind of." She's like, "Oh, that's too bad. *I* have you now."

With a long line of waiting customers at the cash register, Cecilia felt trapped. She wasn't sure how to deny the customer's request without creating a fuss. "I never know when they're going to have a conflict. I hate dealing with that. . . . I'm just like, 'Oh, my God. Why?'" The volatility of service interactions demands that workers be constantly smiling and constantly alert. Kathleen (Black) similarly states: "They were too demanding. 'Can you go get me that? Come on, *girl*, go get me . . .'" In Kathleen's account, it's uncertain if the demanding request "girl" is racialized, but it's clear this staffer was treated disrespectfully.

Such accounts of commandeering customers came primarily from women of color, although Glenn, who is white, reports a similar trope when he suggests that some Abercrombie Kids customers are "very rude." "'I need this, I need this,'" he mimics before describing one "very abrasive" Abercrombie Kids mother "who was angry because we didn't have this one item in her daughter's size." Glenn then repeats, "And she was very angry about it for some reason." And yet he remains an outlier; these accounts are consistent among women of color and relatively absent in accounts from other workers. Logically, this may imply that customers are more demanding with women of color or that women of color, as a group, are more alert to customers' unreasonable expectations and the possibility that they may become aggressive. This pattern reflects both gendered and racially discriminatory stereotypes; other research suggests that consumers in many domains may be more likely to treat Black, Latina, and Asian women workers as subservient.[31] Without institutional recourse—let alone organizational policies aimed at redressing discriminatory practices—these workers are left to deal with hostility in the workplace. Just as workers of color are less likely to feel close to their managers and coworkers, they may also have more distant and potentially conflict-ridden relationships with customers.[32]

Uncertainty about whether a situation will turn sour leads to workers being hypervigilant. Complicating matters, customers are often angry about issues beyond workers' control and ability to solve. Patrons become frustrated about out-of-stock items, for instance, but ordering is often based on fast-fashion corporate metrics; even frontline managers cannot always solve the problem if popular sizes are frequently in short supply.

Frances and Veronica give examples of just this situation. Veronica, who is Black, says that customers at Gap, "always expect you to have their size. That's why when they're looking . . . a lot of people, they do get aggravated when you don't have their size. Yeah, they don't understand that we can't help it." At Abercrombie, Frances (multiracial) confirms, "Some customers, they want this shirt this size [and if] you don't have it, you just ruined their day. . . . They're angry now. That's that." Veronica and Frances are aware there's little that they can do to assuage irate customers' feelings, especially when corporate practices help create that anger: an advertised sale attracts a flurry of customers, so popular sizes sell out. Customers react to such shortages with anger and derision directed at workers.

Frontline managers can be called upon to deal with angry customers. Two Black women in our study, Tia and Kathleen, recounted such moments. At Forever 21, Tia says, "Some people would be angry, some people would be yelling and screaming and stuff. I don't deal with that. That's not my problem." Kathleen recalls that boutique managers trained her in how to respond:

> Some customers who were . . . overly aggressive, sometimes. Don't ever argue with the customers. . . . If a customer's yelling, then walk away. Don't

even try to calm them down. If you see the person is really yelling, don't calm them down, just walk away from them.

Directing upset customers to on-site managers shelters workers from protracted, emotionally draining interactions, though crucially, the practice isn't actually about concern for workers. It's a reflection of their limited agency within the organizational hierarchy. Few sales workers can redress customer complaints; they can't, for example, override the cashier system to change prices or grant returns, so frontline managers *have* to step up.

We did hear a few accounts of white men sales associates intervening when irate customers attacked a woman coworker. David, for example, reports that at Abercrombie, "if someone would get mad at one employee, I'd be like, 'Yo, what's the problem? . . . What's going on here? Can you please calm down your voice? You wanna talk to the manager?' Right away I was—like we would step in." Lance (white) states that if a Hollister customer becomes aggressive, coworkers "come and help them out, give them a break, like, 'We'll deal with them,' something like that." Hannah (white) provides a confirming account of male allyship at Aeropostale:

> I remember one time, there was this woman who was yelling at me for something that had to do with jeans. I was standing at the cash register and one of the, one of my guy coworkers came . . . up beside me and was talking to her, and was like "Is there a problem? What can I help you with?" And he pretty much took over the situation for me.

A display of masculinity may disrupt customers' aggression toward women workers. Both white men and white women hint at gendered intervention. Although Black women relay many, many accounts of antagonistic customers, they do *not* mention coworkers intervening to assist. Managers step in to deal with irate customers, but coworkers rarely do this for their Black women counterparts. Race and gender intersect in all aspects of life, including these retail workplaces; all workers face conflict with shoppers, but their access to workplace solidarity and mechanisms to disrupt some of the worst dynamics of customer service is decidedly uneven. Thus, Black women's experience of customer aggression is not mediated and exacts a deeper toll.

CONCLUSION

Like most workers, the retail staffers we interviewed want to make a positive difference with their work.[33] Customer service can be satisfying, such as when workers support shoppers in feeling good about themselves and happy with their purchases. Yet employees also understand their jobs are mired in negative interactions and expectations that they will perform emotional labor, controlling their responses when customers are rude or aggressive.[34] Workers describe experiencing a range of emotions in the workplace—feeling variably rewarded, frustrated, debased, flirty, and annoyed—as they try to project feeling happy and calm. How their emotional labors play out varies by race and gender.[35]

Our data suggest that some staff attempt "deep acting"—trying to truly make themselves feel deeply happy in the workplace—but nearly all perform "surface acting," like smiling in the face of angry shoppers. Notably, this emotive dissonance evokes the most jarring accounts from white men, who see this labor as particularly taxing. Our research suggests that the experience of emotional labor may be racialized and gendered, not only by workers in different jobs but among workers in the same position.[36] This departure reflects gendered and racial experiences with surface acting outside of the workplace, where women and men of color are more accustomed to acting in ways that are incongruent with how they feel.

Racial and gender differences also emerge in workers' accounts of interactions with customers. White workers emphasize how shoppers treat them in ways that are tinged with class-based condescension, revealing how unaccustomed some whites are to encountering disrespect in public spaces. Asian, Black, Latina, and some multiracial women convey experiences with *unusually* unruly customers, when these customers feel service has fallen short and their specific desires—*this* shirt in *this* size, for instance—have gone unmet. White men appear to enact masculinity and "step in" when customer interactions with a woman coworker go awry, although it is unclear whether women of color receive such support. Racially uneven actions to disrupt harsh customers from berating women workers reinforce isolation, disaffection, and inequality for women of color within the service quadrangle. White workers experience advantages of solidarity and recognition by coworkers and frontline managers in navigating customer encounters, accentuating the white dominance of most retail spaces.

Finally, many mention tensions between providing good service to their customers and following the expectations of the store and corporate managers. The corporate imperative to maintain store appearances weighs heavily on frontline retail workers, who too often find themselves unable to complete their tasks due to corporate labor practices that undermine frontline manager autonomy. In stores with enough workers on busy shifts or more lenient policies, employees feel that they can provide better service. Such situations allow for more enjoyment and meaningful connections.

Low-wage retail clothing workers labor under contradictions: customers expect quality customer service, even as managers schedule too few workers or schedule workers so rarely that they cannot keep up with the constantly changing "floor sets" and fast-fashion merchandise. Workers search for meaning and take pride in providing shoppers with the service that they would expect for themselves, while also struggling with customer demands, rudeness, and even aggression. Consistently, race and gender shape workers' experiences, such that women of color describe regularly dealing with customer anger and doing so without reliable support from coworkers or managers. Visible workers are central actors—and objects—in clothing retail, as we discuss through the lens of aesthetic labor in the next part of the book.

PART III   Aesthetic Labor

5 Beautiful Bodies on the Sales Floor

"THEY BASICALLY LOOK FOR PEOPLE THAT LOOK LIKE THE POSTERS"

Born and raised in the New York City metropolitan area, Kathleen participated in a fashion modeling club in high school. After a short stint at a department store, Kathleen got a job at a boutique selling clubwear, jeans, sweaters, tank tops, and other form-fitting, vibrantly colored clothes to teenage and twenty-something women.[1] The boutique's mannequins displayed throughout the shop are all white, and except for Kathleen (who is Black) and a few friends hired through her, so are the boutique's employees. She says all the sales associates were attractive, with "big breasts . . . brown or blue eyes, and blond or really dark brunettes. . . . It was never a regular girl. . . . It was just weird." Kathleen recalls that her managers saw her as possessing a great look, standing about 5 foot 6 inches tall, with shoulder-length, wavy black hair, unblemished medium-brown skin, and a full-lipped smile of straight white teeth. When retail clothing employers hire people to work in stores whose brand targets teenagers or twenty-somethings, their bodies usually reflect broader beauty standards that entail racialized, classed, and sexualized ideals of femininity and masculinity.

Kathleen was a top seller, surprising her store manager, who confessed that Kathleen was the boutique's first Black employee (see chapter 1).

That surprise may be traced to the ways hiring managers—like so much of society—discriminate against women of color, particularly darker-skinned Black women, though in this case specifically because they're assumed to be unable to represent the brand. Kathleen's experience as the first "Black girl" at the boutique illuminates how race, gender, and class co-constitute the aesthetic labor process that, for the stores in our study, produces a white-dominant brand. However, her success at selling and at getting her Latina and Black friends hired suggests that these racialized practices may shift to diversify or exoticize the brand (even as they continue to reproduce white-associated beauty ideals, like long, flowing hair).

In the next chapter, we discuss how employees wear the merchandise as their "uniform," but here, the focus is on the ways workers' bodies (apart from clothing) are regulated. Across the industry, particularly in stores oriented toward teen shoppers, workers' bodies are a core part of constructing the brand. Thinking about her coworkers at Hollister, Claire, who is white, tall, and thin, with straight blond hair and blue eyes, points out that they all looked alike:

> Every single person there was above 5′6″; [the staff are] white . . . and attractive. . . . There was no one that was Black or heavier. They all looked like clones of each other. We all like fit in the same size clothing. It was just really . . . that kind of threw me off.

When Claire considers Hollister's expectations for "natural" hair, nail polish, makeup, and clothing, she notes that when everyone is that uniformly dressed they "look middle classy." The company's body rules about makeup, nail color, hairstyle, and clothing require staff to reproduce—or at least, to hew as closely as possible to—an implicitly white, middle-class femininity or masculinity.

Beliefs about desirable body shapes for women and men inform this aesthetic labor. Claire recalls her Hollister coworkers as "really petite girls . . . really skinny, really skinny legs" and the men as "built, so they weren't as skinny, but still not heavy . . . just some very defined lines." During her employment, Claire fell ill and was hospitalized. She lost a considerable amount of weight. As she recovered and began regaining that weight, she noticed her frontline managers subtly critiquing her:

It wasn't [them saying] "You're fat, go away," but . . . they'd put innuendos . . . like, "Do you need like more jeans?" . . . And I would say, "Yes, I do," and they would ask if I want the same size jean as before or "do you want *bigger* ones?"

Even though Claire knows that she embodies the store's beauty ideals, she also recognizes these gendered and racialized beliefs about desirable body size as troublesome and unhealthy.

Managers' beliefs about what constitutes being cute and stylish help determine hiring choices in this sector of the branded service economy. Some of these workers enjoy their aesthetic value, knowing that others— including their employer—appreciate their looks and fashion sense. Kathleen took pleasure in the boutique's focus on beauty ("I enjoyed what I did.") while also describing managers adjusting workers' bodies when they arrive for a shift to maximize their allure. The service panopticon focuses not just on sales-related metrics and theft prevention but also on policing workers to ensure they look their best. If anyone was "not on point," frontline managers were ready to help:

> You're walking in, it's like, "You have Chapstick on; put lip gloss on." If you just ate, they had in the bathroom . . . dental floss, toothbrushes for everybody in there . . . brush, hair comb, hair grease in the bathroom, hair spray, perfume, deodorant, everything. You had to make sure you always smell good. You have to look good. . . . The bathroom was full of all that stuff. . . . When you clock back in, it's like, "Open your mouth," just to make sure there's nothing in your teeth. You go clean out your teeth if you have any food in your teeth.

As subjects of the branding process, workers' bodies are under the constant gaze of customers, managers, and, to a lesser degree, coworkers. Managers intimately touch their employees and do beauty labor to cultivate their fulfillment of the company's multisensory aesthetic from looking good to smelling nice. Kathleen tells us that once a manager at the boutique "really did some girl's hair over," even at the expense of keeping the store closed to do so:

> We were supposed to open at 9, she didn't open until 9:30, because she had to curl the girl's hair, because the girl's hair was too flat. . . . They put a blow

dryer to her hair, and they curled her hair in the store. We opened 30 minutes late because of that.

Sales workers remain hypervisible throughout their shifts. Amplifying their beauty serves to boost the store brand's overall aesthetic appeal, while also reflecting the frontline managers' attentiveness to the company's image-centric priorities.

Kathleen didn't protest when this gaze turned on her. Instead, she says, she "didn't mind them doing my hair. I don't want to do my hair myself, so they did it for me." She reminds us that work-required primping can be tedious, time-consuming, and costly.[2] She also demonstrates that this industry's consistent hyperfocus on appearance is either already the norm for workers (a number of them detail practicing extensive beauty work even before they were hired) or becomes the norm. Still, though Kathleen initially framed these forms of regulation as reasonable and even helpful, later in the interview, she reflected: "It didn't seem that bad when I was working there, actually. Now that I talk about it, it does seem bad." Away from the job, Kathleen looked back and saw the potentially intrusive nature of this hands-on aesthetic management.

Aesthetic labor processes entail both pleasure and pain. Kathleen shares other concerns related to the beauty appraisal system: the boutique had an almost all-white workforce and only sold small sizes, and the managers singled out some workers for poor treatment:

> There was this girl who everybody . . . I felt bad, they called her ugly, and they used to make her stay downstairs in the basement. She had to do all the stock, running around. That would be the girl they always send downstairs to get extra sizes to bring up. . . . I didn't think she was ugly.

Kathleen enjoyed "looking good" and knowing she was seen as a living, breathing extension of the boutique's brand, but also recognizes the degradation of her coworker. For Claire, the beauty ideals weighed on her self-esteem. Internalizing the corporate beauty appraisal system made Claire, unlike Kathleen, question herself and doubt her attractiveness: "I didn't know why they hired me; like, I can't look as good as these people." Indeed, aesthetic labor may include sexualizing workers to make the store more appealing to customers, even in an era when managers are increasingly careful about sexual harassment.[3]

In this chapter, we analyze how workers experience their aesthetic labor as sales models, including their attempts to resist bodily expectations. We examine their performance of aesthetic labor in how they wear their hair, makeup, and jewelry, as well as how managers persistently surveil and regulate their bodies. As in other chapters, we demonstrate the salience of race, considering that beauty appraisals inherently include skin tone and other racialized phenotypical markers, sometimes in the "plus" column, sometimes in the "negative." Workers' bodies become part of the labor process—in how managers style workers to help maximize their brand embodiment, how customers comment upon their bodies, and how managers and customers sexualize sales workers as commodities.[4] The racial, gendered, and classed beauty hierarchies propagated in the lifestyle branding of most clothing retail reflect and reinforce the belief in a superlative beauty that is white (and lighter-skinned), gender normative, and "middle class."[5] These troubling beauty evaluations compose corporate branding work to sell "good looks" and "good lives" using workers' bodies as marketing vessels.

BEAUTY AND THE BRAND: UNDERSTANDING THE AESTHETIC LABOR PROCESS

Aesthetic labor is especially prevalent in stores targeting tweens, teenagers, and "college kids."[6] These retailers implement labor practices that use workers as models for the store's signature "look." They hire people seen as visually "fit" to represent the brand and mold them constantly, treating them as walking mannequins.[7] Sociologist Ashley Mears explains that through this labor process, "service employees become part of the products being sold."[8] Thus, when it comes to "onboarding" new employees, appearance is more important than experience and qualifications.[9] In this chapter, we explore how managers use workers as in-store models.

As part of the service panopticon, company appearance policies encourage store managers to hire based on very specific criteria related to "attractiveness" and constantly monitor workers' bodies. To keep their jobs, workers also learn to manage their appearance, thanks to regular interactions with their managers about their looks. Corporate policies largely appear to reproduce a particular classed, racial, gendered, and sexualized beauty aesthetic found in mainstream society and popular culture.[10] Beauty, which is socially constructed, is a form of symbolic capital; workers' bodies help signal their status.[11] Hiring workers who fit socially constructed beauty ideals allows these fashion stores to tap into some of that symbolic capital for their brand. Clothing retailers seem to believe that maintaining a cadre of "gorgeous" staffers attracts impressionable customers.

The clothing retail industry's focus on beauty imposes *body rules* as another dimension of aesthetic labor.[12] Sociologist Eileen Otis conceptualizes "body rules" as "the expectations for bodily presentation and displays . . . shaped by historical and cultural norms of behavior for categories of identity including sex, age, race, ethnicity, and class."[13] Labor scholars have examined the salience of workers' bodies across various occupations, including clothing and cosmetic retail, hospitality, aesthetic services, and the restaurant industry.[14] Throughout, workers use their physicality to create part of the service rendered. Most of these jobs consist of beauty "display work," whereby workers' bodies are treated as objects to view, such as fashion models, adult entertainers, and sex workers.[15] Clothing retail combines display work with interactional labor, in which customers and managers focus on attractiveness, dress, and workers' demeanor, especially in branded firms that emphasize the performance of certain social tastes, manners, and sounds. We focus on workers' embodiment of the body rules pervasive in this sector as another dimension of the service panopticon, which operates as a corporate arrangement to reinforce brand-based classed, gendered, sexualized, and racialized ideals.

Not all clothing retail workers perform aesthetic labor or follow specific body rules. Jobs occurring mostly in the back-of-store stockroom don't create aesthetic value. Instead, these workers—like Kathleen's poorly treated coworker at the boutique—remain largely invisible as they unpack shipments, attach price tags and security sensors, and move merchandise to the sales floor. Stella, who has work experience at Forever 21 and Macy's, points out that both stores divide the labor between these more and less visible positions. Men, particularly Black and Latino men, tend to receive stockroom assignments, along with "a couple Hispanic women." Stella, who is multiracial, pauses, adding, "It's so rare if you ever see a white woman stocking our shelves. . . . It's almost all white women who do the pricing and signing, which is weird." In her experience, managers assign mostly Black and Latino men to occupy the least visible, creative, and customer service–oriented positions. Other workers confirm similar patterns of race- and gender-based division of invisible and visible labor in line with their organizations' racial beauty hierarchies.

Aesthetic labor is required of the visible sales associates, who model the merchandise as the stores' walking mannequins. Their beauty and appealing physiques form their "body capital," which adds symbolic value to the brand. Corporate endeavors to treat them as "brand representatives."[16] Cultural theorist Pierre Bourdieu conceptualizes how the human bodies of laborers are assigned value in social interactions based on the performance of the appropriate and mutual cultural markers.[17] Their bodies take on value through social relationships, in which individuals perform, assess, reward, and/or diminish each other accordingly. Aesthetic labor stems from appraisals of workers' attractive and stylish appearance.

Class saturates this labor. Abercrombie stores, for instance, reflect a series of expectations about "upper-middle-class" (implicitly coded as white) aesthetic performance; Forever 21, on the other hand, has a lower price point and an extreme fast-fashion focus that aims at affordability, so it doesn't require the same type of aesthetic labor from its staff. Somewhere in between, an "edgier" and "artier" look is cultivated by higher-price-point Urban Outfitters, leading to aesthetic performances that reflect not only class privilege but also different notions of how class should be performed. We find that while workers at stores with a lower price point were given greater latitude regarding body rules than *some* of the higher-price-point stores, like Abercrombie & Fitch, price does not determine the aesthetics expected of workers. Indeed, J. Crew, at a higher price point, allows workers to enact their own style within a somewhat looser set of aesthetic rules, perhaps because they market to a wider age range of potential customers.

Gender is enacted quite explicitly in aesthetic labor, as women are expected to perform femininities and men to perform masculinities.[18] Gender isn't "natural," but an achievement; we learn how to stand, walk, dress, and otherwise perform gender.[19] Aesthetic labor tends to emphasize gendered bodies, and previous research on retail points to how women workers' clothing, makeup, and body shape are central points in the service they provide.[20] As sociologist Lynne Pettinger argues, "the use of women's bodies to sell the product makes clothing retail a paradigm case of a complex gendering process whereby markets both construct and make use of broader cultural forms of feminization."[21] Yet relatively few studies have explored the masculinities that retail workers enact.[22] Labor research broadly suggests that men emphasize the masculine nature of their jobs in women-dominated occupations, such as men flight attendants emphasizing their role in ensuring the security of the flight, or men teachers emphasizing that they work in a gym.[23] Our study allows us to explore how men retail workers navigate the gendered performance of aesthetic labor.

In stores oriented toward tweens, teens, and twenty-somethings, corporate and store managers sexualize workers. While workers at stores aimed at a wider age range, such as J. Crew or Old Navy, suggest that workers' bodies are less regulated, at youth-oriented stores, workers report sexual attractiveness as key to the job. As labor scholars Chris Warhurst and Dennis Nickson point out, it is important to understand "how employee sexuality can be turned into a labour strategy."[24] Existing research tends to focus on women's bodies being sexualized, as well as on women's resistance to these processes, for example, among service workers in hotels, sex workers, or workers in "breastaurants" that advertise themselves as featuring sexy waitstaff.[25] Our interview respondents include both men and women, allowing us to consider how both men and women workers navigate this sexualization.

The Abercrombie stores, again, reflect a particularly sexualized location, with a history of positioning shirtless men models and skimpily dressed women as greeters. Indeed, until 2003 Abercrombie published a "magalog" filled with near-nude soft porn pictures of men and women, aimed at attracting primarily white gay as well as straight readers.[26] The homoeroticism and whiteness of Abercrombie's marketing was part of what brought us to interview workers diverse by both race and gender. Our interviews, however, demonstrate that the sexualization of workers isn't confined to the Abercrombie stores, even though it's heightened in this location. Also, the men we interviewed were not eager to discuss how they are sexualized by managers and customers or through the images in the stores; women were much more likely to discuss these experiences.

Sex sells, the adage says, and that's very much on display in clothing retail. Kristen Barber finds, for instance, that hair salon managers mobilize workers' "heterosexual identities and heterogendered appearance to enhance both their corporate brands, and their clients' social status."[27] Understanding how retailers strategically use workers' sexuality in similar ways is important to understanding the dynamics of aesthetic labor at play in our study.[28] Given that clothing retailers display both men's and women's bodies, the aesthetic labor process sexualizes both men and women in this work.

Workers thus display and perform gender, sexuality, class, and race, in keeping with the norms or "beauty standards" for their stores.[29] Sociologist Pei-Chia Lan reports, for instance, that cosmetic retail managers discipline their sales workers to develop the desired, embodied performance of class, gender, and heterosexual norms. In her study, managers expected women workers to wear clothing in "the fashionable colors being promoted that season" and impose managerial and discretionary disciplinary techniques to maintain certain hair and makeup styles.[30] Thus, retail workers within beauty industries often perform particular types of racialized and classed femininities.[31]

Race is crucial to aesthetic labor. Most mainstream US-based clothing stores value white-associated beauty ideals: narrow facial features; relatively pale skin; light eyes; and long, shiny, straight, or wavy hair.[32] These practices establish what we refer to as *racial beauty hierarchies*. In this context, the most salient is a tri-racial beauty hierarchy, in which white dominance and anti-Black racism are mediated by valorizing and exoticizing certain people of color—usually those with lighter skin tones and/or white-associated phenotypical traits.[33] Race scholars Eduardo Bonilla-Silva and Karen Glover contend that such tripartite racial hierarchies retain the power and advantage of whites and the subjugation of Blacks by placing "honorary whites" into a middle, buffer group in which they have relatively more value than Blacks because of their proximity to whiteness.[34]

Skin color, hair texture, and style, as well as other corporeal traits, form the bedrock of racialized beauty evaluations in clothing retail. Retail managers appear to enforce colorism, preferring white and lighter-skinned Black, Asian, Latina, and multiracial women over darker-skinned Black women in customer-facing roles. In our fieldwork, the beauty ideals displayed in teen-oriented clothing retail branding clearly gave preference to tall, white women and lighter-skinned women workers of color, often with light eyes and slender builds. Men workers generally had Adonis-like athletic builds—muscular and broad-shouldered—and a wider range of skin tones. Centuries-old colorist beauty ideals are reinscribed when these white-dominant institutions prefer and promote lighter-skinned workers over darker-skinned people, especially darker-skinned women.[35]

Branding includes images and symbols inside the store, such as posters, music, merchandise, mannequins, and staff members, as well as advertising found outside of the brick-and-mortar stores (that is, billboards and websites).[36] Corporate marketing dictates these displays, often through highly standardized guidelines that specify exact folds for different items and which outfits go on which mannequins. That is, corporate marketers realize and emphasize the importance of visuals for establishing what their brand is and is not. Rachel, who is multiracial, regularly dresses mannequins at American Eagle. The directions for dressing these "bust forms" include clear dictates regarding the display of white and Brown mannequins:

> They send me pictures of where the bust forms have to be. And, in the pictures in that area, if it's a Black bust form and a white bust form, it matters. [The managers] go in and they check to make sure that you put the right clothing on the right color. And, they don't call them Black. They call them "spice," which to me is more offensive than Black.

Here, the company is treating "spice" mannequins as racial variations in otherwise exclusively white displays. Its euphemisms cannot cover the racial hierarchy—the white supremacy—that American Eagle reinforces through its routinized design techniques.

PERFORMING THE LOOK

Aesthetic labor practices mean recruiting and maintaining a sales staff with the requisite symbolic capital to perpetuate the branded allure of the models on the posters mounted on each store's walls. Many of the teen-oriented stores give workers clear instructions about how to represent the brand, including directives regarding hair, jewelry, makeup, piercings, and tattoos. The standards differ from store to store. Corinne, who is Asian American, compares two stores: at Abercrombie, everyone is "very fit and stood up straight and had really nice, clean, natural faces, whereas [at] Forever 21, you could be more expressive, wear crazy makeup or crazy clothes, and it was just a different type aesthetic." At both stores, workers' aesthetic labor aims to express and enliven the store's specific style.

Hollister's managers told Liz (Black) about their look-centered expectations right up front: "When I applied there, I had a nose ring, and they were like, 'You can't have that.' I had my nails done, and they're like, 'You can't have that.'" The immediate notice of these body rules forced Liz to self-impose the company's expectations. Though she was hired primarily for a stockroom job, Liz altered her image to better align with the store. For Frances (multiracial), it's "funny" to see her coworkers' appearance after work. Upon finishing their shifts at their Abercrombie in a predominantly working-class town's mall, workers engage in a form of code switching, or the process of displaying cultural capital in ways that align with another audience. On the sales floor, Frances explains, "We all look clean-cut, with the guys and no facial hair . . . and girls with their natural hair and no makeup. . . . When we get ready to leave, we put on this new look . . . it's like, 'That's the same person! Holy crap!'" Once their shifts are over, workers like these can consciously choose to opt out of the company's style rules. Aware of being hypervisible and subject to the gaze of managers and customers, workers who don't identify with the brand quickly abandon it for a more authentic style.

Abercrombie refers to its regulations about attire, hair, jewelry, makeup, and body art as a "Look Policy," while other stores include these expectations in their training manuals and employee handbooks. Managers express clear body rule expectations and reinforce these expectations within the service panopticon that focuses on workers' bodies, in addition to the sales and theft prevention we discussed in part 2 of the book. Claire describes Abercrombie brands like Hollister and Gilly Hicks as requiring a "natural" look:

> They were very strict about the rest of our appearance so, like, we couldn't wear nail polish and we had to look natural. A lot of us wanted us to wear

makeup but our makeup couldn't look "unnatural," so we had to do natural makeup and we couldn't dye our hair or do stuff to our hair. There were certain hairstyles we had to wear.

We return to explore the racialized politics of hair later, but for now we can contrast this Abercrombie brand "family" policy with the looser expectations and enforcement at other chains. Those selling to broader populations, such as Old Navy, don't appear to regulate nonapparel aesthetic choices. Department stores more simply promote a "professional" appearance, rather than indicating specific rules about workers' bodies. Employee codes, handbooks, and posters communicate and cultivate a store's branded "look" more explicitly when the target customer and target staffer are both younger.[37]

As our interviewees note, managers appraise workers' physical appearance starting in the hiring phase. Charlotte (white) states that beauty inspires all recruitment efforts. According to her, Hollister managers want workers who resemble the models and fulfill the company's "type":

> Tall, thin. If you're a guy: tall, *built*. Long blond or brown hair. It used to be when I first started a ton of blonds everywhere, and when I went back last year I was like, "Whoa, brunettes everywhere!" ((Claps.)) So they definitely changed; it doesn't really matter, like long, nice hair. Nice facial features without enhancement, without makeup. . . . They basically look for people that look like the posters that are up all throughout the store.

These expectations intersect across gender, race, and class. Although Charlotte doesn't explicitly define the "type" in racial terms, her emphasis on the noticeable change from more blond white workers to more brunette (and still white) workers hints at the store brand's racial aesthetics. The gendered idealization of women having "long, nice hair" also suggests a preference for middle-class and white-associated finer hair texture and straightened styles.[38]

Our observations in clothing stores confirm the ubiquity of white-looking, lighter-skinned, and/or racially ambiguous models in branding and displays. Many workers add that beauty expectations emphasize "perfect" bodies, which are either white or racially ambiguous; are lighter-skinned; and fit within small-sized, middle-class aesthetics. Composing the bulk of the clothing retail workforce, white women perform most of the aesthetic labor these companies seek out, yet some women of color feel included in these rules. Lori (Black), who worked at a store with a more racially diverse staff, offers positive sentiments. She likes the Wet Seal brand and notes, "I usually like to look cute when I go to work. I look like I'm going out." In examples like Lori's and Kathleen's (whose experience was discussed at the beginning of this chapter), we see that, like whites, workers of color sometimes enjoy their embodiment of the brand and the appreciation of their "good looks," especially when they like the clothing and identify with it as a consumer.

Yet workers' sentiments about aesthetic labor vary within or across racial groups. For example, Liz, who is Black, experiences alienation in her attempts to embody "the look" and identify with the brand. Despite her firm's pro-diversity campaign, she still perceived a persistent exclusion of darker-skinned Black women:

> Hollister, not just Hollister, a lot of places, too . . . want to promote an idea that they accept like all races, which is good. But then their ((air quotes gesture)) "Black" girl will be a girl that is, from the looks of it, she's probably not fully Black. She's got the curly hair, but she's not my skin color. She's extremely lighter than me, and so I kind of feel like that's their way of being, "That's somebody that looks like you." It's like, no, that's not somebody that looks like me. She's not me at all.

Even white-dominant brands seeking positive associations with diversity portray colorist ideas about desirable forms of Blackness as they erase darker-skinned women.

These racialized processes can be complex, as when racially "diverse" workers are prized for their racial ambiguity rather than for representing a wider array of beauty ideals. Corinne (Asian American) notes that her Abercrombie coworkers included many people who, "Although they were diverse, they were very racially ambiguous. . . . They could be half, they could not, like they were very. . . . I don't know what the proper word for it [is], but they were like Americanized." Such workers represent the "middle" group in a tri-racial hierarchy. Gwen, a white woman who was formerly a Hollister manager, describes hiring decisions in ways that reveal the shading of colorism:

There are always the debates and things about how people are promoting diversity, but they won't go with the very black African Americans. They'll go with the lighter. Or, like I said, maybe half of our staff was nonwhite, but they look Caucasian still so you wouldn't know their actual, you wouldn't know their nationality unless you asked.

Her account—and the conflation of "nationality" with racial groups—implies that stores select workers whose bodies signify "more desirable" versions of racial and skin color difference (note that half the staff was nonwhite but "white looking"). Valuing racial ambiguity in these ways fits neatly with tri-racialism and reinforces whiteness as the beauty ideal while also nodding to a corporate appreciation of diversity. Skin tone seems to be the most prominent racialized phenotypical feature in these beauty appraisals, though other physical markers of "racial difference," such as hair and nose, lips, hips, and eye shape, also come into account.

Black women's experiences attest to the tri-racial ranking of clothing retail workers. For example, an Abercrombie store manager recruited Denise to work as a sales associate "model" in Atlanta. Denise's slim, 5-foot-9-inch figure mirrors the models displayed on the Abercrombie walls, websites, and shopping bags. She has medium-dark brown skin, high cheekbones, and an eye-catching smile; her relaxed hair is long and wavy. Denise sees her job offer as part of Abercrombie's diversity campaign:

> I know they've had issues in the store as far as like marketing because you do see a lot of white faces. . . . So, I felt like it was a smart move for them to try to recruit more people that are Black, Hispanic, those kind of things.

Denise interprets the recruitment of Black and Latinx workers like herself as an acceptable business strategy given the discrimination lawsuits the company had settled and the "diversity and inclusion plan" it released in response, as explained in chapter 3. Although she took the job, the brand isn't appealing to her: "It's not really my style."

This is to say, store brands commodify cultural visions about what is desirable, including paying lip-service to diversity *and* favoring white-proximate phenotypes. Signature looks that encapsulate a brand reflect the gender, sexual, racial, and class notions shaping ideals of beauty, coolness, sex appeal, and so on.[39] Cultural goods, like branded clothes, are produced by the store and interpreted by consumers. For Denise, Abercrombie is a brand for more affluent and white consumers:

> Nothing about it is urban, nothing about it is affordable. . . . So, to me, who they are selling to and who they are targeting are middle-class, upper-middle-class whites . . . because that's who is in a lot of their advertisements and their billboards, and this kind of easy, carefree living. And, that's not true—especially in this country—for minorities, so I would say that what they are selling isn't necessarily for a section of the populace.

Using the racially coded term *urban* to imply that this store excludes representations of more socioeconomically and racially disadvantaged people, Denise communicates that white-dominant branding strategies largely omit representations of Black American cultures. Further, she recognizes that the Abercrombie "look" is classed: unaffordable for most people and aimed at those with "carefree" lives. The appearance aspect was, for her, the worst part of the job: "Having to conform to the style, definitely. I felt like—I don't know." Lowering her voice, Denise sums up: "I just didn't like it."

THE POLITICS OF HAIR

Mary (multiracial), having memorized them, can recite the Abercrombie rules about women's hair

> because it's . . . on every single bulletin board in every single store about how you can wear your hair. . . . [No] up-dos, like prom up-dos . . . no French braids, no tight braids, if you're gonna wear a braid, it has to be a side braid, very loose. . . . If you're gonna wear your hair wavy, like it has to look natural and beachy, and straight hair's fine.

"Straight hair" and "loose braids"—these are classed and racialized rules that privilege white-associated styles and bar Black-associated styles. Denise learned that, at Abercrombie, her hair needed to be "straight down, and behind my ears or curled, just like really simple and clean cut," adding, "nothing too flamboyant."

Hair politics are incredibly salient for Black Americans.[40] They are central to racialized beauty hierarchies that place the highest value on straight, shiny, long tresses for women.[41] Across occupations, workplace dress codes enforce such white-dominant, anti-Black body rules onto employees. Black women are the key informants explaining these practices. Antonia, for example, identifies straightened hair as important to fitting into the Express workplace. Racial stereotypes and perceptions of hair cleanliness, she says, absolutely shape this policy: "It honestly comes down to what people perceive from the media because some people see [dread]locks who's like, 'That's dirty, you don't wash your hair. . . . That's not what we want in our store,' type of thing." "Unprofessional" is a frequently evoked term understood by many Black workers as coding disrespect for their natural hair. Liz, working at Hollister, conveys palpable frustration about racialized hair expectations: "That's the look that they want me to have, and the hairstyles that they want me to do. My hair doesn't do that."

Pauline, who is also Black, explains that micro-braids were once prohibited by Abercrombie stores but were eventually permitted: "Before, that wasn't something [we were] allowed to have. But because they wanted to show that we're ethnically diverse, you can have micro-braids if you want to." Pauline insightfully ties the company's attempts to appear diverse with the rule loosening, but the fact that the rules still dictate the size and style of acceptable braid types signals only a shift in *which* types of Blackness the store accepts as being on-brand. Leah notes that Hollister's hair policies still discriminate between

> certain types of braids[,] and your dreads had to be a certain size. . . .
> I remember over the summer because I usually braid my hair and I was like,
> "Forget it; let me just put it in a ponytail." . . . But you know cornrows? They
> didn't want those. Over the summer, I just put those in my hair to make my
> life easier but they were like, "No."

By banning or limiting Black-associated hairstyles, these body rules explicitly racialize the store brand using workers' bodies. Beauty appraisals of workers cast more Black-centric femininities as less desirable at the same time that they overlook the time and money required for Black women to maintain the desired white-adjacent look. It is a particularly classed femininity that clothing retailers desire.

Figure 13. Sales clerk helping a customer. SOURCE: iStock.com/monkeybusiness images.

Abercrombie brands, as we have seen, enforce especially strict, clearly communicated instructions regarding work-appropriate hairstyles. Claire, who is white, laughs about how this issue played out at Hollister:

> I always had to plan so much time because I had to shower and blow dry my hair; and like you could not come in with wet hair, it was not acceptable, and they preferred it to be down and in its like natural state. . . . They just were about it not being natural, but it looking natural; and then you had to do your makeup to look natural, and get in your flip-flops and trudge through the snow.

As Claire emphasizes, requirements to "look natural" to express the brand's aesthetic did not mean actually "being natural." It required an enormous amount of beauty work to thread this needle. Corinne (Asian American) complains about the inordinate preparation time needed to work at Abercrombie: "It was just extra time that I had to put into . . .

work for working a three-hour shift. So, it was more tedious on my part, it just felt more draining to come to work." Performing beauty ideals meant working unpaid overtime, exacerbating other complaints about working in fashion retail.

Men aren't immune to hair rules, particularly those governing facial hair. At Abercrombie, Frances notes, "Guys are not allowed to have facial hair at all. At all." Glenn confirms that, at Abercrombie Kids, "Guys can't have facial hair. . . . No one can have extreme haircuts or anything like that." Bryan and David, also at Abercrombie, detail the importance of appearing "baby-faced," getting regular haircuts, and styling to fit the brand. David says that, according to the hair rules, "I can't put a lot of gel in it. So, I try to put some wax to make it look natural, cause it has to be as natural appearing as possible." Again, "natural appearing" stands out as a directive. Given Abercrombie's intensive Look Policy, which promotes a cultivated "natural" look, men working in this brand family report spending more time on styling than other men we interviewed. Gabe says that at American Eagle facial hair "had to be groomed . . . any other guys that had worked there, they never had outrageous styles, like they didn't have a mustache that curled off to the end." Yet even this varied. For example, Brendan laughs, "At Pac Sun, if you had a grizzly beard, they wouldn't care, they would be like, 'Awesome, man.'"

Managers control men's hair by directing workers to change their hairstyles or shave to conform to the body rules. Jason (multiracial) generally likes working at Abercrombie but finds body rules irritating: "Having to be clean, clean, clean-shaven every single time. That was annoying. I got yelled at that a couple times, a good amount of times actually. You couldn't have little stubble even. . . . They would make you go in the back and shave." Gwen, a Hollister manager, described monitoring workers' tresses within the service panopticon:

> The manager makes small suggestions like . . . "your hair really doesn't look natural like that, I could tell that you straightened it, or I could tell that you're using too much product," that kind of thing[;] guys would come in with like five o'clock shadow, and they'd be given a razor and told to go to the bathroom.

Workers come to exercise self-regulation and impose the known body rules on themselves, as part of the service panopticon.[42] Managers actively reinforce these rules, asking employees to wash their hair if they used too much product or to shave their faces before beginning their shifts.

Only one worker recounts resisting hair regulations, highlighting the tenuous character of worker-manager relations within the service quadrangle. Pauline, who is Black, redirected her Hollister managers, who asked her to dye her hair all one color because her hair was dyed in an "ombre" style, where the tips of the hair are noticeably lighter:

> I was just like ((sarcastically)), "Oh, because I'm a beautician and I can just go back and dye my hair right now." I was just like, "No. My hair color will change once I get paid and I go to the hair salon. Till then we're just going to look at this all together." But I did try to do my best and I'd put my hair like in a fishtail braid, so it wasn't as obvious. . . . [T]hat was the best that I could do.

Pauline hadn't realized that her ombre style broke the rules, and she refused to immediately acquiesce to managers' directives. She sought a compromise by styling her hair to disguise the dye job until she had earned enough money to change her hair color. Given her low pay, Pauline was unwilling to immediately spend more money simply to meet the look requirements, no matter how much the managers wanted to maximize her aesthetic value to more fully embody their brand's look.

ACCESSORIZING THE BODY FOR THE BRAND: COSMETICS, JEWELRY, AND BODY ART

Store managers also regulate workers' visible uses of makeup, jewelry, and body art or "modifications" (that is, tattoos and piercings) in ways that similarly project ideals of white, middle-class femininity and masculinity. At the Abercrombie stores, the signature look was "natural beauty." Gwen explains Hollister's basic policy on cosmetics: "You weren't supposed to wear makeup . . . mascara was the only thing allowed if it didn't look too overdone." She details:

> You kind-of are expected to look naturally good, so you know, no blemishes or bags under your eyes. Cover it up with a little bronzer, so you look natural, but you can't be putting on like purple eyeshadow, or dark blush and that kind of thing, where you clearly have makeup. It's just kind of like the

natural earth tones, where you're like, "Are they wearing makeup, or do they just have a good complexion?"

Blemish-free skin is ideal, given the company's strict cosmetics policy, but it means wearing makeup without being seen as wearing makeup.

Charlotte puts these body rules in the context of employee recruitment efforts: "If you saw a really pretty girl walk in the mall and she had a ton of makeup on, [Hollister] wouldn't recruit her because they don't know what she looks like without any makeup on." Hiring managers only consider potential sales workers whose "look" already conveys what they view as a healthy, middle-class vibe that will attract the right customers. Corinne mentions that the rules about makeup were challenging for her sister, who worked at Abercrombie: "[S]he loves top liner . . . sometimes she would just like wear it to see if she would get away with it. . . . But like they would definitely tell her like 'you can't wear eye liner.' . . . They regulated it more for sure." Workers must sacrifice personal style to meet their workplace's body rules.

The cosmetics category includes nail polish, to the frustration of many workers. Some stores are relatively flexible about it; at American Eagle, for instance, "You can have nail polish [but] you don't have to. I know girls have fake nails," Tara says. "We don't really have any strict regulations against that." But again, the Abercrombie brands are more restrictive. As Frances (multiracial) observes with a frustrated sigh, "You can't have your nails painted . . . any bright colors. They'd want you to have a clear coat or beige, tans. Natural colors." Leah confirms this at Hollister, an Abercrombie brand extension: "Nail polish, you could only have it on your toes and it has to be like red, white, or pink. . . . So, you can never have your hands painted. And I remember one day I actually painted my nails by accident, but I just hid them." Aware that she had broken the body rules, Leah avoided the discipline by keeping her hands out of managerial view for the whole shift.

Carolyn recalls forgetting to remove the nail polish on her toes one day. Her Hollister manager reminded her, "'I can send you home for that,' and I was like, 'I'm sorry. It will be fixed by my next shift.'" Other instances require immediate changes. At Gilly Hicks, Hannah recounts a shift when "I looked like I had eyeliner on, so they asked me to go wash my face, or the girl who had a feather in their hair, they asked her to take it out." As we heard with facial hair and hairstyles, workers told us their managers repeatedly insisted that workers adjust their appearance in line with brand expectations before they could do their jobs.

Adornments, including jewelry, are tailored to further cultivate the gendered, racial, and class-specific aesthetic of each store. Many women complain about being limited to, for instance, wearing one set of stud earrings, one ring, one bracelet, and a watch. "I have this necklace that I always wear, and I wore it to work," Claire remembers, "and they said, 'that's not Hollister-issued. You're going to have to take that off.' They would go up to you and say it." These abrupt moments of regulation were seen as distracting and annoying. Liz removed her nose ring and triple ear piercings for each shift in the Hollister stockroom, summarizing the body modification rules as one pair of lobe earrings "or nothing. No tattoos, no piercings. None of that." In line with the specifically gendered nature of the job, men are even more restricted when it comes to accessorizing. David explains that for "accessories, you're limited to a watch. You can't even wear a necklace—or a ring," though during fieldwork we saw some men wearing leather cuffs sold by Abercrombie. Other workers confirm that "if [men] have earrings they have to take them out," as Charlotte notes for Hollister.

Body art is subject to surveillance. Constructing its middle-class preppy, "all-American" brand, Abercrombie stores do not hire people with visible ink or nontraditional piercings. Glenn says this is absolute at Abercrombie Kids: "Tattoos, you wouldn't get hired. Absolutely not if they were visible." At other Abercrombie brands, Lance says: "Tattoos, you usually had to cover up." Pauline works at Hollister, too, and tells a story about a coworker who showed up with a lip piercing, which managers made her remove before it could heal. Many corporate expectations about jewelry and tattoos support a notion of white-associated, middle-class masculinity and femininity, as well as the depersonalized, dehumanized role of their sales staff in profit making.

Yet not all retail workers report rules about tattoos and piercings. Carl, who had worked at both Abercrombie & Fitch and the upscale J. Crew, notes that one of his J. Crew managers "has a tattoo right on the back of his neck, and it's plainly visible." J. Crew markets itself as staid, and so this seems like a departure, but many workers at stores with less preppy, more class-varied, and punk-influenced brands emphasize that tattoos and piercings could be a positive. Sherrie comments that "luckily Pac Sun is really laid back, if anything they love tattoos and piercings [and] crazy funky hair colors." Because these looks reflect the specific store brand, managers celebrate rather than police them. Sabrina, who worked at Urban Outfitters, describes another setting in which tattoos, piercings, and unusual hairstyles were regarded as positives:

> All my managers had that kind of thing . . . a store manager had like a chunk of bleach blond hair in the front where her bangs were, and she had tattoo sleeves. [Another] had tattoos and gauges, and I think actually pretty much all of my coworkers had visible tattoos. Yea, and piercings were really common too.

Lauren, another Urban Outfitters alum, describes the atmosphere as "very open about tattoos, and piercings," offering examples: "[O]ne of the store managers has like a ton of tattoos, and another one has like a ton of piercings. So, that part is really cool, just because they are very open about that." Tia discusses a heavily pierced coworker at Forever 21 who had "a chain that would hang up and come up to her ear and stuff. And, she had tattoos all over her body. So, it didn't really matter to that store." Julian, an H&M manager, reports, "You can have tattoos, you can have facial piercings, you can have crazy makeup, colored hair. . . . There's a pretty open door with that. It's cool."

While we observed workers at Urban Outfitters who looked like they could be employed at Abercrombie—as well as those who did not—we didn't see workers at Abercrombie who had a more varied look. So, we see that while workers at the Abercrombie stores had strict "look policies," those at other teen-oriented stores seemed to have more discretion about their personal look and how it benefits the brand. This means fewer middle-class body rules and less employer-directed beauty work; instead, these workers produce aesthetic value by self-directing their beauty work, sporting the hairstyle and accouterments that they choose. Thus, the service panopticon can in some settings be looser, with less restrictive expectations for aesthetic labor, although it's more rigid in other settings.

Body rules regarding cosmetics, jewelry, and body art tend to be confined to more upscale stores, or to the Abercrombie brand, which conveys more middle-class ideals. For example, Kathleen claims that, at her boutique, "They don't want you ever to put too much makeup on. . . . You always have to have a natural look." Wearing the appropriate amount and style of cosmetics is a balancing act in which workers attempt to interpret and reproduce the desired signature look with their bodies and resources. Jill argues, "They want us to reflect the store [Forever 21], and they're all for fun makeup because it's not like a very pristine, upscale store, so it's not hair in a bun and like a blazer or clean makeup." She suggests that "fun" is more acceptable at a store catering to a wider class range.

Workers in other teen-oriented stores replied to our questions about makeup and hair requirements quizzically. Risa responds that, when it comes to makeup and hair at Zara, "That just varied from worker to worker. I mean, sometimes I would go in with no face on. Sometimes I would go in with makeup on. So that didn't matter." We were even met with shock at the idea of rules governing hair and makeup; Carmen, who had worked at Free People and other clothing stores, recoils, "Oh, God. No. That's awful! No, never that, honestly!"

The varying degrees of aesthetic labor reflect each organization's aim to create and maintain *racialized beauty hierarchies* that signal a classed, gendered, and racialized market to consumers. And this labor comes at some cost to workers: loss of personal style, increases in preparation time, and discrimination against what may be their preferred but are corporate-deemed "undesirable" markers of lower-class and/or Black-associated aesthetics. In stores where the brand is more eclectic, workers' aesthetics are regulated and disciplined less heavily.

BEAUTY AND BODY SIZE

Beauty and body size are intimately connected within Western beauty ideals. With variations around, say, muscularity and curvaceousness, early twenty-first-century US beauty norms privilege thinner, lighter-skinned women. Managerial discipline can come in the form of hinting, such as when Claire, whom we discussed at the beginning of the chapter, began to regain weight after an illness, but it starts at the point of hire. Denise (Black) says about Abercrombie,

> I don't even think that you'd get an interview if they didn't feel like you weren't. . . . I don't even think you'd make it for callbacks. . . . For the models it was kind of like, "Yea, we want a certain look, and you have that look."

She continues, explaining that she "would say that my coworkers were all very good-looking . . . and you could tell that they were chosen for a reason. . . . The guys were especially . . . cute, and I guess that was the goal." Corinne expands: "At Abercrombie, definitely everyone had to look this way. And I think it was unspoken that everyone should look this way."

Since Express "caters to people that are a certain size," Antonia recalls, workers had to fall within that size range to perform their role as walking mannequins.[43] Charlotte says much the same about Hollister: "The clothes are fit to fit smaller people. So, if you don't fit into the clothes, you're not going to be able to brand them, and work the floor." Managers hire people who could wear the merchandise (as we discuss further in chapter 6), and Hollister workers are frank. Leah claims the company "want[s] slimmer people. . . . Their sizes don't even run that big either and [the workers] were mostly fit." And Liz indicates workers feel pressure to *stay* within Hollister's body expectations: "They definitely feel some sort of responsibility to work out and look like they're very fit and in shape. . . . I do think there is an expectation to like stay slimmer and like smaller."

"They rate you on your looks, they have a rating system," Patricia recalls of her experience with Hollister and Gilly Hicks. "And that's really what it's about. They just care about how you look." Women workers from the Abercrombie stores frequently expressed distaste about the importance of physical beauty and attractiveness. Charlotte says her Hollister managers "are very concerned with looks and you can tell that right when you walk into the store because all of the people on the [sales] floor are good looking." The workers' scrutiny often focuses on the way these rules mean some staffers accrue benefits due to their perceived attractiveness. When clothing retail workers refer to their employers as "very into looks" or "very concerned with looks," they often criticize the narrow understanding of beauty.

Men are more neutral, such as James, who observes about the Nordstrom staff, "I don't know if that was just a coincidence, but there [are] big guys, 6'4", 6'2" that worked . . . attractive and handsome guys, beautiful ladies." Trent, an assistant manager at Express, refers to his store manager: "Sometimes she says things that aren't necessarily like the most inclusive thing ever like, 'Oh. We can't hire them because they're not so pretty.'" Although Trent joins in cultivating his own and his workers' aesthetic labor, he acknowledges that these practices can manifest in harsh ways. Not all who participate resist this dimension of the industry, but many find it at least disconcerting to explore the aesthetic expectations.

Women workers often point to a focus on very thin women, mirroring a broader gendered and racialized body project.[44] Patricia describes sales associates at Abercrombie's now-defunct lingerie store, Gilly Hicks, as "skinny, perfect shape, they're just like perfect girls . . . looked like Victoria Secret models, definitely what they were going for there." Standing about 5 foot 6 inches, Patricia might be considered a smidge too short to be a Victoria's Secret "angel," but she otherwise has the same look as the managers who hired her: slender with symmetrical facial features, blond hair, and blue eyes. Hannah confirms that Gilly Hicks managers "preferred really tall and skinny girls," and Corinne says that at Abercrombie "no one in the store was like bigger than a [size] two." Corinne adds, "Everyone was just like tiny and thin, tall, athletic."

Gwen pegs Hollister sales workers as wearing sizes ranging from "o to 5, maybe o to 3." A size two correlates with a woman weighing approximately 100 pounds, although less than 5% of eighteen-year-old women in the United States weigh less than 103 pounds.[45] This suggests frontline managers choose a skewed population to represent their stores. Indeed, Kathleen states candidly about her boutique: "They won't hire you if you're fat."

Again, this size discrimination was not true of all stores, including some aimed at teens. Among the Urban Outfitters staff, for example, Lauren recognizes more body size variation: "Some of [the workers] would be really petite and some of them would be on the larger side, or some would be more bulky, and some of them would be lanky." At Forever 21, the workforce includes "bigger girls, really tiny, tiny girls, and everyone in between," according to Stella.

Some of the women workers with more curves found it challenging to wear store clothing. Patricia, who is white, was uncomfortable with how she had to style her clothing at Gilly Hicks, pointing out: "I have big boobs and their shirts don't fit me right; they're not flattering for my body type. But I still had to wear them, which sometimes is weird, they make you unbutton a certain amount of buttons sometimes and style it a certain way." For Patricia, the body rules feel like they sexualize her since the clothing she's required to wear is designed for a less shapely figure. Liz is also bigger than an extra-small. Comparing herself to Hollister coworkers, she says that some "wear tank tops and the little skirts that come up to the waist, and like they'll tie it, which is not bad. But if I were to wear that, I have thighs and meat. So those skirts would be significantly shorter on me than they would be on the very slim model." Liz gave considerable thought to her body as a size deviation from the Hollister norm:

> I don't consider myself skinny, but I'm not . . . chubby. But I am probably one of the bigger workers. Yea, I'm one of the . . . I might be the biggest girl. And, "big" is a weird term, because I'm not even big, but like that's how I feel looking at everyone else. And it's just like, "Oh. So, they've got to be tiny."

As a darker-skinned and curvy Black woman, Liz feels her body fundamentally differs from those of the store's models, featured on the shop floor, walls, shopping bags, and company website. She is keenly aware that she departs from the brand's idyllic worker-consumer and marvels at how this ethos affects her: "Sometimes it's like, 'Oh my God, I never felt so like big before,' in terms of looking at everybody that I'm working with, and what they want me to look like." For Liz, even though she describes wearing small sizes, she feels bad at work, where it's painfully obvious that she isn't what "they"—the store managers—want their workers to look like. She is, as it were, the exception that proves the rule, and that can be profoundly isolating.

For men, body size expectations are tied to athleticism and height. At Hollister, Lance states, "all the workers were in shape, I was a three-sport athlete," then reasons, "if you think about the work, the people who come in and shop want to see the workers in shape, they don't want to see out of shape [workers]." Men's discussions about the appearance aspects of their jobs suggest a certain acceptance. David, for instance, acknowledges that men working at Abercrombie tend to be "tall and handsome" and notes the overarching importance of being attractive: "As long as you're not fat or you don't have a beer belly, and you're decently good looking, you know, they'd hire you. I'm not saying that they do judge by appearance, but a lot of it is appearance." His words seem to contain some ambivalence; he claims "a lot of it is appearance" and references being "decently good looking" and "not fat," while also trying to avoid the idea that workers are "judge[d] by appearance." It appears that men recognize looks and body shape are part of why they are hired, yet tend to have less-developed critiques of these practices than their women coworkers.

Recall that Abercrombie stores do what they call "casting": searching for advertising models among their sales staff. The "casting" process demonstrates frontline and corporate management investment in workers' appearances. Patricia details this operation:

> The first day you work at Hollister you get a picture taken. . . . The head manager . . . comes and does the picture, so it's kind of like an interview. And like I didn't think it was a big deal but my manager prepped me for it and kinda did my hair a little and she was like, "Don't worry, he's going to love you." She was really nervous and then afterward, she was still freaking out, she was like, "Oh my god, he *loved* you."

Based on the photos, corporate managers may then decide to "cast" workers in advertisements. Mary, who is multiracial and lighter-skinned, criticizes casting at Abercrombie: "All employees have to get their picture taken. . . . We've only had one girl to actually get picked . . . in our entire store of fifty employees, cause they're like super picky, they have like really weird images of how girls and guys should be."

Men workers' accounts of Abercrombie's casting practices seem more matter of fact. David, for instance, describes the picture-taking process differently than Patricia:

> I don't wanna say that . . . you have to be a Barbie doll to work there, but . . . what they do is, before you start working there they take a picture of you, and if you're good looking, then you become "cast of." You have to get approved by the DM [district manager], and then the DM would . . . recommend you to someone else and you become "cast of." And [then] . . . they can call you in, and if they want to model you for some clothes that they want to promote, they would . . . take a couple pictures of you, have like a mini photoshoot, and they would pay you time-and-a-half and give you a free pair of jeans.

David's emphasis on the transactional nature of the process—being paid (in overtime wages and merchandise) to model clothing for the retailer—seems to confer legitimacy on this body "display work" in clothing retail.[46] Another Abercrombie model, Jason, outlines the opportunities of the program:

> You get invited to different photo shoots and different opportunities and then you build; you work your way up. So, you'll get invited to a district shoot where there'll be "cast of" members from the district, and then if you passed the cut then you make it to the region, you know, and then you work your way up. . . . "Cast of" members at the store, they would always be in the front. Like me, for example, I was always in the front.

Although less critical than Mary and Patricia, David and Jason confirm that attractiveness determines who is "cast" as a more valued model sales associate.

Managers sometimes assign workers they deem less attractive to jobs in the stockroom (consider Kathleen's "ugly" coworker, relegated to non-sales-floor work) as they send those perceived to be more striking to the front of the store. Abercrombie stores differentiate between staff on the sales floor ("models"), who workers say tend to be more attractive, and back-of-house staff ("impacters"). Mary talks about a coworker: "He's pretty good looking so they always have him out on the floor. . . . They definitely looked for built guys that were strong," but also states, "if someone applied, . . . [the managers] were like, 'mm, he's not that cute. I think I'm just gonna put him in the back.'" Mary witnessed several instances in which managers discussed moving workers to the back when they didn't quite match the store's standards for attractiveness. At times, Charlotte recalls, too few Hollister "models" would be working on a busy shift, and so "impacters" would be brought out of the stockroom. But she points out, "You'll notice that they'll stick them at the back of the store. Betties Three is where it would be," referring to the "room" farthest from the store entrance.

Therefore, not only do managers hire certain workers, but they also carefully stratify workers into visible and invisible jobs. The difference between models and stockroom workers appears to be primarily appearance based. Gwen, a former Hollister manager, refers to the models up-front as "cookie-cutter" in their looks, suggesting that the people in the "back of the house" are more often racial minorities, especially Black and Latinx workers. She acknowledges that "if you interviewed for model, but they wanted you as an impacter because you weren't totally attractive . . . they would . . . tell you 'sorry you didn't get it, but if you want you could interview for an impacter,' so there is definitely sifting."

Some managers, particularly district managers, made their preferences regarding workers' bodies crystal clear. Mary recalls an unpleasant interaction with a district manager at Abercrombie & Fitch. The manager instructed her to set up a rack of clothing in the back room using the current line of merchandise, which workers are supposed to buy and wear during shifts:

> She said, "But I only want you to take smalls and extra-smalls in the shirts, and I only want you to take, like, oo, o, only up to size 4 in bottoms." And like, I'm a medium in shirts, and I'm not a size four in pants. She said this to me and I was like, "okay". . . this is my district manager, and I could tell my manager was looking at me like, "oh my God," cause I think she felt bad . . . when my district manager left, she's like, "Mary, I'm sorry, that's so dumb. I'm not a size small." Which obviously she is, but . . . she was really offended by it, and I was a little offended by it.

Mary emphasizes that the frontline managers are "very sensitive to the whole thing because . . . they're humans, too. I don't think they agreed with corporate's rules." District managers seem more likely to bluntly enforce the store's body rules on workers, revealing their important role in maximizing aesthetic labor productivity. They're a step removed and won't need to deal with the interpersonal discomfort of a store manager directing a staffer—maybe even a longtime worker or a friend—to be *smaller*. Corporate management's demeaning treatment of workers, however, can put frontline managers in awkward positions as they try to defuse the situation.

Gwen outlines a different sort of appearance policing at Hollister. She recommended hiring a disabled woman, who was very enthusiastic and fit the look policy, despite an evident disability. Although her store manager did not support the hire, when Gwen cited the Americans with Disabilities Act, corporate approved the hire. Yet once the woman was on the job, the district manager constantly reprimanded this worker, asking her to perform tasks that weren't feasible given her physical difference. Gwen had felt good when she made the hire, but

> over time, I think that [corporate managers] were trying to phase her out. She came up to me crying one time. . . . It didn't make me feel good [watching the worker treated badly]. . . . [S]he didn't last long. I almost think that they can kind of control if they don't want someone there . . . they might not tell them "don't work here" but they'll make it a lot tougher on you if they don't want you there. I think that might have happened with her.

Gwen, who thought that this worker was an excellent employee, wondered in retrospect whether she had done the right thing in hiring someone whose "look" her managers rejected. As a hiring manager, Gwen experienced other moments in which she was chastised if staff members fell short of corporate expectations: "Your district manager comes in and is like, 'Why is that girl on the floor? She doesn't fit the look policy.' . . . And you're like, 'Well, I thought she did.'" Because Gwen subscribes to a broader vision of attractiveness, she stood at odds with her superiors.

Managers also want men and women to meet specific beauty ideals, although women workers tend to be more critical of the emphasis on workers' bodies and attractiveness. This difference may be because, based on media, schooling, and everyday life, women cultivate a more robust understanding of sexism and develop vocabulary regarding the exploitation of women's bodies.[47] Men, especially those who are cisgender and straight, may also be less likely to draw attention to the way their job exploits their attractiveness if they appear to gain value from being viewed as "built." Women, too, enjoy the symbolic capital of having a job where they are recognized as beautiful, but it appears to be a more complex, even contentious bargain for them than for their men coworkers.

SEXUALITY ON THE SHOP FLOOR

Aesthetic labor practices sexualizing the retail workforce demonstrate the cultivation, discipline, and extraction of use-value from workers' bodies as sexually alluring branded objects.[48] Clothing retail companies' approaches to worker sexualization differ across race and gender. For example, companies may use darker-skinned and/or racially ambiguous people to exoticize the brand.

Sexualizing the visible sales workers often begins with setting up the store in ways that emphasize provocative images. "The way my store was laid out is that like you walked in and saw the big picture of the half-naked man," Carl remembers. Indeed, Abercrombie & Fitch generally greets its shoppers with a massive poster of a young white guy, mouth slightly agape. He poses shirtless, his Abercrombie & Fitch jeans slung low to reveal more than a swath of skin below his navel. The poster models' faces and stances vary over the weeks, seasons, and years, while their chests remain eternally hairless, their faces blemish and beard free, and their torsos muscular. At Hollister, Gwen points to the disjuncture of selling clothes using "half-dressed pictures of men with no faces even, not any of the clothes." One poster she describes was

> right behind the register [depicting] a scene of about six men playing volleyball. And their heads are all cut off, but you see their bodies; you can tell that they are wearing short cut-off jeans, like that I don't see many men wearing these days, it's like six inches above their knees, and they're playing volleyball, and they're like, we don't sell anything like that for men in there.

This imagery forwards a sense of men-only bonding as well as gay eroticism, reflected in other Abercrombie posters and to some extent in their controversial catalog, *A&F Quarterly*, which featured nude and seminude photos.[49] Frances is also puzzled by the advertising photos:

> Mostly guys without a shirt on. And that's the whole photo sometimes I've noticed. It's like, where are the clothes? I remember there was one where the girl wasn't wearing a shirt at all, she's like holding herself up [partially covering her breasts], no shirt on at all. What are we trying to sell here? Nothing? What are we doing? I thought that was crazy.

What exactly is the store trying to market with these promotional images? David mentions that some Abercrombie customers even mention finding the posters inappropriate: "A lot of complaints do happen by mothers because the pictures are a little explicit to them."

Cheryl, who works at Victoria's Secret, acknowledges that the company's promotional focus seems to be on models' sex appeal rather than the functionality of their wares: "We have a lot of pictures of girls in the outfits. A bunch of posters that are huge with the [Victoria Secret Angels] models in them and the different underwear." Workers indicate that these images reinforce appearance-based hiring, beauty norms at work, and the sexualization of the brand in ways that hint at the sexuality of the workers themselves.

Retail clothing workers, in other words, are meant to be embodied versions of these young, skin-bearing bodies displayed throughout the store. "Shirtless greeting," a now-discontinued Abercrombie & Fitch practice, is a prime example of sexualized labor. [50] During big shopping events and regularly at stores in major cities, men workers would pose near the storefront wearing only Abercrombie & Fitch jeans and flip-flops. Sometimes a woman stood between a pair of shirtless men, modeling Abercrombie's newest miniskirt or crop top. Shoppers greeted these workers with fanfare, posing to take pictures with the "model" staffers. Jason, who is lighter-skinned and identifies as multiracial, was recruited by his managers for this particular duty:

> "Hey, are you interested in doing Black Friday shirtless greeting? If you are just meet up with me after [your shift] and we'll take a picture." And you take your shirt off, take a picture in the back of your whole waist up. . . . Then the district manager would approve you for shirtless greeting.

Photographing workers in this way was similar to the "cast of" practice, allowing management to evaluate their employees' bodies. Managers standardize the shirtless men representing the brand and welcoming customers into the store.

Bryan reports that to be chosen for shirtless greeting, which came with a pay bump, "You just have to have the look . . . the right body type, cut and jacked for men. . . . [They make you] take your shirt off to make sure you have the right body for it." The women who accompany shirtless men greeters needed to have the right look, too: "thin with a butt," Bryan says. Leah elaborates: the women workers chosen for shirtless greeting events can be dressed in swimwear, standing outside the store to perform display work and letting customers take pictures of and with them.[51] "I was like, 'This is really awkward,'" she remembers.

These practices amount to obvious, visible sexualization of sales associates. Mary characterizes them as "really hotly debated. Because, personally I think it's dumb. They get a $100 bonus and then they get paid hourly wage just to stand there," commenting, "It's just really a shallow thing." Charlotte, who is white and worked at Abercrombie's California-themed brand Hollister, agrees. She was chosen to accompany the shirtless greeters and received a free $200 outfit: a miniskirt, tank top, leggings, Hollister's letterman cardigan, scarf, and leather flip-flops:

> It was the dumbest looking outfit. And the guys got a pair of Hollister red bathing suit shorts and a whistle. And they were cold. Yeah, from midnight to 7 a.m. I got paid to stand with those guys and say, "Hey, how's it going?" for like however many hours. . . . So, appearance-based, everything. I wouldn't have gotten that job if I wasn't 5′5″, blond hair, blue eyes, tan at the time.

The beauty-based reward system and uncomfortably sexualized role both made Charlotte uncomfortable.

Shirtless greeting is less common at smaller-scale stores or outside of special events. That is, most workers appear fully clothed while welcoming and interacting with customers. Yet these encounters also demonstrate heterosexualized aesthetic labor practices by situating workers so that they are likely to interact with customers of another gender. In our observations, we saw that in Abercrombie stores, women customers usually interacted with men workers, and vice versa. Men primarily work in the first room of women's clothing, where women shoppers are most likely to begin browsing. Brendan says about Pac Sun:

> They played off the different sexes. Cute girl brand representatives would be at the guys' denim wall. They would flirt with them. I would be at the girls' denim wall. I would basically flirt with them. And it was basically just known all around that you just have to be nice, kind of have fun with it, that kind of thing.

Even if managers don't specifically ask workers to flirt with the customers, the workers understand flirting is a job expectation. The gendered and sexualized positioning indicates purpose: workers should interact with customers in ways that customers regularly interpret as sexually inviting.

Figure 14. Shirtless greeting at Abercrombie. SOURCE: iStock.com/Massimo Merlini.

Indeed, customers frequently stare at and sometimes "hit on" the workers. Charlotte even overhears their conversations: "There's a lot of like teenage boys will come in and be like, 'Oh you see that girl in the front?' And just talk about the girls all the time because you know they're all good looking. . . . And guys will come in and hit on you and stupid stuff like that." Kathleen refers to a similar pattern at her boutique store, "Boys would walk in. . . . They would just try to talk to the workers sometimes, just being annoying and stuff like that." And Hannah sighs about annoying Gilly Hicks customers, noting: "'We hear in the store, girls walk around in lingerie.' I was like 'Nope, that's not what happens.'" Hollister customers often tried to flirt with Claire:

> A lot of times, especially on like Friday and Saturday nights, big groups of people would come in and groups of guys would be like messing around with you and just saying pickup lines and all this stuff. . . . Obviously when you realize "they find me attractive" that's a good feeling, but then you're like, literally this isn't what I look like; I'm wearing this natural makeup and these clothes I don't usually wear and all this stuff; this isn't me. I don't know.

Claire understood that she was rewarded with status from men shoppers because, on the job, she represented the attractive ideal preppy white woman aesthetic. Yet she also knew this was an inauthentic look for her, and thus the praise, too, was inauthentic. Mary reports that men get approached at Abercrombie, though women workers receive more of the unwanted attention: "I think a lot of pre-teen girls walk in and they're like, 'Oh my God, he's so cute.' But I don't know, it just seemed to like, revolve way more around women, which I thought was kinda weird." To workers, these sexually charged interactions were unnatural or "stupid."

Some went further, describing these situations as embarrassing and objectifying. Jason comments that he was "a pretty modest person" who had to get used to the dynamic at Abercrombie:

> At first, it was embarrassing. . . . I would blush and just laugh it off. And just say, "Oh, you know, blah blah blah, can I help you with something?" . . . Over time it just, you know, I had women come in there and talk about my feet one time, I was wearing flip-flops, like "you have the most beautiful, gorgeous feet in those flip-flops." . . . A bunch of random things, when you work there for a while, you hear it all.

Customers ask to take pictures with him. Some even ask him out. Jason thinks the "most annoying" customers are the "little girls" who would "just like huddle in a group and then one would come up and ask a question and they'd all be laughing in the background, that happens all the time." Embarrassed with the treatment, Jason has identified approaches to deflecting the attention. Over time, he's come to take this aspect of his job in stride.

Workers also sometimes felt encouraged to dress in a sexualized manner—to become sexual objects. Patricia, who is a blond, blue-eyed white woman, said about working at Hollister, "I always felt like kind-of an 'item' to them. Weird. . . . I remember like that they made me unbutton [my shirt], and like you couldn't have bra straps [visible]. And, I was like their Barbie sometimes I felt like, which I didn't really like at all." Producing a sexually provocative aesthetic value for a clothing store can be demeaning for workers. Hannah describes the very short skirts and tiny tank tops that managers asked her to wear while working at Gilly Hicks, noting, "When I would go out on my break, I would put on sweatpants and a sweatshirt because I didn't like walking around the mall like in that. . . . I don't know if you'd wear [that outfit] out or not."

Claire recounts a story about her manager asking her to wear short shorts in the middle of January. She responded saying, "'I'm 5'9", these shorts just don't fit me. They're going to be way too short.' They were like, 'Well, that's the Hollister look, and you need to have the Hollister look.' I don't know. I just did not like it at all." Claire also tells a story about a Hollister coworker who wore a see-through sweater without a bra or camisole underneath it, so that "you could see everything." She felt that there should have been repercussions, but the manager simply said that this coworker "looked hot." For Claire, while she understands the store's aesthetic around appearance, "People were to the point [that] it was inappropriate." Two days later, Claire quit her job. Claire felt that her managers controlled her look in ways that made her uncomfortable, displaying more of her and other workers' bodies than was appropriate. And so, she quit.

It's not simply that these stores employ "good looking" people, but that they stratify, regulate, and sexualize their workers. This sexualization also has particular outcomes for workers of color, who may not be recognized as "attractive" enough due to racialized beauty hierarchies, and who receive less institutional support when customers treat them inappropriately. Managers monitor workers' bodies, facilitating their perpetuation of the brand for customers' gaze and enjoyment, but rarely understand the racialized outcomes of these practices.

Repurposing workers' bodies to promote a given brand of sex appeal is often lumped into a general sense of expectations about service industry employers "looking good" and "sounding right" in their workforce. This illuminates some aspects of discrimination and harassment that stem from embedding the "look" onto retail workers' bodies. Sexualization of workers may continue to subject employees to discrimination and alienating appearance-based practices in an attempt to create "cool" teen-focused brands.[52] Abercrombie & Fitch's recent shift away from sexualized models and shirtless greeters does suggest that change is possible.

CONCLUSION

The aesthetic labor process rewards and demeans workers through evaluating, surveilling, and controlling their bodies. The service panopticon ensures that not only are workers upselling customers and selling credit cards, but they're also representing the store as models, through gendered, classed, sexualized, and racialized performances. Many of the workers we interviewed detail the body rules they must follow through self-imposed beauty work. The aesthetic labor arm of the service panopticon thus matches these companies' general combined use of internal and external control techniques, as managers also externalize regulation of their staff's bodies to turn them into in-store models. Endeavoring to maximize their workers' aesthetic value for the brand, they direct employees to remove unsanctioned makeup and jewelry, shave, style their hair differently, or change their body size. Well aware of their role as "brand ambassadors," workers indicate their agency in creating and maximizing their aesthetic value. Some resist, while most regard the nonattire appearance expectations as reasonable.

However, workers also criticize the values projected within the brand's vision of beauty and coolness. The tri-racial beauty hierarchies that reinforce colorism and binary gender performances reproduce a middle-class and white-dominant understanding of desirability across the bulk of the US retail clothing market. White-associated features are upheld as a gold standard, with racial ambiguity and/or lighter-skinned looks valued next, and Black-associated aesthetics are policed and even banned. Body rules also signify class dimensions, emphasizing "natural" and "healthy" looks that diminish bright makeup, body art, and piercings. The focus on thin women workers and muscular men workers also supports particular cisgender notions of attractiveness. The aesthetic labor process is therefore inherently discriminatory; managers do not discern who is "good looking" in a vacuum. Instead, corporate and store management reify racialized, gendered, and classed visions of beauty in selecting, cultivating, and disciplining workers' bodies.

Sexualizing sales workers goes a step further in commodifying aesthetics. Abercrombie stores offer numerous examples; the "cast of" model program, shirtless greeting, and expectations about flirting within the "party" atmosphere of the stores all stand out. Both men and women workers recognize that their employers purposefully use their aesthetic value and sexual allure to sell clothing. Unlike previous studies of cosmetic workers and hair salon workers, we argue that both men and women are sexualized in these workplaces.[53] As they perform similar tasks, they experience them differently. For instance, all workers note that it can be a "boost" to be judged attractive, but women voice more simultaneous discomfort. This pattern may reflect the importance of women's maintaining dignity in these workplaces and the lesser threat of sexualized work to men's dignity.[54] Either way, look expectations reinforce inequalities by race, gender, and class in ways that may go undetected because few workers escalate their ambivalence to formal complaints. Fitting the look is understood as part of the bargain, from recruiting and hiring to primping, removing piercings, and standing out front shirtless, flirting with teens browsing the mall.

6 Modeling the Merchandise

"THEY ALWAYS CHECK YOU, FROM HEAD TO TOE"

Denise, who is Black, was shopping with her younger sister when an Abercrombie & Fitch manager recruited her to become a "model" (a position commonly referred to as "sales associate" at other stores). Over the next two years working in the store, Denise says, "I helped wear the clothes, and if there was an event, I'd go to that, and also I had floor duties, not only greeting customers, but also helping to keep the [sales] floor neat, folding things." Modeling the merchandise was central to the job; greeting customers and folding clothes were secondary tasks. "You're not only selling the clothes," she insists, "you're selling the look."

Abercrombie corporate and store managers bar workers from wearing other brands when they're on the clock. "They really did try to stress that 'we want you to wear the brand, we want you to be in uniform,'" Denise explains. Some sales models receive free clothing as compensation, though most workers have to pay, albeit at a discounted rate, for their own "uniforms." Denise had "tops and two pairs of jeans, so it was kind of mix and match" across work shifts because she refused to buy additional items. When she quit, "I ended up giving it all to my [little] sister," Denise comments, pointing out that she is "really not an A&F person."

Managerial surveillance of workers' appearance is, as shown throughout this book, a pillar of the clothing retail work experience: "You could tell—kind of like inspecting you, looking to see if you're in uniform, and I mean that they would tell people 'you're not in uniform today.'" Denise continues, "I could always tell that they were checking. I could always tell.'" Managers might give workers who weren't in uniform something to wear, ask them to buy clothing on the spot, or send them home. As Denise reasons, "Because I mean, you're not in uniform, you wouldn't necessarily be helping [the company sell]. . . . The first time they'd let it go, but habitually, it's like 'now you're not really doing your job,' So uniform was important." Denise recalls that managers would scold staff for not wearing the brand, reminding them, "When you accepted this job these were the terms that you agreed to." Managers use these "terms" and formalized, corporate-crafted "dress codes" as cudgels in exercising technical, routinized control over their workforce. Requiring each employee to conform to a standard set of body rules both establishes an ethos of embodying the brand and normalizes disciplining workers' aesthetic labor output to maximize its use-value.

Since Denise defines the job primarily by its "model" title, she is unsurprised that managers expect employees to wear the merchandise. She remembers how the body rules intensified in preparation for district manager visits:

> It would even get more like serious, to make sure everyone was in line . . . they just needed to make sure that everything was together, so of course you were looked over that day, you know, kind of checked out. . . . It was actually a little more tense because you know those people who you know maybe had a few dress infractions in the past, they're looking to them to make sure.

Denise's experiences are comparable to those of the other workers in our study, particularly those at the Abercrombie stores (Abercrombie & Fitch, Abercrombie Kids, Hollister, and Gilly Hicks). Many workers describe themselves as "walking mannequins," modeling the clothing as real-life, interactive mannequins.

Like some of her counterparts in chapter 5, Denise affirms being valued through her aesthetic labor: "Modeling and having people look at you, or compliment you . . . was fun, because you get to be outside of yourself for like a couple hours." Treating the job as distinctly beauty-centric allows Denise to appreciate the pleasurable aspects of her labor. Yet she also acknowledges the ugliness of being prized for her physicality and self-presentation: "I just feel like it's very superficial. . . . I'm just kind of like a prop, basically." Workers experience aesthetic labor in complex ways, especially the women who, across race, articulate a keen awareness of the negative dimensions of racialized beauty hierarchies.

WEARING THE CLOTHES

In the previous chapter, we considered how managers regulate workers' bodies, treating them as models. In this chapter we focus on how managers regulate workers' clothing, treating them as consumers. Modeling the company's clothing is central in stores oriented toward teenagers, twenty-somethings, and high-end shoppers.[1] While workers ring up customers, fold clothing, and police the stores for shoplifters, they model the merchandise and thus embody brand consumption for onlookers within the service panopticon. This practice embeds "the self-presentation and other personal characteristics of the worker" in "the work process and the work product," as labor scholars Cameron Macdonald and Carmen Sirianni contend.[2]

Aesthetic labor is central to workers in retail clothing jobs.[3] Organizational scholars John Allen and Paul du Gay argue that retail managers encourage workers to "deploy their own experience and identity as consumers in their paid work of providing 'quality service.'"[4] This performance connects workers to customers, as we have also shown in earlier chapters. Sociologists Christine Williams and Catherine Connell emphasize that employers regard workers as "brand representatives," who both "personify" and "embody" the brand, for example by wearing the store's merchandise.[5] These researchers theorize a hybrid "worker-consumer" in retail stores, workers who identify with and enjoy being associated with the brand, regarding themselves as "knowledgeable consumers."[6] Yet over time these workers become disillusioned with the degraded work they do, stop identifying with the brand, and leave these jobs.[7]

Body rules in youth-oriented stores require that workers wear the merchandise (or similar clothing that doesn't advertise competitors) as a condition of employment. However, because the stores don't usually provide the clothing, some ambiguity exists around how managers uphold these rules.[8] Employers treat workers as a captive market, consumers required to purchase store products as part of the job despite their low wages.

The previous chapter considered how employers develop and discipline their workers' bodies to perform aesthetic labor that often reifies existing beliefs and ideals of social difference (that is, race, class, gender, and sexuality). In this chapter we extend that analysis to examine how employers use aesthetic labor to maximize the brand's symbolic capital through workers wearing merchandise as "uniforms." Within the service panopticon, managers use encouragement, rewards, surveillance, and discipline to exercise control over workers' bodies and maximize their value as the brand's in-store models and worker-consumers.

Self-imposed and managerial enforcement often entails sporting the (most current) merchandise to produce symbolic capital for the brand and, in some cases, for individual employees. But that also means a shift in the labor process: lines between workers and customers are blurred when the rules force employees to become a market for each season's new line. By now, readers will expect that these practices reinforce gendered expectations, too: women workers receive rewards for embodying normative femininity and men for performing normative masculinity.[9]

The walking mannequins frame further urges us to consider that customers are also encouraged to engage with and critique staffers' bodies. Customers look them over, ask them about their sizes, and may insult them; sales staff use their bodies to try to encourage customers to find clothing that fits them. Workers experience complex feelings about how retail organizations use their bodies to consume the brand and to entice sales. Consuming the brand and modeling the merchandise extends the panopticon, encouraging shoppers to intensify their gaze of workers' bodies and even openly discuss workers' bodies.

REPRESENTING THE BRAND

Many fast-fashion, teen-oriented retail companies refer to sales associates as "brand representatives" to make expectations clear. Workers are supposed to convey the store's signature look to customers. Based on his experience at Pac Sun, Brendan translates this expectation to generally mean that workers "had to be representative of the type of style, culture, clothing, or whatever they sell." However, there are variations in how companies communicate and regulate these expectations. Lauren, who worked at both Urban Outfitters and Gilly Hicks, emphasizes that Gilly Hicks managers "are a lot more strict on presentation and expectations." Thus, the meaning of "representing the brand" differs based on the organizational context.

Stores hope to influence lifestyle even beyond the brand.[10] Influencing a lifestyle—shifting customers' understandings of their own identity and the degree to which a certain brand will help them communicate that identity—has the potential to lead to substantially more sales as Gwen, a former manager at Hollister, explains:

> They pride themselves on: "We're not promoting a brand, we're not promoting a style, we're promoting a lifestyle." They want you to walk into Hollister and be like "I want to live in California. I want to listen to music all the time/ I want to wear the hippest things, look the best, and all this stuff." . . . They are not just trying to change what you wear, they're trying to change what you like and what you do and what music you listen to, and that kind of thing.

The process involves not only recruiting sales staff but also stratifying sales workers into visible positions and invisible positions (like those in the store's stockroom; see chapter 5).[11] "Models," workers occupying visible roles, must always represent and sell the store brand. Claire (white), who worked on the Hollister sales floor, clarifies:

> When you're wearing their clothes, you're obviously advertising their clothes. . . . That's why they really are stressing who is standing in the front because you want the most relatable, attractive-looking person in the front so people would see if she . . . looks nice, then I could look nice in Hollister clothes.

The "greeter" position is another high-visibility role. These workers represent the store's look and its newest merchandise for passersby. David (white) reasons that wearing the clothes could encourage customers to buy the items "'cause it looks good on us." Models serve to sell merchandise by showing off how great they look. Indeed, Charlotte (white) connects the workers' modeling of the store's apparel to the pale mannequins: "Whatever's on the mannequins themselves is what we wear, too. And that's definitely what goes the quickest." Thus, customers entering the store to buy clothing are reminded, wherever they turn, of the latest looks and can use mannequins and workers interchangeably to make purchase decisions.

Even at stores that don't use the nomenclature of "model," workers identify with modeling, such as Tia (Black), who pronounces, "If you work for Forever 21, you have to look like you could model for Forever 21." Sabrina (white) discusses the frontline managers who "encouraged you to wear things that you bought from Urban Outfitters, especially if it was still in the store. Because, the thought was that if a customer sees you wearing it, and they like how it looks, then they are more likely to buy it, which makes sense." Workers across a wide range of youth-oriented stores pointed to this idea that customers are more likely to buy clothing that looks good on the sales staff, and all of the workers in teen-oriented clothing stores described selling the brand as an essential part of their job.

Selling the brand sometimes undermined their autonomy by asserting control over their bodies. Kathleen (Black), who worked for the boutique store oriented toward teens and twenty-somethings, attests to the extent of the service panopticon. Even when she was off the clock, managers "didn't even let you eat lunch outside," Kathleen explains, "because they were scared of what you would be doing in the neighborhood. You had to get lunch and bring it in. . . . They didn't want to see a [boutique] girl sitting in McDonald's. It's just weird." Despite making wages too low to afford all but fast food, Kathleen did not contest managers' expectations about meal breaks. She only saw them as a "weird" part of the job.

Dress code rules are less specific in stores focused on adult customers; they usually don't require wearing the store's clothing. Frank works at TJ Maxx, where the dress code is "business casual," allowing him a fairly flexible wardrobe, although he cannot wear blue jeans, shorts, or shirts with large logos. He notes, "They want [us] to look professional. I don't think they're encroaching on anybody's civil liberties." At Nordstrom's, James reports, "You had to look nice, but you can wear what you want, which was cool." And Joyce mentions that Macy's employees must simply wear all black (although the sales associates in the young men's and junior's departments have to "dress fashionably"). Variations in expectations for attire in stores that target customers across age ranges suggest that standards of cleanliness and professionalism are the sales staff's priorities, not mirroring the mannequins. Only in more teen-focused shops and areas of department stores do employers expect workers' clothing to reflect the "trendiness" of the merchandise. This also means workers in teen stores are subject to a more severe panopticon.

Julian, a manager at H&M, identifies some limitations within the company's "pretty lenient" dress code, such as more revealing apparel. He further opines:

> I'm kind of glad that we're not like Abercrombie & Fitch, where you have to wear [their] clothes and you have to wear what's current. So, for me personally, I just get dressed comfortably. Sometimes I feel like dressing a little nicer so I dress a little nicer. But yeah, there's . . . really [no] requirement.

This flexibility appears significant to frontline managers (and more entry-level workers), given that their jobs limit their autonomy. Carl also reports that although he couldn't wear logos from other stores, J. Crew had relatively few rules about clothing: "The only thing that guys have to wear from J. Crew is a J. Crew tie. And the reason is because we get free ties, so they're thinking, 'Well, if we're giving you this for free, you obviously have one to wear.'" Carl, and a few other employees who received free items, had no problem wearing merchandise to work. But many others resisted buying their own "uniform" again and again. Fast-fashion seasons change quickly, even every few weeks. Keeping up, even with a discount, is an expensive prospect that makes workers, who may be scheduled for relatively few hours each week, feel exploited in yet another dimension.

CREATING A CAPTIVE MARKET OF WORKER-CONSUMERS: MERCHANDISE AS UNIFORMS

Wearing store merchandise helps sell those items, while also serving as a potent labor mechanism to assert control over workers' bodies.[12] As Denise describes at the beginning of this chapter, managers often emphasize the importance of being "in uniform," or wearing the brand. Yet legally the stores cannot require workers to wear their clothing, unless they provide it, leading to a somewhat mixed message. As Tara, a shift leader, says, "It doesn't have to be American Eagle, but it's better if it is." Workers express substantial frustration, especially with the expectation that they pay for their own uniforms. They suggest that clothing retailers, who can presumably access such clothing at cost, should be able to outfit employees if that's a priority.

Between broad-scale retailers like Old Navy and department stores, with less rigid dress requirements, and the Abercrombie stores, which exemplify the most regulated approaches to worker attire, we see a range of worker-customer configurations. Contrasting her work experiences at each end of this spectrum, Hannah notes that at Aeropostale, as long as her clothing was not branded, she was okay, but at Gilly Hicks, "I *had* to get a pair of their flip-flops, and I *had* to buy a skirt and one of their tank tops. And that's what I would wear to work."

Strict dress code requirements could also create physical discomfort. Flip-flops were standard at Abercrombie stores, but workers were critical of them because the beach shoes offer little in the way of arch support or warmth. Pauline remembers her manager insisting that she change out of her Vans (closed-toed shoes that Hollister also allowed) into her flip-flops in the middle of winter: "She was like, 'Can you put them on then, instead?' I was just like, 'but it's freezing. My toes are still warming up.'" Gwen mentions that as a manager, she would have a nine-hour day in the shoes: "We're required to wear flip-flops. . . . You go home and your knees and back are killing you, you have no support, there's no sort of back support in flat rubber sandals." Leah also remembers the flip-flops: "I would hurt so, so bad." A style choice meant to convey a corporate brand of cool, that the store is a place where customers can feel free to hang out, causes workers discomfort and pain. This may seem like a small thing, yet workers at stores that allow them to choose the shoes best suited to working on their feet were less likely to complain about the physical strain of their jobs overall.

Quite a few workers discuss "getting into trouble" for wearing the wrong shoes, or more accurately, for wearing shoes that allow them to work comfortably. Brendan, for instance, was scolded for wearing the wrong footwear at G. H. Bass, but he had chosen those shoes because he knew he would be unloading goods. At Sears, Carmen remembers a similar exchange with a store manager: "One day I wore sneakers, like black Vans with white laces, and, she was just like, 'Oh, you're not supposed to wear sneakers.' And I was like, 'Sorry.'" She continued, detailing how supportive shoes would alleviate the fatigue of long shifts spent standing: "They're the comfiest thing I own, and I'm going to be on my feet for seven hours. I'm sorry I chose to wear sneakers." Workers express frustration that stores don't recognize that workers need to wear shoes that reflect their working conditions. Workers who have to stand on hard floors for hours at a time, or unload trucks, suffer when wearing the "cute" shoes the stores wish to advertise. Workers know that their bodies get tired and are vulnerable to injury on the job—unlike their plastic mannequin counterparts.

Most of the teen-oriented retailers ask that workers wear either the store's clothing or lookalikes with no apparent branding. Echoing Frank at TJ Maxx, American Eagle employee Gabe recounts, "It has to either have the American Eagle or no logo at all. So, I could wear just a plain shirt from Gap, as long as it didn't say Gap across the chest." If workers wore the wrong clothing, Lillian stresses, there would be consequences: "There was actually one girl who came in with Hollister jeans, and she had to buy jeans from American Eagle right away." Gwen, a Hollister manager, explains that it could be difficult to find items without other store's logos:

> You can't wear something that says Wet Seal on the tag, but you also can't wear something with distinct pockets, like Lucky jeans . . . so you have to wear a pair of jeans that doesn't have any type of design, any type of anything. . . . Those jeans are very hard to find.

Even when the rules don't force workers to buy the brand's apparel, dress codes turn workers into a stable consumer base. When the company's dress code is so specific that only the brand's clothing line meets that code, workers become a captive market, regularly purchasing clothes. Even at Aeropostale, Hannah "bought one or two jeans just because all my jeans had stitching in the pockets [indicating they were not Aeropostale], so I didn't have anything else to wear." As Gwen and Hannah convey, requiring "unbranded clothing" challenges workers since subtle style differences could be read as branding. Many workers resort to buying jeans from their store to avoid any possibility that managers will view their jeans as "branded" for another store. By disrupting the lines between consumers and workers, the rules may even impede workers' ability to recognize their labor power and therefore erode potential on-the-job organizing.

The expense of maintaining a work wardrobe arose regularly during our interviews. Claire (Hollister) is indignant, "Your whole first paycheck just went. . . . It was stupid," while Tara (American Eagle) comments, "I know a lot of the new people come in and they just spend hundreds of dollars . . . but I don't have too much money to spend extra." Heather observes that new hires would end up with a "whole new wardrobe":

> You're just surrounded by clothes, so you just succumb to buy it. You're just like instilled that this is the style, so why don't I have it? I should be wearing this. . . . And then their check is going to buying things at Forever 21 so it's like, "what is the point of me working here if I'm not even making money?"

Without intending to, as Heather recounts, workers sometimes return the lion's share of their paychecks to their employers. Carmen doesn't know how her Free People coworkers "were affording it," but buying and sporting the store's clothing gave them something "in common with the manager."

Gabe, who didn't shop at American Eagle before working there, says, "After I got the job I would leave my paycheck at the store." He remembers managers urging him to buy clothes. They did so "more often" upon realizing that he "was susceptible" to this pressure:

> There was a time when I had like eight or nine pairs of jeans, which right now I have like maybe two or three. When I think back about it, it was kind of insane. Just the amount of T-shirts I had. Something about working there that just made me want to stay up-to-date with the style.

Corporate sales goals for each store location work in tandem with corporate body rules to compel frontline managers to treat workers as consumers. Brendan, like Gabe, laughs about his consumption during his tenure at Pac Sun: "I spent a lot of money there . . . an average of three articles of clothing, three or four, a month." Kathleen also remarks about her work at a boutique: "I didn't have a paycheck. I'd pick up my pay, I used to give them back the money because I used to buy all my clothes there. It was so bad." Surrounded by merchandise and managers encouraging them to buy and wear store clothing, men and women report leaving a large portion of their paychecks with their employers. Managers treat workers as captive consumers; keeping a large labor force of workers, even if most are scheduled for relatively few work hours, improves the store's bottom line.

Workers earning minimum wage try to navigate the costs of their "uniforms" and dress code compliance through a range of strategies. David (white) rarely buys Abercrombie clothes, saying, "The last time I bought something was this shirt [tugs on collar of gray button-down shirt] which was . . . $39 with my discount. Pretty expensive but, I just figured I haven't bought anything in a while." David indicates that the clothing is costly, even when discounted; men, whose clothing tends to be less visibly seasonal, may be able to avoid buying, as he does while continuing to fit the store's branded look. Among women, the strategies may tend toward purchasing the least expensive options available with each new "season" of merchandise. Antonia (Black), for instance, avoids purchasing higher-priced items at Express: "I bought a few T-shirts, little simple things. I wouldn't really buy the shoes or the pants or something like that."

Pauline (Black) explained to her coworkers why she would bring her "work clothes" and change into them immediately before the shift and change back out of them before leaving Hollister:

> I was just like "I have other clothes besides this, I need to put this away because I'm going to wear the same thing tomorrow. I'm not going to buy anything else new. I will do laundry but don't think I'm going to buy a new shirt from you guys."

Workers thus resist consuming the brand and acting as a "brand representative" outside of paid shifts. Mary (multiracial) contends that most Abercrombie workers would "penny pinch," saying, "usually I would just find one thing and wear it every single day 'cause there was no way I'm gonna spend $40 [each] for five shirts, I'm just not." These workers wear the same outfit every shift or rotate between a scant few outfits to limit the costs of performing aesthetic labor.

Organization scholars Leanne Cutcher and Pamela Achtel argue that requiring sales associates to buy merchandise to wear as work uniforms with their paltry earnings may lead to disaffection with the brand.[13] Our interview data support this argument. For example, Charlotte (white) "was obsessed with Abercrombie" in junior high. She explains that "Hollister was kind of like new. . . . When I started shopping there, one of the couple of times, I got recruited." A few years later Charlotte wouldn't wear the Hollister clothing anywhere else, so that she could maintain their pristine "look" for as long as possible, refusing to accumulate more Hollister items.

Others resist the captive market intention directly and refuse to buy from the store. This was particularly prevalent among workers of color. Liz, who is Black, bought clothing that would fit the work rules since she didn't already own the attire they expected her to wear, but "it wasn't [Hollister] clothes, because I was not trying to spend over $40 on two things." Liz found cheaper clothing elsewhere that met the managers' expectations. Carmen, who is Latina, sarcastically recounts working in sales at Free People: "Ask me if I ever bought anything from there while I was there? No." Corinne, who is Asian, also refused to buy clothing at Abercrombie. She recalls, "I don't think I bought a single thing when I worked there," and, "I just didn't see the point of like buying a flannel [shirt] for 50 bucks. So, I just wore a white T-shirt and jeans every single shift." That Corinne and Liz both had stockroom positions likely minimized the managerial pressures regarding branded embodiment expectations. Still, such approaches subvert the captive market dimension of aesthetic labor and the service panopticon that seeks to control workers' bodies and spending habits. Some workers suggest that refusing to purchase the merchandise means being less likely to be scheduled for shifts.

Workers find the central expectation among clothing retailers that they will both purchase and wear the store's merchandise demeaning.[14] They recognize frontline managers as purposely upselling workers and customers alike. These decisions reflect economically exploitative aspects of this industry, namely that purchasing merchandise detracts from workers' meager earnings and blurs the distinction between consumer and employee.[15] Yet these choices also reflect race and class. Some workers emphasize that the stores they work for don't fit "their style." For example, Frances, who is multiracial, emphasizes that after workers clock out at Abercrombie: "Guys have the baggy pants now when they leave, instead of having their pants around their waist . . . and put on their Nikes instead of their Converse or something. Where they dress completely different." Workers of color tend to report not buying merchandise, perhaps because the styles target white consumers and idealize white identities. Staying within the body rules without becoming captive consumers may, in this way, be read as a subtle expression of racial pride.

KEEPING UP WITH THE TRENDS

Retailers direct workers to stay "up to date" and model the most current line of merchandise. This intensification of aesthetic labor demands means workers purchase clothing regularly, with each new "season," despite not getting reimbursed. Abercrombie corporate management allowed workers to use higher-than-usual employee discounts on about five different outfits every season. The company refers to these items as the "Triple-As." At Hollister, Carolyn notes, "We have winter Triple-As, fall Triple-As, and summer Triple-As, and once they flip over, your wardrobe has to flip over, too." As Frances points out: "Whatever they put on the mannequins, they put in this book. And that's what they want their employees to wear."

Both women and men workers describe this system, though men seem less pressured to buy these promoted items. "You *don't have* to buy it," Bryan says of Abercrombie, but "they'd like you to buy it, so they have the new look," which encourages customers to adopt the newest styles as well. At Abercrombie Kids, Glenn recalls, managers also took a subtler approach: "They say it without saying it that you have to buy the clothes. But they have a list in the back of the store that has all the clothes you need to get." Jason also says Abercrombie managers "would highly recommend [buying the Triple-As]," attempting to increase internal sales. Gwen adds to the picture, explaining that management actively monitors workers' purchases:

> There is a record kept [at Hollister] of who buys them, and if you buy them, you're expected to wear them during your shift. . . . They [corporate managers] do have [the managers] stress that [workers] are not required to buy these, because they would have to be free if you were required. . . . They give you the option of buying these things, but if you do buy them, you have to wear them, since you got them at the discount.

Organizational practices like these push workers to buy the items, as corporate managers establish a record of who buys them and frontline managers surveil employees to ensure that they wear the Triple-As. If, for example, a worker bought a discounted shirt from the Triple-As, but store managers wanted to prevent them from buying the cheaper clothes for friends, they'd request the worker wear that shirt to their shift. Indeed, one attorney leading a lawsuit against Abercrombie & Fitch alleges that although the company had a disclaimer that workers didn't need to purchase these clothes, "many employees saw their hours cut, and/or were sent home when they arrived in anything that wasn't 'in uniform'—that is, wearing Abercrombie & Fitch."[16]

Resistance to the worker-as-customer ideal appears rather common. When the new Hollister season was released, Pauline remembers the store managers' obvious efforts to encourage employees to purchase the fresh merchandise: "It's all about the language that they would use to remind you: 'Have you checked out our [new line]? Did you get a look at [it],' trying to remind me about it. And I was just like, 'Oh yeah, I saw them.'" Pauline, like a customer faced with upselling tactics, simply ignores managers' sales pitches. Charlotte divulges her frustration with her frontline manager when the season changed at Hollister, and workers were barred from wearing shorts:

> She was like, "You can't wear shorts, [Charlotte]. You have to buy a pair of jeans." And I was like, "I'm not going to buy a pair of jeans, I have every single pair of jeans this store has to offer me. I'm not paying money for it." And she was like, "Well you're not in key look [the current season] and I can't have you be on the floor like that." And I was like, "Are you going to find someone to cover my shift? Do you want me to go home, because I'm not buying a pair of jeans?". . . If I was any other associate, [I'd have said] "Okay," and buy a pair. A lot of them are really timid like that and don't want to say "no" to a manager. But there was no way they were going to make me buy a pair of jeans.

Charlotte preferred to give up a shift rather than buy the newest jeans. She would have, indeed, lost money by staying at work and buying expensive merchandise she didn't need. The fact that her coworkers would buy a new pair of jeans in the situation just made her all the more certain that she should not.

Charlotte's experience illuminates how frontline managers' relationships with workers can splinter through the cultivation of aesthetic value while reinforcing the notion that longer-term workers become disillusioned with the job's more superficial requirements.[17] Gwen, a manager, recalls how her higher-ups pressured store managers at Abercrombie:

> Our district manager always told the managers, "You better make sure that everyone is excited about the new Triple-As." Like in your five-minute meetings, you're supposed to say "Did you get your Triple-As yet? Did you see them?" and if they say "No." "Oh, let me show you the packet; look at this. Oh, you'd look cute in this. Why don't you just try it on?" During hours, we're sending kids in the dressing room, "Oh those look great on you," or "Try this size. This'll look better if you roll the sleeves like this."

Corporate creates an aesthetic labor process in which senior managers urge frontline managers to talk workers into purchases. Indeed, at times workers were sent to try on clothing *during* their shifts. Perhaps unsurprising given the specificity of body rules, these practices nonetheless demonstrate the intensity with which managers scrutinize and regulate workers' bodies to consume and perpetuate the brand—often to the detriment of worker satisfaction, but to the benefit of their sales numbers.

These tactics also occur at other similarly niched stores. Gabe describes how at American Eagle, the "new arrivals," are both placed on mannequins and offered to workers at more steeply reduced prices, so that workers and mannequins advertise the new "look" in tandem. Lori expresses that Wet Seal managers encourage employees to buy and wear certain items: "You don't have to wear the top if you don't want to, but it would be nice if you wore them because it'd be easier to sell it." Sherrie explains how at Pac Sun: "They would basically select an outfit and if you liked it, you could buy like the whole outfit for 70% off, but you'd have to get everything that they suggested. That was their way to push the new items onto the employees." To her, it felt exploitative.

Seasonal clothing could also lead to physical discomfort. Fashion seasons tend to appear in stores well before the clothing is weather appropriate. Claire discusses how Hollister's Triple-A's "would change and you would have to buy the new clothes and wear those and . . . they started making us wear shorts in the middle of January!" Lauren echoes this

Figure 15. Worker in a dressing room helping a customer. SOURCE: iStock.com/gstockstudio.

sentiment about Gilly Hicks, "You would get cold . . . and you would get odd looks too, like it's winter and you're walking around the mall in flip-flops, and they're like, 'What is she doing?'" This might work on mannequins, but workers convey that requiring them to don shorts and flip-flops in winter, as if they were mannequins that couldn't feel cold, is dehumanizing, embarrassing, and uncomfortable.

Inside the stores, we often observed that sales workers wore outfits that matched the mannequins' clothing. We wondered if it was a requirement, but workers explain that this coordination is coincidental. Pauline shares about Hollister: "There would be times where like I walked in, and everybody was wearing the same flannel shirt. And I was just like, 'This is a problem, guys.'" Having all of the workers in the store—as well as the mannequins—sporting a particular shirt is a sort of absurdist end point of the requirement to purchase from a limited range of new clothing. Gwen explains:

> They'll give you four or five plaid shirts [in the Triple-As], and four of them will be hideous, and everyone's like, "There is no way I'm going to wear that,"

and there will be one very cute one, so everyone is going to buy that one. So, they give you this list, but there are only a few that you're going to choose. And I don't think they do that on purpose, they obviously think that [all of the outfits are] great, but yea, just that's why, when you walk in, everyone's wearing the exact [same outfit].

Mary confirms: "There's a limited list of what to pick from and certain things are more popular than the other things. . . . All the girl coworkers are like, 'Oh, that's a cute sweater, I want to get that.'" Identifying a narrow selection of new merchandise perpetuates the repetition of the clothing displayed throughout the store, on workers and mannequins alike. Carl, who has work experience at both Abercrombie and J. Crew, explains that identical outfits are unlikely at J. Crew because their "60s list" (comparable to Triple-As, but 60% off) includes "20 shirts, and ten different pairs of pants and twelve different pairs of shoes, and it's so, so much" merchandise. Thus, corporate policies at youth-oriented stores that focus on only a few items of clothing lead to negative unintended consequences.

Workers at stores with more flexible policies are generally happier because their employers don't stress constant consumption and thus they can communicate their personal fashion sense. Aesthetic labor can be pleasurable and creative, especially under less intensive surveillance from managers. For example, Sabrina remembers that Urban Outfitters managers

> really encourage you to develop your own style. . . . We had one professional skateboarder who was working here, and he would always wear his skateboarding stuff. And [the manager] would be like, "I'm a dancer, so I wear a lot of my dancing clothes." And so, everybody has their own unique style.

Sabrina appreciates this opportunity for employees to explore and express themselves at work. Part of the Urban Outfitters sales staff herself, Lauren says, "They say just to have some taste in it, and just not be casual." Urban Outfitters adopts a laxer dress code than the Abercrombie stores, but similarly engineers its rules to showcase the brand through worker bodies and styles.

Forever 21 is also more relaxed, as Jill conveys: "It was casual. They were like, 'Okay, we have a few rules, but for the most part it's up to you, and we want you to reflect your own style.'" Tia adds, "Actually one of the requirements of being an employee of the store [Forever 21] is to dress trendy. So, you have to have your own style, and you have to have your own way of dressing." These workers feel encouraged to draw upon their fashion sense in dressing for work; they also complain less about the high cost of clothing. The only exception is Lillian. Comparing her two clothing retail jobs, she feels

> less pressure dressing up for Abercrombie, because they have specific and really strict rules for what I can or cannot wear, like what kind of hairstyle and everything, but American Eagle was more lenient, so I went on their store website and tried to match what kind of style looks American Eagle.

For Lillian, Abercrombie's stricter body rules at least made it easier to identify her employer's expectations; moving to American Eagle made it more challenging for her to decide what to wear. Lillian's account acknowledges the conscious labor workers put forth to meet employer expectations about on-brand appearance.

Stores provide discounts to partially mitigate the costs of their work uniform and to entice employees to make purchases. These discounts, however, don't fully redress the injustice of paying workers very low (and stagnant) wages. Instead, the requirement to model the merchandise, especially the most current items, facilitates more frequent spending. Workers at stores without requirements to "stay current" or buy the merchandise tend to see dress codes as reasonable; they view their managers as asking them to dress professionally. However, workers at stores with strict appearance codes express substantial frustration, both with the costs incurred and the sense that managers reward aesthetic labor with additional shifts and better hours. Aesthetic labor has a now-you-see-it-now-you-don't quality among this workforce. While employers do not *tell* their workers that they *must* wear store clothing, it's clear that those who comply with the rules stand to benefit.

Clothing retailers may argue that they are forced to require workers to cover this expense due to the tremendous turnover in their frontline sales workforce. This turnover, however, reflects the no-win proposition of balancing regular job-related expenses with low wages. If uniformity is the goal, then investing in workers' aesthetic labor by providing them with store clothing would be more effective. At the same time, workers appear happier when they consume as they please and convey their own sense of style in the workplace, so lifting strict dress codes might be a better concession.

REGULATING THE LOOK

Most workers at stores that enforce body rules emphasize that they regulate their appearance and obey without being prodded. Self-regulation is a key element of worker control within the service panopticon, especially visible within aesthetic labor performances. Lori feels that the need for income helps ensure that workers at Wet Seal and Justice follow appearance policies: "If they send you back [home], you don't get paid. So, I feel like everyone [knows] you've got to come to work appropriate."

Surveying and adjusting workers' attire are important store manager responsibilities. Lillian highlights the excessive detail corporate management provides about styling the merchandise as work uniforms: "Sometimes the Triple-As would tell you how you should roll your jeans or how much sleeve you could roll up, it was really ridiculous." Corporate management relies on store managers to ensure that the staff follows those specifications. In turn, Jason remarks, Abercrombie managers check each employee as they arrive:

> When you walk in, they always check you, from head to toe. "Hey, tuck the left side of your shirt in. That's right. Let the belt show. Cuff your jeans. Unbutton, button up one more." That was my biggest one, I'd always have to button up another one; it'd be too low.

The strictness of Abercrombie's body rules entails a hands-on approach from store managers. Abercrombie employees, like Mary, recall managers' "styling" techniques:

> One of my managers would actually come over to me at the beginning of my shift and look me up and down and then get down on her knees and start rolling my jeans, and then, "Back up, back up. Let me see," and then just be like, "Tuck in your shirt."

Frances interprets this styling as managers teaching staff (and onlookers) how to wear the clothes appropriately. According to Frances, the managers would say, "Don't worry about it, it's okay. People make mistakes but just do it this way right now; fix it."

Most workers make occasional mistakes. Managers usually handle these infractions by reminding them of the policy and telling them to keep it in mind for their next shift. During one shift at Gilly Hicks, Hannah "forgot because the backs of the tank tops were kind-of racerback, and I forgot to wear a racerback bra, and my bra straps were showing." Her store managers warned her "how [she] shouldn't do that again." Hannah knew that managers regularly assessed her appearance, but felt they mildly enforced the body rules since they primarily cautioned workers about transgressions and asked them to conform to the dress code. Trent, a manager, says he tends to deemphasize clothing rules at Express unless his district manager is visiting; we see again how multilevel management is key to the service panopticon. Frontline managers exercise some autonomy in their role of cultivating and conforming workers' aesthetic labor, but usually only do so in the absence of their corporate superiors. David hints at this managerial discretion at Abercrombie: "As long as you don't do it every time you come in they'll be okay with it, they'll let it slide."

Other times, managers require workers to immediately redress the problem by altering their appearance or send them home for violating the body rules. Leah relates an interaction with a store manager at Hollister in which she "was wearing my belt and was just minding my own business and a manager" approached to ask, "'What's up with that belt?' And I was like, 'I have to wear it with my pants.' And he was like, 'No, you have to take that off.'" Leah followed his instructions. Lance suggests that if Hollister workers wore the wrong shoes or clothes, his manager would say, "Change it. Go to the store and buy some." Many regard these adjustments as an unsurprising part of the job but also find such enforcement abrupt, arbitrary, and costly.

As Stella says about Macy's, "There's one manager who will write people up if they're not in dress code, but that's only if he's having a bad day." Stella excuses this manager's behavior, noting that he inconsistently enforces the dress code. Most workers reason that on the rare occasions when staff members were sent home, they had made fairly serious errors and the managers' reaction was appropriate. James, who worked at the more upscale Nordstrom's, states that managers sent home employees whose garb departed from the dress code, and "if you were doing that regularly, you're going to get canned." He emphasizes that managers clearly communicated these rules, warning workers about coming in without the right look, and so he feels it is appropriate if workers lose their jobs for ignoring the dress code. Workers like James internalize the body rules, leading them to both self-impose the regulations and normalize punitive measures that management doles out for infractions. Thus, the service panopticon operates to encourage workers to self-regulate as well as succumb to external reprimands.

Frustration with the ways managers capriciously enforce body rules is palpable in our interview data. For example, store managers reprimanded Heather at Forever 21:

> I came in one day in overalls and a shirt, you couldn't see any part of my body, you could see the top part of my back and I got in trouble for it. And I was like, "What dress code am I breaking here?" And they were like, "Your back's showing." I'm like, "What?" And then some girls would come in in tank tops and their whole stomach would be showing.

Heather felt embarrassed for being called out, with the implication that she showed more skin than her coworkers in an unbecoming way. Tia, stating that some of her Forever 21 coworkers were dismissed for not following the dress code, comments: "They never did that to me though because I definitely would not have [gone] home and came back. I would have been like, 'All right. Bye.'" Tia identifies that she had her limits and could successfully resist extreme forms of managerial punishment.

Corporate visits raise the stakes regarding the body rules. Stressed frontline managers endeavor to ensure that their staff meets corporate specifications—to the degree that almost all of the workers at teen-oriented shops tell stories about dressing more carefully when corporate managers visited. These preparations are consequential, and workers are disciplined more commonly around visits from the higher-ups. At American Eagle, Gabe notes, when "someone got sent home [for an appearance violation], it was usually because the regional manager was there, and they would make the executive decision. And the days and weeks following that, then managers would be more strict on appearance." Frontline managers warn workers about upcoming upper-level visits. They emphasize the importance of following the dress code, or being "extra polished," as Antonia says. Jason explains about Abercrombie, "The previous shift before [corporate] would be coming in, they'd say 'oh, they're coming in Tuesday, Look Policy 100%, be on top of your game.'" Tia laughingly describes the anticipation before Forever 21 corporate manager visits: "That was like, you know, 'Oh my God, the president is coming.' That was how they acted.... If you're not wearing something nice, go home. Don't even bother, just go home." Bringing corporate surveillance into the store itself intensifies the rule-bound gaze for frontline managers and workers alike.

Store managers become more insistent that workers sport the newest merchandise when their bosses arrive. Frances says that her Abercrombie "managers let us know ahead of time, [saying] like 'by the way, our DM's [district manager] gonna be in tomorrow, so make sure [you're wearing] your Triple-A's . . . from *this* time.'" David comments that he was once chastised by a regional manager for wearing an out-of-season shirt at Abercrombie: "The district manager actually came in, he's like, 'That's not in the Triple-A's this year at this time, so you're not supposed to be wearing that' and I'm like, 'Wow, okay,'" leading David to recognize that "appearance is a lot." Officially and legally, managers cannot require workers to buy merchandise, let alone new clothes every season, yet they regularly reprimand those who aren't "in uniform," especially when higher-level organizational representatives are watching.

Although part of management, store managers generally don't admit to subscribing to all of the body rules that corporate managers tout. Trent, for instance, describes his discomfort:

> Our district manager is like, "You have to dress Express, you have to shop at Express, you know, at least once a month. You need to be doing this." And that's what I don't feel comfortable with. I don't feel like that because you work in a retail store you need to shop there like every single week because you're . . . just asking for more money. That's just not . . . how I feel, but when our district manager comes, we do dress our nicest, so I'll always wear whatever's the latest kind of newest thing that I've purchased from Express.

Although Trent feels that he and his employees shouldn't be expected to consistently buy new clothing at Express, he does toe the line when district management is expected and encourages his staff to do so. District managers, of course, are also policing the managers' looks, as Gwen explains about Hollister: "The district manager is not going to be happy if you're wearing a pair of white jeans and you're promoting dark jeans, so the managers are always expected to be wearing Triple-As." For Trent and Gwen, their manager status does not mean that they have greater flexibility regarding the dress code. Instead, they feel held to high standards both personally and in terms of regulating their workers.

GENDER CONFORMITY IN APPAREL-RELATED BODY RULES

Many of the stores reinforce gendered clothing distinctions, requiring workers to conform to binary gender norms in their presentation in the workplace.[18] In some stores, corporate management limits the use of employee discounts to within-gender purchases. In other words, men workers can apply their discount to buy men's clothing and women can do so to buy women's clothing, but workers have less latitude to purchase or sport cross-gender clothing. Some of the stores also set different rules for men and women governing which items they can wear. Although relatively few workers complain about these practices, a few men suggest pushing back against the limitations on their clothing choices.

Two of these men are gay, and another man is "primarily straight"; the other eight men we interviewed don't make these claims. Carl, an assistant manager at J. Crew, gripes that if he wants to buy women's clothing, he would get the lesser 30% "gift" discount rather than the 50% "worker" discount: "I complain all the time because there are actually like several pieces of women's clothing that I want to buy that are more gender neutral and I'm [like] 'Why can't I use a 50 on this?' Because all the women can. So, I'm arguing on that one." Carl sees these rules as unnecessarily restrictive of his gender expression. Trent, an assistant manager at Express, agrees that these gendered body rules control his embodiment of the brand:

> This is what I have a huge problem with: it's different for gender. So, for instance, women can wear like open-toed sandals but me as a man, I can't; and I have a problem with this so much because most of the stuff I do buy in

> Express, I buy women's clothes that look good on me. . . . I believe in gender-bending . . . but the things that I wear are not necessarily how it is.

While Trent can buy women's items for the same discount that he receives on men's merchandise, he is not allowed to wear many of those items at work. These apparel-related restrictions reinforce a sense of binary gender performances presented in how the store organizes and markets its merchandise.

Julian, an H&M manager, explains, "There's a differentiation between what tank top a guy can wear and what kind of tank top a girl can wear. That's something that's always bugged me a little bit because I'm like, 'How can you make that, that differentiation?'" Such practices aim to control how employees represent the brand, showing that companies try to limit the presentation of their workers' gender and sexual identities and performances to those that align with the brand and appeal to customers. Julian also comments that, as a manager, he suspects he would give a woman wearing shorter shorts more leeway than a man, noting "I'm not saying that's fair." For these men, the dress codes are biased because of the gendered distinctions in what they could wear to work or for which items they could get their employee discount.

Workers sometimes observe the ways apparel-related appearance policies are unfair to women. Carl, for example, argues that the J. Crew dress code holds women to higher expectations than men, as women are not allowed to wear jeans:

> I usually wear jeans and like shirt and a tie and a cardigan, like something really easy. Especially the women's personal shoppers, they are just layered and layered and have jewelry on and shoes and skirts. . . . I feel like their routine must be a little bit more difficult as far as getting ready for work. . . . Their [dress code] is more strict. They have to have more accessories than we do.

Carl acknowledges that women's sales associates could select some more casual outfits, still emphasizing the stricter and more demanding expectations for women's dress than those for men.

Others say that when both men and women must conform to dress codes, these policies often reflect distinct gendered expectations, so that women are sometimes said to get more leeway than men and other times are described as being held to more elaborate dress standards. Although we didn't interview enough straight and gay men to be able to generalize, within our sample, the men who don't define themselves as simply "straight" comment on the unfairness of expecting them to buy and wear only men's clothing, when some of the women's items better fit them or their sense of style. Their experiences reflect how queer workers must uphold heterosexual and binary gender norms in the workplace.[19]

SELLING WITH BODIES

In addition to purchasing and then modeling the merchandise, customers, corporate, and frontline managers expect workers to regard their bodies as selling tools. Women workers, in particular, are accustomed to shoppers commenting on and referencing their bodies. Clothing retail asks workers to engage in a unique form of "bodily labor"; sociologist Pei-Chia Lan refers to this performance as "the mirroring body," whereby workers use their bodies to display appearance ideals.[20] In the case of clothing stores, frontline managers urge sales workers to try on the merchandise and prepare themselves to discuss the fit of particular items. For example, Sherrie says at Pac Sun:

> When the store wasn't busy, they'd have us try on all the different styles of jeans and find the one we thought was the best fitting, or you know compare them. So then when we talked to customers, we could be like, "Hey, I just tried on those jeans. You know, they're awesome." Or you know, "You might want to go up a size in those, they're pretty tight."

Workers' bodies serve as mannequin-like display objects, a source of interactive consumer-based advice to help sell the clothing. Stacey explains this practice as making the customer service interactions authentic and personable: "[Old Navy managers] want us to be like, 'These jeans fit me really well. They want us to be really genuine." For some workers, such embodied labor might improve the service they provide to customers. Yet others experience more ambivalence.

Most accept that customers ask about their personal size and fit, seeing it as a natural way to operate as a sales associate. Nora outlines this process: "They'd be like, 'Would this fit you? Because my daughter looks probably about this size.'" She laughs, remembering, "one time I actually tried out an outfit for a customer at American Eagle." Sociologist Lynne Pettinger argues that the aesthetic labor of workers wearing the clothing sold in the store is distinct from the customer interactions, though both are important components of the labor and branding processes.[21] Veronica references how these requests at Gap made her feel helpful: "We'll ask her, "Is she my size? Is she a little smaller?" Carolyn says, "that happens a lot" at Hollister, when customers remark, "'Oh, my nephew or my niece is your size; like what size do you wear?'" Antonia doesn't mind this, so long as her Express customers avoid open criticism:

> For example, jeans, "Oh, my girlfriend has a butt kind of like yours, blah, blah, blah." That type of thing. "What would you suggest I get her?" It wasn't really like, "Yeah, why are you wearing those jeans when you know that you have a flat butt?" At first, I was like okay, you definitely checked me out. But all right, whatever . . . thanks for the compliment . . . and then you just help them out.

Customers' body comments might feel awkward, but when they are not explicitly negative, workers can see this as simply part of the job. Tia also asserts that this isn't a problem at Forever 21, noting, "I like the way I look. . . . I would say, 'Oh yeah, I'm a size. . . .' I never took offense to that." Praise and admiration constitute clear perks of the job for some, making the explicit consumer gaze involved in performing aesthetic labor more fulfilling.

While also a teen-oriented retailer, American Eagle sells apparel in a wider size range than some competitors. Rachel, who is mixed race and light-skinned with blond hair and blue eyes, mentions how she uses her body to market American Eagle clothing to similarly shaped women:

> Since I'm a half Middle Eastern . . . I have a lot more curves than the average white person would. I've actually drawn a lot of attention from other minorities, specifically Black females and Latina females. . . . They will come to me and be like, "What jeans do you buy here? Because we see that you have more curves." And it's because I wear clothes that accentuate mine. It has worked as a benefit for the company.

Figure 16. Women examining merchandise. SOURCE: iStock.com/monkeybusiness images.

Rachel interprets her performance of aesthetic labor as extending the brand's appeal to include Black, Latina, and multiracial women, who are more often associated with curvier bodies than white women. She says, "They realize that if I can fit in those clothes, then they can, too, instead of thinking that it's 'just for the white girl.' Just a huge critique of Abercrombie."[22] Her experience as a multiracial twenty-something shows how the clothing industry may commodify racial ambiguity to appeal to a more racially diverse clientele (see chapter 5).

Rachel also demonstrates that some workers enjoy embodying the brand—it can even present an opportunity to critique stores that only carry smaller sizes. Rachel mentions her willingness to even initiate an explicit discussion of her body if she thinks customers are regarding her body as a mannequin:

I will be almost forthcoming with talking about how things fit me. If I see somebody's staring at kind of the way that [the clothing] fits me and wondering, comparing in their head. Not trying to be vocal about it. I'll be the

one to say something . . . . I have no problem talking about how anything in
the store would fit my body.

Emphasizing which clothes fit her curves to American Eagle customers isn't troublesome for Rachel, who embraces the sense that she can
positively impact others by openly communicating about her own body.
Racialized beauty hierarchies shape the women workers' experiences and
often shine a light on personal sentiments about body size and sexuality.
Rachel relates selling the brand to her experiences with body size norms
imbued with racial and gender significance. She identifies the importance
of helping customers feel better about their bodies, confiding that two of
her friends are anorexic and that she once dreamt of being more narrowly
shaped:

> As far as I'm concerned, if I had somebody in fifth grade [tell me] that even-
> tually, I was going to love the way I look, I would've laughed at them, but it
> would have been helpful. And so, that's why I try and be helpful. No one's
> comfortable in their body ever. Nobody feels 100% about the way that they
> look. I never did.

Rachel's past experiences make it crucial for her to support customers
in their search for outfits that make them feel good. In stores with more
narrow visions of beauty and correspondingly small size selections, her
efforts would be wasted. Thus her aesthetic labor feels, to her, like a form
of implicit resistance.

Others find customer comments on the fit of their clothing far more
intrusive. Workers describe interactions with customers that seem the
inverse to how they attempt to politely and sensitively provide customers
with feedback on clothing. While, as we note in chapter 4, workers devise
several approaches to avoid even the appearance of criticizing customers'
bodies, women workers in particular describe impolite and even insulting comments on their bodies. These critiques occur because the workers
are wearing the merchandise; customers appear to treat them as being as
unfeeling as the mannequins wearing outfits in the windows.

Asking workers their size to determine what size to buy for another
person is "not kosher . . . not polite," in the words of Angela at Old Navy.
Angela feels these questions are insensitive, whether the size they ask

about is large or small. Even Rachel, who generally feels comfortable discussing her body with shoppers, has limits. Rachel recounts a memorable experience with an older white woman who went out of her way to criticize Rachel's body:

> [This customer] goes, "Yeah. I'm looking for jeans for my granddaughter." I'm like, "Okay, do you know what size she is?" She goes, "She's not as fat as you." That was her response. I was like, "Okay, well unfortunately, that's not helpful to me. . . . That's not a number, that's not a size." So, she goes, "I just told you. She's not as fat as you. Find me a jean that's not as fat as you." At that point, I was pissed. It was Christmas Eve. I was not messing with this lady. So I proceeded, I looked at her and said, "I'm a size two, which is considered pretty skinny in the jean world. So um, is your granddaughter like a size zero, double zero?"

Fat shaming and other negative interactions reveal another dimension of the ugly underbelly of aesthetic labor: it makes workers vulnerable subjects to potentially harsh gazes from customers and managers.

Within the service panopticon, it can be hard for workers to rebuke an insulting customer or extricate themselves from the interaction. Tara describes dealing with these situations at American Eagle:

> It's not the best feeling. . . . "I'm shopping for my daughter. She's built like you, but she's a lot skinnier." And [sales associates] are just like, "Thank you." But it's not the best feeling in the world, but I mean, you're not going to say anything and be like, "Okay," and try and help them the best you can. You're not going to yell in their face, like "That's rude!" I mean, you want to, but you can't.

The emotional labor requirements of their jobs require frontline workers to display emotions that may be contrary to how they feel. These tense situations around body talk appear unique to aesthetic labor. We heard a variety of exchanges like these. Joyce describes Macy's customers referencing her size in discomforting ways:

> Whenever I'd work in the plus-size section. I'd get a lot of customers asking me like, "Why would they put a skinny girl like you back here?". . . I'd say, well, there's men that work in women's departments, too. You don't have to wear the merchandise to work in the department. Or . . . they'd come out of a dressing room saying, "I couldn't wear this, but you can because you're

skinny," and pointing out things to me like that, like almost kind of making it personal.

Although referring to Joyce as "skinny" might not seem quite the same insult as "she's not as fat as you," these comments similarly induce negative, even demoralizing sentiments. This evidence fits with sociologist Kjerstin Gruys's ethnography of a plus-size women's clothing store, where managers attempt to limit the non-plus-size workers' interactions with customers.[23]

None of the men in our sample shared these sorts of unsettling conversations with customers, but a large subset of women recounted such stories. This pattern suggests a gendered dynamic in which customers feel welcome to openly criticize women workers, putting them in more difficult positions when performing aesthetic labor. Importantly, these critiques are so common *because* the workers are wearing the store's clothing. Gendered expectations of women exacerbate these challenges; it is telling that the men we interviewed didn't recount these kinds of encounters. Frontline managers hire and expect aesthetic labor from both men and women, but gendered patterns in how customers respond to and engage with workers make these jobs more intrusive and challenging for women.

CONFLICTING FEELINGS

Women express more ambivalence about the aesthetic labor they do, including wearing the merchandise, while men appear to be more matter of fact, defining it as simply another part of the job. For example, Charlotte refers to Hollister as "corrupt and superficial. I gotta stick with 'superficial' because I can't think of another word that describes that, so." She recognizes that beauty appraisals drive the workplace's reward structure: "I benefit from the fact that they favor me, but that's just not fair." Charlotte knows that she reaped rewards from Hollister's appearance-based labor practices but disagrees with their practice. Gabe on the other hand says that he "felt fine" about embodying the American Eagle brand in the ways managers and body rules directed.

However, managers struggle with the superficiality of aesthetic labor, too. Gwen worked amid this tension at Hollister:

There would be kids who help us when we're very short on hours and no [other workers] can do it and always jump in and volunteer and then . . . they are passed over [for more shifts] because they're not one of the better-looking people. . . . They value appearance over . . . more important things, like work ethic and reliability. . . . I've never found looks to be a deciding factor for anything, so it just it would kill me to interview someone who I felt would be perfect for a job, and then know I would get in trouble for hiring them if I put them on the [sales] floor.

Most businesses might reward the most efficient or helpful workers. Gwen reports that Hollister's business model instead rewards the "better looking people." She reflects upon the contradiction between her own orientation toward valuing workers for their nonaesthetic output, stating that the job involved "ignoring a lot of my personal values in order to maintain the values of the company" and led to a "personal struggle, a lot of the time." She wasn't alone; many managers we spoke with acknowledged and voiced discomfort with the differential treatment of workers based on appearance.

Women workers, across race, frequently mention the stress of constant appearance-based judgment and surveillance. Also, because managers hire and judge staff in these ways, workers suggest that they compete to look better than their coworkers. Claire (white) talks about Hollister's physical environment as intensifying the company's beauty-centric ethos:

I was working in the front a lot and stuff, there are giant mirrors that are right where you have to stand so that the whole time. . . . You're just kind of looking at yourself in the mirror wondering what if I don't look like you're supposed to. . . . It's just like really pressuring, and I felt self-conscious all the time. . . . Everyone's basically wearing the same clothes, they're dressed as you, and it's like, "Wow, what if I don't look really good? Are they going to fire me because like I don't look like that?" It was just really stressful. I didn't like it.

For Claire, one of the biggest challenges in the workplace was being part of a lineup of women all wearing the same clothing and wondering whether she measured up. Under such circumstances, it makes sense that women working in jobs that emphasize attractiveness speak about how work challenges and sometimes increases their self-worth.

Patricia, who is white, also conveys ambivalence, mentioning that she would never refer to herself as a model at Hollister on social media, even as she reveals that working near the store entrance and modeling the merchandise can be a "little boost" to her self-esteem. The symbolic capital created during the aesthetic labor process can provide workers with an internal perk. When a customer identified her as what Hollister workers are "supposed to look like," she describes her reaction: "To be honest, I'm not the most confident about my body image. And I feel like there they were making it seem like I was. I never felt right, I mean when the guy said I'm the definition of a Hollister worker. I was just kind of like 'Uhhh, no.'" Patricia expresses a disconnect in how others see her and how she sees herself: "I did feel the need to make myself look good to fit in." Liz (Black) is similarly ambivalent:

> It sounds so superficial and bad. . . . They promote this thing, the CEO of Abercrombie was like, "Oh well, we don't want people wearing our brand, because they're not the cool kids," or whatever. And as bad as it sounds, it's like, "They hired me. Maybe I am a cool kid." And it's just kind of nice, just to feel wanted.

That pride tinges her experience makes Liz feel pangs of guilt:

> I feel like Hollister reinforces all the negative things about that, in terms of like how women should look, or how girls should look, or how guys should look, too. And, that we should all just be really tiny, or really buff. . . . If you don't look like that, then you're not cool. . . . It just definitely makes people who can't afford or fit into their clothes, that don't fit into their ideal, feel bad about themselves. And even though I work there, it's still . . . it's just sad.

Liz, again, is a darker-skinned Black, curvy woman who worked for a brand that promotes a narrow sense of how people should look, by class, by body size, and by race. Yet her contribution to broadening the beauty ideal at Hollister was extremely limited, as her tenure was in the stockroom.

Men return in their comments to the positive reinforcement they get through aesthetic labor. Modeling the Abercrombie & Fitch merchandise simply made Bryan, who is Latino, feel good:

> They [customers] like something that I'm wearing. That makes you feel good. Yeah, because they're not like, "Look at you—terrible. You're disgusting, like what are you wearing? Terrible outfit." Yeah it's not like that. But it's

a good feeling, but I don't really, I try to be humble as much as I can. You know? But yeah, really, I just feel good.

With his style and attractiveness celebrated, Bryan could appreciate the ongoing recognition of his symbolic capital. Glenn (white) qualifies his valuation of the cultural rewards reaped from modeling at Abercrombie Kids: "I know it sounds bad, but it meant that I had the status and I was one of the cool people." When one customer told him, "you definitely look like you work at Abercrombie," he recounted, "Again, I know it sounds bad but that made me feel good." That their connection to a status-bearing brand amplified Bryan and Glenn's sense of being valued highlights the dual composition of symbolic capital in the aesthetic labor process: they could gain positive appraisal by the company for perpetuating the brand as well as "cool" and "cute" status from peers and shoppers for being associated with the brand. Though Glenn indicates that he knows it's not all good, perhaps signaling some critical awareness, these men voice less discomfort and more pride in aesthetic labor and the accrual of symbolic capital than do their women colleagues.

David (white) was among the very few men to respond to sexualized aesthetic labor with concern, forthrightly criticizing Abercrombie's appearance-based focus. Framing it as an almost ethical opposition, he tells us he would never work as a shirtless greeter because "it's not in my morals to do something like that. I would hate to stand in front of the mall, ((ick sound)) people everywhere." However, David remained less troubled by other aesthetic labor requirements.

CONCLUSION

All of the teen and twenty-something niche clothing stores promote themselves as a lifestyle brand and aim to employ people who embody that brand.[24] Employers regulate worker looks in ways that advance their product, especially by demanding they model the merchandise.[25] Workers are aware of their employers' dress codes and recognize that they are being judged based on their ability to meet brand-oriented expectations.[26] Attire-related body rules are not merely confined to wearing store merchandise, which workers regard as a "uniform" they should purchase, but also extend to modeling the newest trends. As such, workers aren't simply hired to interact with customers or keep the shelves stocked. Their aesthetic labor may be a less obviously onerous set of tasks than, say, constantly refolding T-shirts or unpacking shipments, but the detailed body rules and accompanying disciplinary practices evince the centrality of cultivating workers' beauty and brand embodiment within the clothing retail labor process.[27]

Frontline managers play a crucial role in controlling workers' aesthetic labor. As visible in-store models, frontline managers are also subject to the aesthetic expectations of the panopticon. They use their own bodies to exemplify expected aesthetic labor, while surveilling, monitoring, adjusting, and disciplining their workers. The degree to which managers remind workers of body rules, arrange their clothing, ask them to change, or send them home for not following rules is amplified before visits from corporate management. This brand-focused surveillance is particularly clear in managers' insistence that workers buy and model the newest merchandise. Aesthetic labor performances thus reflect the uneven power relations visible in the service quadrangle and extend the panopticon.

Attempts to maintain a captive consumer market among the companies' entry-level retail workers can foster a frustrated workforce and undermine potentially fruitful frontline manager-worker alliances. Despite its negative impact on employees, this tactic appears to be relatively successful for retail companies, based on how much merchandise the workers we interviewed admit to buying. Resistance to the apparel-related body rules, particularly the frequent changeover in the newest fashion "season," seems to occur most frequently among "veteran" workers, for two reasons. First, over time, workers accrue enough merchandise (or clothing similar enough to comply with the dress code) to have the uniform over their months and even years of employment. Second, employees become disillusioned with the brand and the constant encouragement to buy.[28] Many express a keen awareness of the expense of purchasing items, even with their discount, and wish to maximize their take-home pay. Resistance is more challenging for the constant influx of newer workers, who may not yet own the items that management desires them to wear at work. At the point of hire, employees may be nearing their peak of consumer interest in the brand, leading them to literally buy into aesthetic labor demands.

Gender mediates corporate management regulations and inspections of worker uniforms. Men and women face different rules, giving men more leeway in certain ways and women more leeway in others. Either way, management requires most employees to conform to hegemonic binary gender aesthetics, reflecting gendered bodies and styles in conventional ways.[29] Customers add to the service panopticon as they openly surveil women workers' bodies. They may stare and ask questions and even shame workers for their body sizes; this is in direct contrast to the care that workers take in providing feedback to customers. Because workers explicitly model the store's clothing, their work puts them directly in the line of fire for inappropriate comments from customers.

Many of the women describe discomfort with how their managers and company body rules (hetero)sexualize them, although men are less visibly concerned about this process. We expected that men would feel more discomfort with being sexualized in these overt ways, though scholars understand that men challenge appearance-based norms less frequently than do women. Sociologist Tristan Bridges suggests that men may engage in "practiced indifference," salvaging their masculinity by appearing "relaxed, content, and at ease with an increasingly varied range of gender performances."[30] Women, however, have developed some rhetoric against appearance-based work, and in almost every case expressed at least ambivalence about performing such labor. Men convey concern less frequently, though customers and managers evaluated their bodies in the most exposed situations, like the shirtless modeling now out of fashion at Abercrombie brands.

This chapter and the last have shown how aesthetic labor plays out in clothing retail chains. Department stores may expect workers to dress professionally, but the aesthetic demands of teen-oriented retail clothing stores are substantially more challenging. Requiring regular apparel purchases turns workers into customers, further reducing already low pay. At the same time, aesthetic labor means that workplaces continue to reinforce inequalities by gender, race, and class, valorizing particular classed notions of whiteness, femininity, and masculinity while exoticizing or flat-out demeaning certain forms of racial "Otherness." Although these tensions aren't confined to clothing retail, this industry makes the intersection of race, gender, and class in twenty-first-century workplaces extremely, intentionally visible.

Conclusion

Capitalism's ceaseless search for markets and profits has included the rise of a "fast-fashion" model in which manufacturers constantly produce new items, retailers incessantly change their product lines, and workforces turn over at a dizzying pace. The organization of youth-oriented retail clothing work involves minimal training and demanding emotional and aesthetic labor, performed for low pay, with little advancement opportunity, unpredictable scheduling, and scant job security in hierarchies that reflect racial, gender, and class inequalities. Youth-oriented retail clothing workers thus provide a lens through which to understand the changing economy—and may help plot a course toward a more sustainable and just arrangement.

Technology has only further degraded conditions and diminished opportunities for those working low-wage retail jobs. Workers are under near-constant surveillance by customers, frontline managers, and corporate managers. Corporate managers make decisions based on real-time "metrics" that poorly measure reality; frontline managers lose autonomy despite their experience; and workers recognize instantly that their workplace does not value hard work, loyalty, or even a high level of customer service. Surveillance technologies expected to cut labor costs and boost profits demoralize workers and frontline managers while often alienating customers.

Youth-oriented clothing retailers may be a more "extreme" case than other retailers, as corporate managers focus less on maintaining long-term relationships with their customers and dedicate more resources to creating brands for new cohorts of tweens, teens, and twenty-somethings to embrace. Yet we believe this case also reflects the increasingly frayed relationships between employers and workers, as also exemplified by the gig economy.[1] Indeed, these jobs look remarkably like "gig work," despite being performed within regular, nonplatform workplaces. Employees' part-time and constantly changing schedules are but one prime example of the similarity.[2] Understanding the structuring of these jobs may help workers, labor organizers, and policy makers respond to a broad array of changes in the service industry.

Changing technology also plays a role in the changing fortune of retailers; as more and more shopping moves online and social media advertisements increasingly drive sales, brick-and-mortar stores and the vast shopping malls that house them are emptying out.[3] Indeed, the COVID-19 pandemic hastened a move toward online shopping and closure of brick-and-mortar locations, as consumer spending nosedived for a time and customers have increasingly adopted online shopping for all of their needs.[4] Approaches such as Kohl's Snapchat Virtual Closet allow customers to shop by entering online dressing rooms that allow them to mix and match different products and to include friends in the shopping experience.[5] Brick-and-mortar stores may be replaced with cyber vendors that guarantee customers free shipping and no-hassle returns, even "gamifying" shopping.[6] The future of retail clothing might be that online shopping becomes the norm and in-person shopping is relatively rare, a quaint holdover from the past.[7]

Yet some evidence suggests consumption during the pandemic doesn't signal a complete deterioration of in-person shopping habits. While the pandemic has accelerated the growth of online shopping, consumers still appreciate in-person shopping in ways that boost sales; when they go to brick-and-mortar stores to pick up products they have ordered online, customers are likely to buy additional items, making "frictionless" shopping across modalities an important goal for retailers going forward.[8] Clothing retailers, then, face a set of choices that must be made amid true uncertainty. The long-term health of the clothing industry may require building sales models that differentiate between computer-mediated online shopping and in-person shopping. For example, in-person shopping may be distinguished by a return to high-quality individualized customer service, as well as sales events that draw customers to stores.[9] Another strategy is augmented reality, in which mobile phones provide more information and discounts to shoppers as they walk through brick-and-mortar stores to "enhance real-world shopping experiences," though these strategies may feel intrusive to customers.[10]

Several factors might lead customers to prefer shopping in brick-and-mortar stores. Shopping in person allows customers to experience—touch and try on and talk about—the clothing. It can be more convenient, enabling instant gratification, and save costs for consumers. Many customers also enjoy the social interaction of shopping, especially compared to technology-generated targeted ads.[11] These are all factors that the COVID-19 pandemic may have underlined; in-person shopping and more local and sustainable products may experience something of a renaissance in the postpandemic era, as customers seek out companies that have local and transparent supply chains and more sustainable approaches to making and delivering goods.[12] Customer service is simply different in person than online. Certain sectors of appearance-based retail industries, like clothing and cosmetics, particularly benefit from human connection and immediate feedback. Shoppers ask sales staff for guidance on what's trendy (which, of course, algorithms can also do), but they also get a chance to ask what merchandise and styles would look best *on them.* They see how the clothes look on people with similar body types and get opinions from staffers "in the know."

Encounters between workers and customers have, of course, historically formed a core aspect of retail clothing labor. Staff members draw on their skills to query customers, help them find the kinds of items they want, and reassure them about their purchases; customers benefit from better, tailored, service, while clothing workers can find meaning in their jobs. These interactions also require workers to have product knowledge and perform emotional labor, and corporate-issued, routinized scripts tend to weaken these interactions, particularly when it comes to the satisfaction both shoppers and workers get out of them.

Providing high-quality customer service might strengthen the consumer experience, but it also needs to lead to better treatment for workers. We have shown how in practically every setting, these workplaces mistreat workers: paying them too little, scheduling them erratically, and promoting white, middle-class beauty and service ideals that reinforce inequalities. Workplaces need to dramatically transform, which will require changes to labor law and antidiscrimination law as well as meaningful enforcement of these regulations (with the important caveat that these companies need to adopt policies that do not merely gesture toward diversity but actually create inclusive environments).

THE ORGANIZATION OF SERVICE WORK

Service labor is fundamentally about human interaction. As we have argued, social interactions in the retail realm can lack respect and authenticity, *and* they can foster "real connections" between workers and customers as well as among the staff. Interpersonal relationships can be the best part of the job. Yet the power arrangements between workers, customers, store managers, and corporate management means these relationships can be undercut, such as when customers treat workers rudely, managers create austerity schedules that don't allow workers to support themselves or to develop relationships with customers, or coworkers treat colleagues with disdain.

We extend sociologist Robin Leidner's triangular conceptualization of service work that considers how alliances and conflicts may shift between workers, managers, and customers, considering how corporate management's use of big data and surveillance technologies renders these twenty-first-century workplaces service quadrangles.[13] The corporate level maintains access to, and frequently uses, digitally obtained data to monitor each store location as well as employees' sales, hours, and comings and goings. Remote technologies inform corporate management of the various activities occurring within their retail spaces almost in real time, enabling higher-level managers to direct frontline managers to quickly change staffing levels to match customer and revenue flows. These data, however, tend to be decontextualized and can lead to bad decisions. Corporate managers do not develop relationships with frontline workers, making it perhaps easier to treat them as walking mannequins and their store managers as little more than enforcers of corporate policy. Degrading work in these ways lowers customer service capacity, undermining long-term profitability in favor of unimpeachable metrics.

Store-level managers often work shoulder to shoulder with their staff. Although they occupy full-time positions and earn higher wages than their sales associates and stockroom personnel, frontline managers are still lower in the corporate hierarchy than their regional and corporate counterparts. Like workers, store managers can suffer from edicts such as wearing leather flip-flops throughout eight-hour days, but they often gain from other privileges, as well as higher pay and benefits. Store managers can play favorites in setting staff schedules in ways that perpetuate racial inequalities, choose how and when to enforce aesthetic rules that dehumanize workers, and even divide staff through job and shift assignments.

Workers, meanwhile, insist that they require a certain level of autonomy to provide tailored customer service. Leidner shows, for instance, that routinization lowers customer satisfaction and decreases employee morale.[14] Yet employers continue to further routinize service encounters; this allows for a more easily replaceable workforce. Despite knowing that scripted greetings, for instance, are less effective than customized greetings, workers have little recourse; under multitiered monitoring, from frontline managers watching them navigate sales interactions to corporate managers' secret shoppers and customer feedback forms, providing personalized customer service can threaten their job security. Routinization is aimed at lowering labor costs, but it more effectively lowers customer engagement (in ways that cannot be wholly replaced by "lifestyle branding") and undermines workers' ability to feel they are trusted or respected on the job. Instead, they are walking mannequins spouting a pull-cord set of rote scripts about two-for-one sales and seasonal looks.

Scholars of service work often foreground disrespectful treatment from customers; the denial of worker dignity is a core topic in critical labor studies and the sociology of work.[15] Our research reveals further complexities in service encounters: workers, especially women of color, certainly recall being treated disrespectfully by customers, yet they consistently stress that customer appreciation is one of the best parts of the job. When

customers are particularly vexing, the staff hand them off to store managers as a way to resist extreme forms of demeaning treatment.

Drawing on their own consumer identities allows workers to concep-
tualize their role in service encounters. This "golden rule" practice also
informs how they react to the class-based extensions of (dis)respect
between workers and customers and between workers and the different
management tiers. Workers in their late teens and early to mid-twenties
recognize that the lowly status given to retail and similar kinds of low-wage
employment comes with grave symbolic *and* economic consequences—
even shockingly bad treatment. For the most part, the longer they occupy
these jobs, the more disillusioned they become with the organization of
work: the low pay, the unpredictability of schedules, and the pretense that
"the customer is always right."

Individual workers' social locations shape their engagements with
shoppers, coworkers, store managers, and corporate managers, such that
there is no monolithic experience of performing retail work. White men
most often describe the challenge of acting differently from how they feel,
perhaps because women and people of color have more extensive practice
in performing emotional labor (often to appease white men). Across race,
women appear to face more frequent and more involved customer service
requests, with women of color reporting the most unpleasant interactions
with customers and the least connected relationships with coworkers and
managers (unless they work in particularly racially diverse stores). As a
result, white workers more often than workers of color tell us their workplaces are supportive, even if they occasionally have to deal with challenging customers. Racial discrimination is central to the narrative we tell;
workers of color, particularly Black women, in predominantly white stores
consistently find less support among coworkers and managers and face
more aggressive interactions with unruly customers. Black workers also
note the unfair and discriminatory treatment of Black customers, who are
often profiled as shoplifters.[16]

Leidner's triangular conceptualization of alliances and contestations
between workers, managers, and customers made enormous contributions to a literature on work that tends to emphasize the industrial
dynamics of workers versus managers.[17] We expand this framework to
a quadrangle, a tilted, four-pointed power dynamic, in which alliances

and conflicts not only occur between customers, workers, and managers, but differentiate between frontline and corporate managers. We expect the quadrangular arrangement we observe in clothing retail to apply to a range of twenty-first-century service industries. For example, in an ethnography, anthropologist Greta Foff Paules explores how power plays out between a nearly all women waitress staff and mostly men restaurant managers.[18] Not only does corporate management determine standard operations, such as scripts for customer engagement and where the waitress's hemlines should fall, it also inhibits the ability of frontline managers to influence routine tasks and workflow within the restaurant. This organization remakes frontline managers into instruments of upper-level management, enacting scripts and policies just like their workers.

Based on her research on retail scheduling practices, social work scholar Susan Lambert argues that frontline managers are primarily responsible for minimizing labor costs, based on hourly sales ratios.[19] This distribution of scheduling power, and expectations for perpetuating labor practices that treat sales workers as hourly costs, rather than as necessary actors to support daily store functions, put workers and both levels of management at odds. Our study reveals the trying experience of frontline managers attempting to thread this needle (and how their work changes during corporate managerial visits). Store managers acknowledge that stores *need* a stable and skilled workforce that competently performs and self-directs requisite tasks like keeping the sales floor and stockroom neat, assisting customers, and following corporate appearance policies. Many of the managers we interviewed voiced frustration about the practices decreed by corporate managers. Emphasizing the common interests, and thus the potential for alliances, between workers, frontline managers, and customers, appears to hold the most promise for improving labor practices in this sector.

TECHNOLOGY, DATA, AND THE CHANGING LANDSCAPE OF RETAIL

Technological advances allow corporate management to keep an uninterrupted gaze on each store branch, each worker, and each customer. The service panopticon, theorized throughout this book, is a surveillance apparatus stretching across nearly every aspect of the clothing retail industry.[20] From the remote surveillance of various sales metrics through cash registers to mounted video cameras recording the movements within each room and sprinkling the stores with "secret shoppers" to gauge employee friendliness and compliance with mandated scripts, corporate managers keep their collective eye on store managers, workers, and customers. As a panopticon, the surveillance system in clothing shops both reduces the power of frontline managers and requires workers, who know their work is constantly being tracked and observed, to follow company rules.

Technology is also implicated in the restructuring of retail as corporate managers track information about customers, through rewards programs, data mining, and algorithmic analysis of buying trends. As communication scholars warn, Americans need to worry not only about how police and national intelligence agencies use "big data," but also about how retailers track, tag, and tailor communication strategically in brick-and-mortar stores as well as online.[21] Through location-aware apps and programs, customers transmit information to retailers in expected and sometimes unexpected ways. For example, customers may be aware of how corporations use rewards programs to encourage greater sales but may be less conscious of how web browsers' "cookies" provide retailers with ongoing information about their browsing and buying habits across the internet and facilitate targeted advertising wherever they browse.[22] To keep up, brick-and-mortar stores have successfully increased the digital information they gather about every interaction with customers.[23] These technologies tend to mimic previous human relationships in which salespeople recognize repeat customers and tailor suggestions based on conversation and experience, through browser search histories and app interactions.

To be sure, we did not set out to study surveillance technologies. As we began interviewing retail clothing workers and frontline managers, we realized we were gathering fascinating details about how technology had changed their workplaces. This information was impossible for us to ignore. One of the most constant themes from store managers was that, rather than relying on high-stress visits or phone calls, corporate managers now access an enormous amount of real-time data about each store, as well as each of its managers and workers.[24] These metrics are often decontextualized, so workers and store managers underscore that corporate cannot capture the reality experienced in the stores.[25] Customer surveys, generally filled out by unhappy customers, have an exaggerated impact, further skewing corporate's dataset.[26] Rather than producing better decision-making, the technological spread seems, in practice, to produce worse jobs, higher turnover, and poorer customer service.

Surveillance operates in complex ways.[27] We argue that the clothing retail sector creates a matrix of multidirectional controls to cultivate the company's value both monetarily and symbolically: workers watch customers to prevent theft; workers self-regulate their bodies and engagement with shoppers to adhere to corporate rules; customers surveil workers' performance of the routinized dimensions of service (e.g., as "secret shoppers" or through shopper surveys); frontline managers style workers' bodies and pat them down after they clock out; and corporate managers monitor frontline managers, workers' bodies, sales, and footfalls in each store. The service panopticon creates such extreme supervision circumstances that some workers quit their jobs. Others stay, yet regularly resist certain desired practices (like scripted interactions and upselling shoppers). Surveillance within the retail workplace is thus both a tool of domination and a catalyst for resistance, extending to the appearance dimensions of this beauty-centered sector.[28]

BEAUTY AND THE BRAND: REBUILDING THE PILLARS OF CLOTHING RETAIL

Beliefs defining attractiveness shape both what management seeks in its workforce as well as how workers experience these jobs. Workers who are considered beautiful and befitting the brand receive cultural rewards, including compliments and symbolic capital for their aesthetic value. Sometimes their "look" brings about material rewards such as more (or regular) hours and even bonus "gigs" with higher pay (for example, the shirtless greeters chosen to entice customers into stores like Abercrombie & Fitch). Sales staff—at least those who gain accolades for their appearance—may enjoy such recognition and draw on aesthetic labor performances to reclaim ownership of their bodies and allure. As the sociological literature on "beauty work" shows, many people (across gender) spend a good deal of time, money, and energy maintaining and/or improving their appearance.[29] From tending to their tresses to paying for professional nail care and spending hundreds of hours exercising, many of the young, pretty people employed by brand-based clothing chains that target teens and twenty-somethings cherish the "looking good" dimension of the aesthetic labor they're paid to perform and seem willing to accept that it means lowering their ability to save the scant money they earn.

This valuation is complex. Even workers who "have the look" and like the appearance-based aspects of their jobs come to understand its ugly side. Caring primarily about beauty is riddled with problems for many of these well-groomed workers. They face unwanted advances from customers. Some feel as if the company has treated them as sexualized props, revealing the discrimination inherent in certain aesthetic labor practices. Also, the superficial nature of this pervasive value system leads many workers to offer critiques on what they view as immoral economic activities. Looking like a mannequin or model has its perks. But it also means that sales staff face the consequences of an institution dedicated to creating and perpetuating beauty hierarchies that demean whole groups of people—including their coworkers.

Race, gender, and class are central to beauty hierarchies. We have argued that predominantly white clothing retail companies in the United States create triracial beauty hierarchies. At American Eagle or Abercrombie, the commercial clothing industry promotes extremely slender women and muscular men; white, light-skinned bodies; and white-associated physical features, such as narrow noses, blue or green eyes, and straight hair, as the ideal. The second tier in this hierarchy includes those who are lighter-skinned and/or have phenotypical traits that are considered racially ambiguous, like curlier hair and browner complexions, as well as the exoticized and fetishized physical features commonly associated with Black, Latinx, Asian, Indigenous, and/or racial "Others," such as fuller lips; oval-shaped eyelids; and curvier, though still slender, female bodies.[30] The third tier, at the bottom of the hierarchy, encompasses a group of racially minoritized, darker-skinned people, considered Black.[31] Hair politics are especially prevalent in the racialized body rules baked into aesthetic labor demands and surveillance practices that create triracial beauty hierarchies in clothing retail. Potential changes may be afoot, with recent laws passed in several states barring employment discrimination based on hairstyle.

Despite modest gains through such legal changes, anti-Black racism continues to saturate fast fashion, much as it does all other social realms.[32] Black workers' beauty is promoted irregularly and remains more subject to exoticization. Black workers are more frequently made invisible (stuck in the stockroom or relegated to less-trafficked spaces within the stores) than other racial groups. And still, the composition of the clothing store workforce is increasingly nonwhite. In 2017, almost a quarter of clothing store workers were Latinx, almost 14% were Black, and nearly 6% were Asian.[33] Successful lawsuits have contested the racial, gender, and religious discrimination inherent in clothing store labor practices, and the industry seems to be shifting to hire more people of color and employ models across racial groups in marketing campaigns. Yet we remain skeptical that stores are deconstructing their white ideals; we observed clear patterns in which companies stratify workers into more visible and less visible jobs and impose more and less stringent control over workers' bodies based on racial and gendered beauty appraisals.

If one of the greatest symbolic and emotional rewards in clothing retail comes from being recognized as attractive and worthy of "modeling" the merchandise, then this major cultural industry needs to put all kinds of people—with different skin colors, body sizes and shapes, hairstyles, and facial features—in prominent positions. The commercial clothing sector could recreate beauty ideals to uplift the notion that anyone is attractive. We contend that *stores can sell clothes without demeaning groups of people and without reproducing racist, sexist, heterosexist ableist, and sizeist beauty hierarchies.* Indeed, we suspect that white middle-class appearance standards that reinforce the gender binary limit retailers' market shares, as they devalue and distance those with "different" looks.

Marketing primarily to white people reflects an industry that has emphasized white consumers, largely by idealizing whiteness and excluding people of color from market research.[34] Meanwhile, Black and Brown customers drive trillions in spending, in addition to trendsetting for whites' spending.[35] Some companies, such as Fenty and Foot Locker, profitably run apparel-related businesses in the United States using more racially

Figure 17. Sales clerk and customer. SOURCE: iStock.com/peopleimages.

diverse marketing approaches. Rihanna's Fenty brands of cosmetics and lingerie, for example, feature a substantially more diverse set of models, including not only by race but also skin tone and body size; the cosmetics company generated $100 million in revenue in its first forty days, substantially more than Drew Barrymore's cosmetics line, which generates about $50 million in revenue per year.[36] Foot Locker Europe has embraced a "social change" narrative, focused on highlighting queer and racial minority communities, clearly focused on drawing "values"-oriented young customers.[37] Research suggests that customers look to buy from companies that align with their values, including embracing diversity, while also benefiting from addressing underserved populations.[38] Additionally, while corporate chains are more likely to be white-owned and emphasize whiteness as beauty, local, independent stores may celebrate a wider array of beauty norms.

These organizations' labor and marketing practices must do less harm and more good. One key focus should be on widening portrayals of beauty so that workers of all body shapes, skin colors, and hair textures can relish the symbolic status of "looking good" for a brand without being fetishized, ogled, or demeaned. Expanding the kinds of models, images, mannequins, and retail workers used to embody these brands might have positive impacts on sales, worker retention, and brand loyalty as more varied "looks" gain equal attention and positive appraisal (even as they continue to promote consumption in troublesome ways).[39]

As critiques of aesthetic labor emerge, we must consider the possible linkages between these labor practices, workers' experiences, and activism. Disrupting the normalcy of exploiting employees as brand objects can be very effective in labor reforms. Consumer- and media-based actions may be other vital ways to expose the industry's exploitative practices and turn corporate brands against themselves.[40] For example, Abercrombie & Fitch's appearance policies have long elicited lawsuits, but it was the broad public outcry following the publication of the company president's comments about wanting only "cool kids" to shop at Abercrombie that created a large backlash and consumer boycotts. Eventually, the firm's leader resigned, and the company announced a new set of workplace policies less intensively focused on appearance.

RESISTING AND REVITALIZING RETAIL LABOR

Public outcries have been effective in changing corporate policies throughout the history of retail labor. Resistance, including social media backlash, deployed against well-known brands has achieved some gains for service workers. But simply "raising awareness" is not enough. The international coffee chain Starbucks offers one such example. During the summer of 2014, various mainstream media outlets like the *New York Times* published stories about the company's use of just-in-time scheduling and how it demands an infeasible amount of flexibility from a mostly part-time workforce.[41] Did this upend service labor practices? Not at all. Despite their promises and soundbites, Starbucks still schedules workers less than a week in advance; some of its staff continue to "clopen," working the closing shift one night and opening shift the next morning, with only a few hours' rest in between.[42] Among the stores we studied for this book, Abercrombie & Fitch brands continue to use on-call systems that leverage corporate-level data to match staffing levels with revenue flow on any given day: "just-in-time" scheduling for the "just-in-time" supply chains that define the fast-fashion industry.

The public has also come to embrace efforts to increase minimum wages and fight wage stagnation against inflation. In recent years, the nationwide "Fight for $15" movement has gained traction in legislatures and across a range of industries. From fast-food jobs that exist as a franchise operation, like McDonald's, to big-box retailers like Walmart, this resistance effort combines tactics to push for increasing minimum pay and rights (through unionization). Fight for $15 has won multiple victories as individual cities have pledged $15 minimums. Target raised all minimum wages in its company to $15 on July 5, 2020.[43] For the handful of Target workers we interviewed for this study, who previously received less than $10 per hour, a $15 minimum wage is a meaningful change. It is also a strategic corporate move that may stave off unionization efforts.

In his study of nonunionized Target and partially unionized Macy's, sociologist Peter Ikeler asserts that Target's paternalistic corporate practices have helped maintain the idea that there is no need to formally organize for labor rights.[44] Ikeler's informants at Target, like our interviewees, witnessed unlawful corporate anti-union campaigns.[45] For instance, like workers at Walmart and other non- or semi-unionized US retail chains, Target makes employees watch public relations videos created by corporate management to argue that forming a union would harm employees. In 2011 and 2014, the now-defunct independent media outlet Gawker posted Target's anti-union videos, which were picked up by various media that portrayed them as discernible, systematic efforts to upend union drives.[46]

The labor movement has long relied on tried-and-true strategies including striking, but the disposability of low-skilled service workers poses challenges to this approach. As employment opportunities in destitute rural areas and increasingly gentrified urban centers remain relatively scarce, management can quickly hire new workers to occupy striking workers' positions. That's one reason retail and other service industries, including hotels and restaurants, try to limit their reliance on worker creativity and autonomy. Constant attrition is anticipated (if not manufactured), and routinization lowers the costs of constant turnover.

The decline of union strength is interconnected with the steep decline in employment tenure in large companies, such as the corporate retail clothing stores we study.[47] Employers are willing to replace even skilled workforces with recently hired personnel. Fight for $15 has successfully leveraged one-day strikes to disrupt regular company practices and, equally if not more importantly, to attract widespread attention.[48] Long-term striking, however, is a less viable option for twenty-first-century workers.

For decades, big business has dealt severe blows to organized labor. In his hopeful discussion of what the labor movement could accomplish in the coming years, labor scholar and sociologist Dan Clawson insisted on the importance of establishing meaningful bonds across various groups of working people.[49] Gains occur through bursts stemming from successful organizing campaigns that create (and maintain) thoughtful social ties built on mutual respect. These campaigns should seek to uplift all those who suffer from our current political-economic system, while also recognizing the specific intersections of class with race, gender, sexuality, and other dimensions of difference, such as ability. Important wins, including commitments to a "living wage," rest on the ability of activists to assert common interests between racial, gender, and working-class groups that have too often been divided by intentional, effective business strategy.

Solidarity between people who consume and work in service sectors that use harmful labor practices, like stagnant low wages and just-in-time scheduling, will be necessary to disrupt low-wage industries. We readily acknowledge that the voluntary corporate adoption of or a federally mandated minimum wage increase to $15 is not sufficient; it wouldn't help the minimum wage to catch up with the inflation of the past few decades, nor would it constitute a decent "living wage" for workers and their families. Yet this campaign has been a boon to the labor movement. It has raised working-class consciousness across the country and shifted consumer perceptions of the wrongful treatment of low-wage workers.[50] Fight for $15 is an important rallying cry that shows, in a concrete way, that organizing workers in low-wage, high-turnover jobs—even beyond service sectors— holds great promise for creating a more humane labor environment in the United States.[51]

Workers and bosses are not the only actors who matter. As we learned from major victories of the farmworkers' movement in the 1960s and

1970s, customers who buy and consume the products of disputed labor conditions can be crucial in forcing management to change its more insidious practices. During the summer of 2020, many retailers responded to the Movement for Black Lives, commonly referred to as Black Lives Matter, which was reinvigorated following the filmed police killing of George Floyd. Other retailers, such as those selling food products, retired explicitly racist brands, such as "Aunt Jemima" and "Uncle Ben's," in response to the movement.[52] Many of the stores that we studied responded to the movement through statements, organizing voter registration drives, and instituting some policy changes.

Extensive statements adorned the websites of many of the stores at which our respondents worked, as did their social media platforms, featuring posts on "Blackout Tuesday" (June 2, 2020). Abercrombie, which, as we've noted, faced a class action discrimination lawsuit that it settled in 2005, posted:

> We're *still* listening. We're *still* learning. We're *still* actioning. Our commitment to equality will not change—we're here for meaningful impact in a longstanding way. With that, we'd like to introduce The Abercrombie Equity Project, our new initiative dedicated to social and racial justice.[53]

Most stores have stated their goals as supporting the movement, but are they substantive? Given the racist practices of these companies and the wider problem of anti-Black racism being a standard facet of social life in the United States, many read their statements as empty attempts intended to appeal to young customers who support Black Lives Matter. Yet cultural commentators emphasize that "performative activism" is less persuasive to young consumers, who look for deeper responses, including more consistently diverse models, more inclusive product lines, and better treatment of workers and customers.[54]

Perhaps the most thorough response came from Urban Outfitters, which owns the store Anthropologie, after workers publicly alleged the racist profiling of Black customers, with workers using the code words "Nick," "Nicky," and "Nicole" to identify (usually Black) customers as potential shoplifters, as well as fewer career opportunities for Black workers.[55] The similarity between these codes and the n-word should not be lost on readers, demonstrating how pervasive anti-Black racism—which includes retail practices of racialized surveillance of workers and customers, as well as racialized violence perpetrated by police and white terrorists against Black people—is in the United States. Although the company initially denied racial profiling, the social media posts and comments of many current and former workers led it to take a series of actions. For example, Urban Outfitters hired a third party to review practices to ensure there was no racial profiling, to conduct diversity and inclusion training to provide anti-racist team education, expand recruiting at historically Black colleges and universities, hire a more racially diverse workforce, better represent the Black community in its models, amplify Black voices regarding racism and police brutality, and support Black communities and nonprofits through programming, advocacy, and donations.[56] It is unclear whether attempts to appeal to Movement for Black Lives supporters will change Urban Outfitters stores any more than Abercrombie's lawsuit changed the experience of Black and Brown workers (given that we conducted our interviews long after the lawsuit was settled).

We believe boycotts may become an essential tactic for those hoping to improve labor practices in the service sector. We do not, however, believe that consumer boycotts and short-term strikes are sufficient to compel corporations to change dramatically. That will require action from a range of stakeholders and the coalescence of an array of various activist strategies. Only then can reformers force legislatures to implement and *enforce* legal, institutionally mandated regulations that empower and protect workers and directly address the racial discrimination that appears to be deeply embedded in these spaces.[57]

Making these jobs decent is another critical step in improving the conditions of retail labor. Unpredictable schedules, low and stagnant wages, and stress caused by understaffing are major challenges for the workers we interviewed. Companies seem willing to accept the low-investment, high-turnover model that requires total flexibility from employees and zero guarantees from employers.[58] But most workers we interviewed fret over their schedules; they need significantly more hours to ensure higher incomes and significantly more regular hours to establish livable careers. A national survey of retail employees, including clothing store workers, finds that open availability is a key factor in determining not only whether an applicant is hired but also whether they will get a chance to advance within the company.[59] Employers' demands for workers to be ever available and accept their constantly changing schedules "overshadow the importance of upskilling to the retail workforce, and disproportionately burden working people with caregiving responsibilities."[60] Absent institutional changes, such as federal laws to eliminate on-call shifts and require two-week-minimum advance scheduling, real, sustained change is unlikely.

The federal Fair Labor Standards Act, for instance, fails to address these problems. New legal protections and expanded collective bargaining agreements (in tandem, naturally, with the establishment of unions through which workers can bargain collectively), including state laws that make similar guarantees, should be the immediate target for reformers.[61] Such protections have powerful effects on the lives of low-wage laborers.

One of the issues retail workers face stems from management's use of metrics and a massive amount of information (or "big data") in determining employee schedules. Research suggests that the best approach is to combine information about the distribution of labor hours compared to sales with frontline managers' insights to ensure that workers receive reasonable, consistent schedules.[62] Sophisticated software, in other words, should inform but not dictate schedules. Still, frontline managers should not have unchecked levels of authority in determining schedules, given the destructive effects of favoritism, which may deepen racial disparities. Worker solidarity and racial progress would instead benefit from fair and consistent scheduling for all workers on the payroll. As patterns of inclusion and exclusion often mirror the racism and sexism of the broader society, we think it is necessary to interrupt common practices that make racial, gender, and class discrimination regular occurrences.

Full-time employment is also pertinent to improving retail jobs. Downsizing the part-time staff by promoting part-timers, who already possess many of the requisite skills and a sense of the organization's workflow, to full-time status would solve the devastating problem of variable incomes. The evidence of racial and gender discrimination in service work leads us to suggest that companies combine fixed criteria, such as employment tenure, to identify which part-time workers would be offered full-time status; building equity via this change will mean offering all employees more opportunities for cross-training and other skill acquisition.[63]

In the pool of workers we interviewed, one person exemplifies how improving the basic working conditions of hours, pay, and opportunity for advancement can make retail jobs decent. Julian has worked at H&M for several years. The part-time staff there receive a benefits package, including health care, vacation and sick time, and a paid birthday off. Entry-level employees, including seasonal hires, receive a minimum wage of $9.90—more than $1.50 over the mandated minimum wage at the time we met Julian. Originally hired as a part-timer—and holding down two jobs to make ends meet—Julian was promoted by his managers to full-time after a year. He is now a department supervisor, with a pay rate of $17.50 per hour and a relatively generous benefits package. While Julian acknowledges a commonly expressed desire "to have a job you enjoy, like everybody wants that," he also points out that "at the end of the day, you're doing it for money." The bottom line for Julian, like many other retail workers, is the paycheck, and his company's policies have facilitated raises and advancement. He's likely to stay with H&M.

The stress of retail jobs is unrelenting. The economic conditions of low pay, variable hours, and few opportunities to advance are enormous stressors, but so, too, are the physical stresses of fatigue from standing for hours on end, wearing mandated outfits including shoes ill-suited to standing on concrete floors, and working extended shifts without being allowed to sit down. Irritable customers, managers, and coworkers are stressful, as are the demands of performing aesthetic labor and being judged and appraised based on appearance. Clothing retail customer service can entail more highly personalized interactions than other retail sectors due to its focus on beautifying consumer bodies, and workers, especially women, need clear protocols for their more intimate customer encounters and the power to exit interactions as they deteriorate. For instance, establishing company-wide protocols in which workers are allowed to tell shoppers they have become rude—to explicitly disrupt the notion that "the customer is always right—and then point them toward the manager, would reduce fear among workers that negative interactions might threaten their employment. These changes would also signal that corporate intends to uphold, rather than undermine, worker dignity.

From the perspective of critical labor scholars, the problem of "service" in capitalist societies has always been and continues to be the way it is

Figure 18. Workers dressing a mannequin. SOURCE: iStock.com/solstock.

conceived as *sub*servience, complete with low wages and poor working conditions.[64] The demeaning nature of aiming to please can be disrupted by giving workers greater power and control, including investment in workers and recognition of the valuable skills that workers bring to their labor. In clothing retail, where the corporation and its multilevel management structure, mediate, and constantly monitor relations between sales associates and customers, managers' trust and support for workers can create greater customer satisfaction; assumptions that workers can be replaced and demeaned clearly do not. In the contemporary consumer society, customers seem to reign supreme; in reality, corporate owners and shareholders almost always do. Developing more personal and human relationships between workers and customers could help challenge a culture of disrespect, while also creating greater customer loyalty to stores. We trust workers, labor activists, and those in the field to best determine the specific changes that will improve these workplaces for those who toil within them.

In this book, we aimed to honor the experiences our interview participants shared as we explored the contours of a particular American labor sector. Workers recognize that employers and shoppers see them as "walking mannequins," hired for their pleasing looks and encouraged to model the merchandise. But retail workers are not simply models or living versions of the plastic display mannequins. They are humans who require reasonable schedules, wages, working conditions, and dignity. They resist upselling customers, pushing shoppers to apply for store credit cards, and becoming a captive market. They remark on the myriad ways clothing corporations attempt to maximize their profits while derailing quality service. Although retail clothing work often reinforces inequalities by race, gender, and class, stores that provide more varied styles and employ more diverse workers may appeal to larger markets. Change is possible, as anyone tasked with an overnight floor set shift can attest. It'll be hard but worthwhile work.

Appendix

RESEARCH DESIGN AND METHODS

We interviewed fifty-five retail clothing workers in the niche market aimed at high school and college-age youth, such as Abercrombie & Fitch and Urban Outfitters. However, we also sampled workers in stores that appeal to a wider customer base, such as Macy's, Old Navy, and Target. Most stores market themselves as "lifestyle retail brands."[1] Previous scholarship suggests that workers positively identify with the brand that employs them, which may introduce compensating differentials despite the low-wage nature of the work.[2] Our research design aimed to focus on clothing retail workers because this group allows us to specifically address questions of identity, consumption, and interactive service work. However, we did not limit our sample to people currently employed in this industry, in order to collect data that reflect a wider variety of experiences.

INTERVIEWS

Compared to the overall population of clothing retail workers, our sample is younger and more educated. The interview sample allows us to speak to the experiences of these particular workers, which may lead to more critiques of the work because many of them identify as temporary retail workers who hope to leave these jobs for nonretail careers after graduation. The median age of clothing retail workers is 28.9 in the overall population and 20 in our sample. The median pay for all US-based retail workers was $10.29/hour in 2012, although clothing

Table 1   Interviewees by Self-Identified Race and Gender

	Asian American	Black	Latinx	Multiracial	White	Total
Women	5	10	2	6	18	41
Men	1	1	1	1	10	14
Total	6 (10.9%)	11 (20.0%)	3 (5.4%)	7 (12.7%)	28 (50.9%)	55

retail workers generally earn less than other retail workers.[3] In our sample, the median pay was $8.25/hour. Table 1 describes the gender and race of the sample. Table 2 summarizes each worker's information, including age, education, and employment, by pseudonym. Skin color descriptors are based on the interviewer's perception. The research team that conducted the interviews included one Asian American woman and two white women.

Although we posted flyers in a range of settings to attract a class-diverse sample, our workers had high levels of education. According to Cardiff, LaFontaine, and Shaw, in 2010, 11% of retail workers had less than a high school education, 38% had a high school education, 31% had some college, 15% had a bachelor's degree, and 8% had an advanced degree.[4] In our sample, 91% had some college, 7% had a bachelor's degree, and 2% had a master's degree. Forty-four of the workers were currently enrolled at a predominantly white public four-year university, which reflects a middle- and lower-middle-class population, who often incur student debt to attend college. Three workers were currently attending a two-year public community college with a more working-class population, who also incur debt but are more racially diverse. Two were students at private four-year colleges that attract more upper-middle-class and upper-class students. The remaining six participants include one worker with a master's degree, four with bachelor's degrees, and one with an associate's degree. Three of those with college degrees were working as managers or assistant managers, and the fourth was lead sales. The worker with a master's degree worked part-time retail in addition to a professional full-time job.

We conducted forty-nine interviews in person and interviewed six people online using video calls. Most participants worked in the Northeast: primarily Massachusetts, but also New Jersey, Connecticut, and New York. We also interviewed participants who worked in California, Georgia, Michigan, and North Carolina.

INTERVIEW DATA ANALYSIS AND PRESENTATION

Interview data analysis occurred in three iterations. We initially coded the dataset using inductively derived codes developed in relation to our theoretical frame-

Table 2 Interview Participant Demographic and Employment Information

Participant	Race	Gender	Sexual Orientation	Age (Years)	Educational Attainment	Current or Former Worker	Store	Position	Length of Employment
Angela	White	Woman	Straight	30	Master's	Current	Old Navy	Sales associate	1 year
Antonia	Black	Woman	Straight	20	Some college	Former	Express	Sales associate	3 months
Ashley	Black	Woman	Straight	20	Some college	Former	Target	Stocker	4 months
Brendan	Asian	Man	Straight	22	Some college	Former	Pac Sun; G. H. Bass & Co.	Brand representative, sales associate	2 years; 1 year
Bryan	Latino	Man	Straight	19	Some community college	Current	A&F	Model	7 months
Carl	White	Man	Gay	23	College	Current; former	J. Crew; A&F	Sales associate, merchandise assistant; model	1 year
Carmen	Latina	Woman	Straight	20	Some college	Former	Sears; Free People; Kmart; Christopher & Banks	Sales associate; personal shopper	1 year; 3 months; a couple months; 4 months

(continued)

Table 2 (continued)

Participant	Race	Gender	Sexual Orientation	Age (Years)	Educational Attainment	Current or Former Worker	Store	Position	Length of Employment
Carolyn	White	Woman	Straight	21	Some college	Current	Hollister	Model	2 years, some seasonal
Cecilia	Asian	Woman	Straight	19	Some college	Current; former	J.C. Penney; Stride Rite; Sears	Service specialist; sales associate	6 months, some seasonal; 2 years; 1 year
Charlotte	White	Woman	Straight	21	Some college	Former	Hollister	Model	3.5 years
Cheryl	Multiracial	Woman	Straight	21	Some college	Current	Victoria's Secret	Sales associate	8 months
Claire	White	Woman	Straight	19	Some college	Former	Hollister	Model	4 months
Corinne	Asian	Woman	Straight	20	Some college	Current; former	J.C. Penney; A&F; Forever 21	Sales associate; impacter; sales associate	3 years, some seasonal; 6 months; 2 years
Danielle	Multiracial	Woman	Straight	18	Some college	Former	Old Navy	Sales associate	5 months
Denise	Black	Woman	Straight	20	Some college	Former	A&F	Model	2 summers
David	White	Man	Straight	20	Some college	Current	A&F	Model	Almost 1 year
Elise	White	Woman	Bi	18	Some college	Former	Target	Cashier	3 months

Name	Race/Ethnicity	Gender	Sexuality	Age	Education	Current/Former	Store	Role	Duration
Frances	Multiracial	Woman	Bi	18	Some community college	Current; former	A&F; Deb	Impacter; sales associate	4 months; unknown
Frank	White	Man	Straight	22	Some college	Former	TJ Maxx	Clerk	4 years (2 years seasonal)
Gabe	White	Man	Straight	23	Some master's	Former	American Eagle	Lead sales, sales associate	3 years
Glenn	White	Man	Straight	18	Some college	Former	Abercrombie Kids	Model	3 months
Grace	White	Woman	Straight-ish	20	Some college	Current	TJ Maxx	Sales associate	1.5 years
Gwen	White	Woman	Straight	22	College	Former	Hollister	Manager, team leader, sales associate	7 months full-time; 4 years, some seasonal
Hannah	White	Woman	Straight	20	Some college	Former	Gilly Hicks; Aeropostale	Model, sales associate	3 months; 9 months
Heather	White	Woman	Straight	21	Some college	Former	Forever 21	Sales associate	2 years, some seasonal
James	White	Man	Straight	20	Some college	Former	Nordstrom	Sales assistant	2 years, some seasonal
Jason	Multiracial	Man	Straight	21	Some college	Former	A&F	Model	3 years
Jill	White	Woman	Straight	19	Some college	Former	Forever 21	Sales associate	3 months seasonal
Joyce	White	Woman	Straight	21	Some college	Current; former	Macy's; Pac Sun	Sales associate	1.5 years; 3 months seasonal

(continued)

Table 2 (continued)

Participant	Race	Gender	Sexual Orientation	Age (Years)	Educational Attainment	Current or Former Worker	Store	Position	Length of Employment
Julian	White	Man	Generally straight but . . .	29	Associate's	Current	H&M	Department supervisor, sales associate	3 years (2 years as benefited supervisor)
Kathleen	Black	Woman	Straight	20	Some college	Former	Boutique; Century 21	Sales associate, head sales associate; sales associate	About 1 year; > 1 month
Lance	White	Man	Straight	20	Some college	Former	Hollister; Abercrombie Kids	Impacter	4 months; 5 months
Lauren	Asian	Woman	Bi	19	Some college	Current; former	Urban Outfitters; Gilly Hicks	Sales associate; model	3 months; seasonal
Leah	Black	Woman	Straight	18	Some college	Former	Hollister	Impacter	4 months, Black Friday
Lillian	Asian	Woman	Straight	21	Some college	Former	American Eagle; A&F	Sales associate; model	3 months; 4 months
Liz	Black	Woman	Straight	18	Some college	Current	Hollister	Impacter	4 months
Lori	Black	Woman	Straight	20	Some college	Current; former	Wet Seal; Justice	Brand representative; sales associate	5 years; 4 years
Marty	White	Man	Gay	19	Some college	Current	Target	Cashier	3.5 years
Mary	Multiracial	Woman	Straight	20	Some college	Current	A&F	Impacter	9 months

Name	Race	Gender	Sexuality	Age	Education	Status	Store	Position	Duration
Melissa	White	Woman	Straight	20	Some college	Current	J.C. Penney	Sales associate	6 months
Nicole	White	Woman	Straight	19	Some college	Former	TJ Maxx; Nordstrom Rack	Sales associate	1 year, some seasonal; 6 months, some seasonal
Nora	White	Woman	Straight	19	Some college	Former	Dick's; American Eagle	Cashier; sales associate	Seasonal; 4 months
Patricia	White	Woman	Straight	19	Some college	Former	Hollister	Model	3 months
Pauline	Black	Woman	Straight	22	Some college	Former	Hollister	Model, impacter	4.5 years
Rachel	Multiracial	Woman	Straight	20	Some college	Current	American Eagle	Sales associate	1.5 years
Risa	Asian	Woman	Straight	21	Some college	Former	Zara	Sales associate	1 year
Sabrina	White	Woman	Straight	20	Some college	Former	Urban Outfitters	Sales associate	2 months seasonal
Sherrie	Latina	Woman	Straight	19	Some college	Former	Pac Sun	Brand representative	3 years
Stacey	White	Woman	Straight	20	Some college	Current	Old Navy	Sales associate	5 months
Stella	Multiracial	Woman	Straight	22	Some college	Current; former	Macy's; Forever 21	Sales associate	1.25 years; 4 months
Steve	White	Man	Straight	28	Some college	Current	Kohl's	Sales associate, stockroom	8 years
Tara	White	Woman	Straight	21	Some college	Current	American Eagle	Shift lead, sales associate	Over a year
Tia	Black	Woman	Straight	20	Some college	Former	Forever 21	Sales associate	2 months
Trent	Black	Man	Gay	22	College	Current	Express	Sales lead manager	5 months
Veronica	Black	Woman	Straight	20	Some college	Current	Gap	Cashier	4 years

works of retail labor, service work, aesthetic labor, race, gender, and sexuality. Subsequent data analysis involved revising and specifying previous codes, identifying new patterns or contradictions that made us consider the findings in different ways.

In the final round of coding, we used NVivo, software for qualitative analysis. We coded the data with twenty-four main codes, such as "surveillance," "scheduling," "emotions," "managers," "customers," and "coworkers." Each of these major codes had many subcodes, for a total of 122 subcodes. So, for example, under the major code "appearance of workers," we had subcodes including "body modification," "body size," "buying clothes," "getting ready for work," "language," "looks," "makeup," "race," and "sexualization." Similarly, under the major code "work conditions," we had subcodes related to "benefits," "career opportunities," "commission," "discounts," "fair," "raises," "tired/body strain," "turnover," and "wages." The first author coded all fifty-five interviews with NVivo, but both authors discussed the coding and the major themes as they emerged.

Coding in NVivo increased the precision of our analysis, allowing us to pinpoint the themes that came up most frequently, as well as the themes that were expressed with the most vehemence. So, for example, workers mentioned interacting with customers 366 times, while they mentioned selling credit cards as a problematic value 75 times. As we worked through the book manuscript, we used the coding to identify key issues that deserved reflection. NVivo also allowed us to run cross-tabulations across themes and subgroups of workers. For example, we examined differences between former and current retail workers, Black workers and non-Black workers, and Abercrombie employees and non-Abercrombie employees. This allowed us to understand how members of different groups understood their work, such as how white men found emotional labor particularly difficult, while Black women were more likely to experience hostility from customers.

Our presentation of these data draws heavily on interview quotes, because workers' voices and their subjective experiences remain underrepresented in the retail scholarship. All names are pseudonyms. We include participants' racial identities when their discussion touches on the racial dimensions of the workplace.

SHOPPER PARTICIPANT OBSERVATIONS

While the fifty-five interviews constitute our main source of data, we also draw on in-store shopper participant observations and two employee manuals to triangulate the labor process and employee experiences.[5] The research team observed Abercrombie & Fitch (three locations, ten visits), American Eagle (two locations, six visits), Hollister (one location, six visits), Hot Topic (one location, three visits),

Pac Sun (two locations, five visits), and Urban Outfitters (one location, five visits) stores.[6] Fieldwork as a retail worker would have permitted prolonged relationships with employees, as well as immersion into the workplace and labor process.[7] Unfortunately, this more extensive participant observation role was not feasible for us.

Notes

INTRODUCTION

1. Besen-Cassino, 2014, 2018; Gatta, 2011; Williams & Connell, 2010.
2. Warhurst, Nickson, Witz, & Cullen, 2000, p. 1 ("embodied capacities"); Williams & Connell, 2010, p. 350 ("a worker's deportment").
3. Carré & Tilly, 2017; Frenkel, 2003; Kalleberg, 2011; Kalleberg, Reskin, & Hudson, 2000.
4. Carré & Tilly, 2008, p. 4; Carré & Tilly, 2017; Grugulis & Bozkurt, 2011; Lambert & Henly, 2012; Williams & Connell, 2010 (US); Du Gay, 1993; Fiscal Policy Institute, 2008; International Labour Organization, 2006; Luce & Fujita, 2012; Presser, 2003 (world economy).
5. Fiscal Policy Institute, 2008; United States Bureau of Labor Statistics, 2018a.
6. Carré & Tilly 2008, 2017; Fiscal Policy Institute, 2008; Henly, Shaefer, & Waxman, 2006; Luce & Fujita, 2012.
7. Farris, Bendle, Pfeifer, & Reibstein, 2010; Head, 2005, 2014; Poster, Crain, & Cherry, 2016, Redd & Vickerie 2017; Van Oort, 2019.
8. Farris et al., 2010; Head, 2005, 2014.
9. Gupta & Zeithaml, 2006.
10. Allen & Du Gay, 1994; Korczynski, 2007, 2013; Leidner, 1993, 1999; Lopez, 2010; Macdonald & Sirianni, 1996; Porter, 1987; Sloan, 2012; Troyer, Mueller, & Osinsky, 2000.

11. Foucault, 1977.

12. Choo & Ferree, 2010; Collins, 2000; Crenshaw, 1989; Ken, 2010; McCall, 2005 (intersectional); Acker, 2006; Amott & Matthaei, 1996; Barber 2016a; Bell & Nkomo, 2001; Branch, 2011; Browne, 1999; Browne & Misra, 2003; Glenn, 1992, 2002; Higginbotham & Weber, 1999; Sokoloff, 1992; Williams, 2006; Wingfield, 2009, 2010, 2012, 2013, 2019; Wingfield & Chavez, 2020; Wingfield & Skeete, 2016 (workplaces); Gruys, 2012; Hanser, 2005, 2008; Kang, 2010; Pettinger, 2005; Williams, 2006; Williams & Connell, 2010 (service jobs).

13. Ken, 2010.

14. Acker, 2006, p. 450; Wooten & Branch, 2012, pp. 294–295.

15. Wingfield & Skeete, 2016.

16. Rosette & Dumas, 2007.

17. Wingfield & Skeete, 2016, p. 63.

18. Braverman, 1974/1998; Marx, 1867/1990.

19. Craig, 2002; Hunter, 2005.

20. Bourdieu, 1984.

21. Lambert & Henly, 2012; Levy & Barocas, 2018.

22. Monahan, 2010; Otis & Zhao, 2016; Tannock, 2001.

23. Braverman (1974/1998, p. 80) claims: "Not only do workers lose control over their instruments of production, but they must also lose control over their own labor and the manner of its performance."

24. Hochschild, 1983.

25. Hochschild, 1983; Otis, 2012.

26. Leidner, 1993, p. 18.

27. Leidner, 1993.

28. Tannock, 2001.

29. Macdonald & Sirianni, 1996.

30. Braverman (1974/1998, pp. 194–195) theorizes the twentieth-century labor-capital relationship thus:

> In this way, the inhabitant of capitalist society is enmeshed in a web made up of commodity goods and commodity services from which there is little possibility of escape except through partial or total abstention from social life as it now exists. . . . In the end, the population finds itself willy-nilly in the position of being able to do little or nothing as easily as it can be hired, done in the marketplace, by one of the multifarious new branches of social labor. And while from the point of view of labor it means that all work is carried on under the aegis of capital and is subject to its tribute of profit to expand capital still further.

31. Crain, Poster, & Cherry, 2016; Klein, 1999; Poster et al., 2016.

32. Allen & Du Gay, 1994; Williams & Connell, 2010.

33. Rhodes, 2010.

34. Barber, 2016a; Hanser, 2008; Kang, 2010; Lan, 2003; Pettinger, 2005.

35. Avery & Crain, 2007.

36. Hochschild, 1983.

37. Poster et al., 2016, p. 12.

38. Frenkel, 2003; Hall & van den Broek, 2012; Hanser, 2008; Kang, 2010; Lan, 2003; Mears, 2014; Nickson, Warhurst, Witz, & Cullen, 2001; Pettinger, 2005; Warhurst & Nickson, 2007, 2020; Warhurst et al., 2000; Williams & Connell, 2010; Witz, Warhurst, and Nickson, 2003; Wolkowitz, 2006.

39. Branch, 2011; Moss & Tilly, 2001.

40. Witz, Warhurst, & Nickson, 2003, p. 50 (emerging subsector); Warhurst, 2016 (key components).

41. Lopez, 2010, p. 260.

42. Warhurst, 2016.

43. Frenkel, 2003; Hall & van den Broek, 2012; Hanser, 2008; Lan, 2003; Mears, 2014; Nickson et al., 2001; Pettinger, 2005; Skeggs, 2004; Warhurst & Nickson, 2007; Warhurst et al., 2000; Williams & Connell, 2010; Witz et al., 2003; Wolkowitz, 2006.

44. Bourdieu, 1984.

45. Frenkel, 2003; Warhurst & Nickson, 2020, Williams & Connell, 2010.

46. Williams & Connell, 2010, p. 368.

47. Otis, 2012.

48. Bourdieu, 1984; Warhurst, 2016; Warhurst & Nickson, 2020.

49. Bettie, 2003.

50. Frenkel, 2003; Nickson et al., 2001; Warhurst et al., 2000; Wolkowitz, 2006.

51. Skeggs, 2004, p. 82.

52. Barber, 2016b, p. 209.

53. Adkins, 1995; Adkins & Lury, 1999; Barber, 2016a; Warhurst & Nickson, 2009.

54. Bhardwaj & Fairhurst, 2010; Cook & Yurchisin, 2016; Martin, Lowson, & Peck, 2004; Nayak, Singh, Padhye, & Wang, 2015; Van Oort, 2019.

55. Martin et al., 2004, p. 367.

56. Martin et al., 2004 (market volatility); Du Gay & Salaman, 1992; Rosen, 2002, p. 181 ("even more frequently").

57. Martin et al., 2004.

58. Ross, 2004.

59. Martin et al., 2004, p. 370.

60. Gatta, 2011; Hanser, 2008; Otis, 2012; Pettinger, 2005.

61. Pettinger, 2005, p. 462.

62. Fieldwork as a clothing store worker would have permitted prolonged relationships with employees, as well as immersion in the labor process (Gruys, 2012; Hanser, 2008; Lan, 2003; Van Oort, 2019; Williams, 2006). We instead conducted in-depth, semi-structured interviews to capture a range of worker experiences across a wider array of clothing retail companies.

63. We also informally asked workers questions focused on resolving tensions in our interview data.

64. Pettinger, 2005.

65. To solicit interviewees, we posted flyers on social media websites and in public places, as well as at a local public university and community college. Each respondent received a $15 gift card to an online merchant and a $5 gift card for referring others. This incentivized snowball sampling approach increased our access to participants. Interviewee networks also allowed purposively sampling more Black and Latinx women and men, most of whom we met through referrals.

66. Pettinger, 2004.

67. Approximately 37% of retail clothing workers in the United States in 2017 were between the ages 16–24, as compared to 95% of our sample (United States Bureau of Labor Statistics, 2018b).

68. Scholars have theorized that younger workers participate in a "different" labor market, experiencing lower-quality jobs with higher turnover (Besen-Cassino, 2014; Osterman, 1980; Tannock, 2001). We spend less time analyzing how age shapes workers' experiences because we are interested in better understanding racial and gender dimensions of aesthetic and emotional labor.

69. As of 2017, 73.2% of clothing store workers were women, 76% were white, 13.8% were Black, 5.7% were Asian, and 23.6% were Hispanic (the numbers do not add up to 100% because Hispanic people may also be listed as white or Black) (United States Bureau of Labor Statistics, 2018c).

70. All three of the workers identified as "Hispanic" or a specific nationality (e.g., Colombian); we use the terms Latino, Latina, and Latinx to refer to this racial-ethnic category. See the appendix for more detailed demographic information about our participants. We asked workers to self-identify and combined certain groups (for example, we labeled African American, Black, African, and/or Afro-Caribbean as "Black," and we grouped Asian American, Asian, and specific Asian nationalities into an overarching "Asian American" category). We also recorded skin color descriptors based on the interviewer's perception, though we recognize that white and Black interviewers' ratings of skin tone are more reliable within their own racial groups (Hannon & DeFina, 2014; Hill, 2002).

71. We received institutional review board approval to conduct this study. We present interview data using pseudonyms assigned to maintain confidentiality and do not present data that might lead to identifying particular workers.

72. These discussions ranged from approximately forty minutes to more than two hours, with most lasting between seventy-five and ninety minutes. Interview questions covered topics such as hiring, training, and interactions with customers, coworkers, and managers. We asked questions about getting ready for work, wages, scheduling, employee discounts, what they liked most and least, and why they quit (if applicable). At the beginning of the interview, the researcher asked, "How did you end up working at [name of store/s]?" We also posed questions

such as: "What was the dress code?" and "How did managers enforce the dress code policy?"

73. By intermittently layering the structured interview guide with reflective probes, we aimed to build rapport with participants and learn about the aspects of their jobs that were most salient to their experiences. Toward the session's close, we posed more contentious questions, such as whether they considered clothing retail to be a good job.

74. We also found that the interviews taught us new industry-specific terms, deepening our understanding of their work experiences. For example, participants explained UPT (units per transaction) metrics as a form of evaluating workers, which meant that they had to encourage customers to "add on" more items to purchases. Our process allowed us to hone our questions over time and ask about issues workers regard as central to their jobs.

75. Interview studies often conclude upon reaching a point of so-called theoretical saturation (Bowen, 2008; Glaser & Strauss, 1999). Toward the end of the second wave, after about forty-five interviews, we began to feel that participants' insights were becoming quite consistent, converging into several streams of retail work experiences. We also noticed that Black women in our sample with skin tones that were medium-dark or dark shared fewer positive experiences in these workplaces. During the final wave of interviews, we searched for further evidence and aimed to interview darker-skinned workers, to illuminate colorism within racialized beauty hierarchies. This enabled us to develop an analysis of aesthetic labor focused on gender, race, and skin tone.

76. Besen-Cassino, 2014.

77. Walters, 2018.

CHAPTER 1. LOW WAGES, LITTLE TRAINING

1. Free People, 2018.

2. Carré & Tilly, 2017; Carré, Tilly, & Holgate, 2009; Fiscal Policy Institute, 2008.

3. Ray, 2018.

4. Marx, 1867/1990.

5. Du Gay, 1993; Braverman, 1998; Ott, 2016.

6. Braverman, 1974/1998; Burawoy, 1979; Smith, 1994.

7. Marx, 1867/1990.

8. Braverman, 1974/1998, pp. 39–40; emphasis in original.

9. Korczynski & Macdonald, 2008; Leidner, 1993; Macdonald & Sirianni, 1996; Otis, 2012; Paules, 1991.

10. United States Bureau of Labor Statistics, 2017.

11. Braverman, 1974/1998, p. 248; emphasis in original.

12. Edwards, 1979; Gouldner, 1954; Ikeler, 2016.

13. Marx, 1867/1990.

14. Hanser, 2008; Mears, 2014; Otis, 2012; Pettinger, 2004.

15. United States Bureau of Labor Statistics, 2018a.

16. Broschak, Davis-Blake, & Block, 2008; Clawson & Gerstel, 2014; Halpin, 2015 (general economy); Henly & Lambert, 2014; Henly, Shaefer, & Waxman, 2006; Lambert, 2008; Presser, 2003; Traub, 2014 (retail).

17. Carré & Tilly, 2008; Carré et al., 2009; Cauthen, 2011; Du Gay, 1993, p. 572; Huddleston, 2011; Luce & Fujita, 2012.

18. Ruetschlin & Asante-Muhammad, 2015.

19. Halpin, 2015; Henly & Lambert, 2014; Henly et al., 2006; Lambert, 2008; Williams & Connell, 2010.

20. Cauthen, 2011; Du Gay & Salaman, 1992; Halpin, 2015; van Klaveren & Voss-Dahm, 2011, Van Oort, 2019. Note: Among retail workers surveyed in New York City, less than one-third know their schedule more than a week in advance; almost half of the workers are scheduled for fewer hours than they would like, have to be available for unexpected shifts, and have their hours changed or reduced without their consent (Luce & Fujita, 2012).

21. Lambert, 2008.

22. Some "part-timers" actually work full-time schedules without the attendant benefits (Fiscal Policy Institute, 2008; Luce & Fujita, 2012).

23. Halpin, 2015; Henly & Lambert, 2014; Lambert, 2008.

24. Halpin, 2015; Clawson & Gerstel, 2014.

25. Carré & Tilly, 2008; Carré et al., 2009; Huddleston, 2011; Luce & Fujita, 2012; Warhurst & Nickson, 2007.

26. Luce & Fujita, 2012; Ott, 2016; Roberts, 2011; Williams & Connell, 2010.

27. Andersson, Kazemi, Tengblad, & Wickelgren, 2011, p. 255.

28. Besen-Cassino, 2014; Bozkurt & Grugulis, 2011; Gatta, 2011; Huddleston, 2011; Williams & Connell, 2010.

29. Besen-Cassino, 2014; Bozkurt & Grugulis, 2011; Gatta, 2011; Huddleston, 2011; Williams & Connell, 2010.

30. Besen-Cassino, 2014; Bozkurt & Grugulis, 2011; Gatta, 2011; Huddleston, 2011; Williams & Connell, 2010.

31. Leslie, 2002; Pettinger, 2005; Warhurst & Nickson, 2007; Warhurst et al., 2000; Williams & Connell, 2010.

32. Besen-Cassino, 2014.

33. Grugulis, Bozkurt, & Clegg, 2011; Halpin, 2015; Henly & Lambert, 2014; Henly et al., 2006; Lambert, 2008; Williams & Connell, 2010.

34. Nickson, Hurrell, Warhurst, & Commander, 2011; Nickson, Warhurst, Commander, Hurrell, & Cullen, 2012; Warhurst & Nickson, 2007.

35. Moss & Tilly, 2001.

36. Durr & Wingfield, 2011.

37. Besen-Cassino, 2014; Bozkurt & Grugulis, 2011; Gatta, 2011; Huddleston, 2011; Williams & Connell, 2010.

38. Luce & Fujita, 2012; Roberts, 2011; Ton, 2012; Williams & Connell, 2010.

39. Leidner, 1993; Warhurst & Nickson, 2007.

40. Halpin, 2015.

41. Tannock, 2001.

42. Nickson et al., 2011.

43. Halpin, 2015; Carré & Tilly, 2017.

44. Bozkurt & Grugulis, 2011; Huddleston, 2011; Williams & Connell, 2010.

45. Williams & Connell, 2010.

46. Marx, 1867/1990.

47. Cauthen, 2011; Halpin, 2015; Henly & Lambert, 2014; Henly et al., 2006; Levy & Barocas, 2018; Van Oort, 2019.

48. Halpin, 2015.

49. Carré & Tilly, 2017; Halpin, 2015; Levy & Barocas, 2018.

50. See also Cauthen, 2011; Halpin, 2015; Henly et al., 2006; Lambert, 2008; Levy & Barocas, 2018; Luce & Fujita, 2012.

51. Cauthen, 2011, p. 6.

52. What makes the "best" schedule depends on individual workers' needs and preferences. Some comment that the best for them is a set schedule of certain days and times, while others emphasize having a regular number of hours each week. Luce and Fujita (2012) similarly find that rather than competing for promotions or bonuses, retail workers compete to be scheduled for enough hours to support themselves.

53. Mulholland, 2011.

54. Besen-Cassino, 2014; Williams & Connell, 2010.

55. Marx, 1867/1990.

56. Braverman, 1974/1998; Halpin, 2015.

57. Bozkurt & Grugulis, 2011; Braverman, 1974/1998.

CHAPTER 2. MULTILEVEL MANAGEMENT

1. Jeremy Bentham (1791) first theorized the panopticon as an institutional building, such as a prison, organized so that there is a central room that looks into each individual outlying room. This design means inhabitants of those rooms know they can always be seen, but don't know if they are currently being observed, leading them to discipline their own behavior as if they are being watched.

2. Foucault, 1977.

3. Khan, 2018.

4. Head, 2005, 2014; Payne, 2018.

5. Braverman, 1974/1998; Ikeler, 2015, 2016; Levy & Barocas, 2018; Mulholland, 2011.

6. Hochschild, 1983; Leidner, 1993, 1999; Ott, 2016.

7. Korczynski, 2007, 2013; Leidner, 1993, 1999; Lopez, 2010; Macdonald & Sirianni, 1996; Porter, 1987; Sloan, 2012; Troyer, Mueller, & Osinsky, 2000.

8. Leidner, 1999, p. 39.

9. Gamble, 2007.

10. Leidner, 1993, 1999; Lopez, 2010; Sallaz, 2002, 2010; Villarreal, 2010.

11. Bolton & Houlihan, 2010; Gamble, 2007; Leidner, 1993; Lopez, 2004, 2006, 2010; Rosenthal, 2004; Sallaz, 2010, 2015.

12. Bolton & Houlihan, 2010.

13. Smith, 1994.

14. Hodson, 2001; Hodson & Roscigno, 2004.

15. In her ethnographic study, Van Oort (2019, p. 1169) argues that despite poor online reviews of customer service at the stores in which she worked, managers coached her to focus on folding and cleaning, rather than on addressing disgruntled customers.

16. Otis and Zhao (2016) find that, in Chinese Walmart stores, managers are not identified on name tags, so workers cleaning and restocking shelves do not always know whether coworkers are also managers; in our settings, workers always knew who had supervisory roles, including fairly low-level "shift leaders."

17. Ott, 2016.

18. Bobo, 2011.

19. Sallaz, 2010.

20. Gamble, 2007; Leidner, 1993; Lopez, 2004, 2006, 2010; Rosenthal, 2004; Sallaz, 2010, 2015.

21. Misra & Walters, 2016.

22. Otis & Zhao, 2016.

23. Leidner, 1993; Leslie, 2002; Warhurst & Nickson, 2007.

24. Otis & Zhao, 2016; Ott, 2016.

25. In Ott's (2016) account of mystery shoppers' interactions with food service workers, he claims that workers could identify mystery shoppers based on timing of visits and the fact that the customer allowed the workers to rehearse the script without interruption—offering clear evidence of the weaknesses of scripted interactions. However, none of the retail clothing workers we interviewed suggest that they could identify mystery shoppers, perhaps because of the different setting.

26. We are indebted to sociologist Eileen Otis for suggesting this explanation.

27. Khan, 2018.

28. Lambert, 2008; Payne, 2018.

29. Workers' reactions in our study differ from Payne's (2018) account of how workers compete over their rankings in store metrics, which may reflect

that Payne's electronics workers see themselves as doing more skilled work, or a heightened culture of competition in these men-dominated stores.

30. Workers show less concern about registering customers for rewards cards. For example, Rachel argues that selling American Eagle credit cards is wrong because customers will "ruin their credit by opening one." But she harbors no concerns about opening rewards cards, since they do not impact customers' credit scores or end up costing them additional fees and finance charges. Thus, surveilling shoppers' habits seems more acceptable to workers, especially compared to the detrimental impacts of store credit cards.

31. Caskey, 1994.

32. Payne (2018) identifies various resistance strategies workers may use, and her ethnographic work gives her a better perspective on how workers may resist these newer technologies; in interviews, our workers did not identify effective resistance techniques, other than, for example, avoiding the cash register.

33. Nordstrom, 2015.

34. Caskey, 1994.

35. Payne, 2018.

36. Inman & Nikolova, 2017.

37. Inman & Nikolova, 2017; Kirkpatrick 2020; Turow, McGuigan, & Marris, 2015.

38. Turow et al., 2015.

39. Levy & Barocas, 2018; Manyika, Chui, Brown, Bughin, Dobbs, Roxburgh, & Byers, 2011; Mayer-Schönberger & Cukier, 2013.

40. Payne, 2018, p. 347.

41. Farris, Bendle, Pfeifer, & Reibstein, 2010; Head, 2005, 2014; Payne, 2018.

42. Nyberg & Sewell, 2014.

43. Head, 2005, p. 70.

44. Bolton & Houlihan, 2010; Lambert, 2008.

45. Gupta & Zeithaml, 2006.

46. Du Gay & Salaman, 1992; Korczynski, 2009; Van der Wiele, Hesselink, & Van Iwaarden, 2005.

47. Hammer & Champy, 2009; Head, 2005; Khan, 2018.

48. Levy & Barocas, 2018.

49. Retailers have used video data more in certain settings, such as in East Asian countries with fewer privacy regulations, to track customers and to identify shoplifters. Beacons, which use Bluetooth wireless technology to capture where customers are based on their smartphones and offer them discounts, have been used by retailers such as Target, but also face privacy concerns (Kirkpatrick, 2020; Otis & Zhao, 2016).

50. In some stores, workers may wear badges with Bluetooth beacons to ensure their movements are not counted as customer movements (Levy & Barocos, 2018).

51. Gouldner, 1954.

52. Bolton & Houlihan, 2005, p. 686; Gamble, 2007; Korczynski, Shire, Frenkel, & Tam, 2000; Lopez, 2006; Sallaz, 2010, 2015.

53. Gamble, 2007.

54. Kirkpatrick, 2020; Levy & Barocas, 2018; Turow et al., 2015.

55. Foucault, 1977.

56. Head, 2005, 2014.

57. Bolton & Houlihan, 2010.

CHAPTER 3. COWORKERS AND BELONGING

1. Besen-Cassino, 2014.

2. Collins, 2000; Durr & Wingfield, 2011; Wingfield, 2010.

3. Demopoulos, 2020; Wong, 2020.

4. Berman, West, & Richter, 2002; Ducharme & Martin, 2000; Harter, Schmidt, & Keyes, 2003; Hodson, 2001; Sias & Cahill, 1998; Sias, Heath, Perry, Silva, & Fix, 2004; Sloan, 2012; Sloan, Evenson Newhouse, & Thompson, 2013; Zelizer, 2010.

5. Morrison & Nolan, 2007.

6. Marmaros & Sacerdote, 2006; Sias & Cahill, 1998.

7. Ray, 2019; Wingfield, 2013; Wingfield & Alston, 2012; Wingfield & Chavez, 2002; Zanoni, Benschop, & Nkomo, 2010.

8. Bell & Nkomo, 2001; Cox & Nkomo, 1991; Feagin & Sikes, 1994; Marmaros & Sacerdote, 2006; Roscigno, 2007; Royster, 2003; Sloan et al., 2013; Wingfield, 2013.

9. In addition to shaping the daily experience of their jobs, friendships can have material effects. For example, research shows racial minorities are less likely to negotiate better salaries than whites, but the race effect disappears for Blacks, Latinx, and other groups, and is greatly reduced for Asians, when friendships with coworkers are taken into account (Seidel, Polzer, & Stewart, 2000).

10. Ray, 2019; Wingfield & Chavez, 2002; Zanoni et al., 2010.

11. Fong & Isajiw, 2000; Lewis, 2003; Sloan et al., 2013.

12. Christensen, 2009; Collins, 2000; Yuval-Davis, 2006.

13. Acker, 2006; Ray, 2019; Wingfield & Chavez, 2019; Wooten & Couloute, 2017.

14. Acker, 2006; Ray, 2019; Wingfield & Alston, 2014.

15. Ray, 2019.

16. Wingfield & Chavez, 2002.

17. McBride, 2005, p. 64.

18. Bello, 2004; Greenhouse, 2004; McBride, 2005.

19. Greenhouse, 2004.

20. Pittman, 2020. Former US president Barack Obama has noted being followed in stores. Experimental studies show that among Black and white customers matched by age, education, build, and attractiveness, Black testers wait twice as long for service; 86% of Black people in one survey indicated that they receive different treatment in stores because of their race (Williams, Henderson, Evett, & Hakstian, 2015).

21. Bay & Fabian, 2015.

22. Demopoulos, 2020; Wong, 2020.

23. Besen-Cassino, 2014.

24. Besen-Cassino, 2014.

25. Williams & Connell, 2010.

26. Marmos & Sacerdote, 2017; Sias & Cahill, 1998.

27. Wingfield & Chavez, 2002.

28. Ray, 2019.

29. Fong & Isajiw, 2000; Lewis, 2003; Sloan et al., 2013.

30. Feagin & Sikes, 1994; Roscigno, 2007; Sloan et al., 2013; Wingfield, 2013.

31. Ray, 2019.

32. Walters, 2018.

33. Demopoulos, 2020; Wong, 2020.

34. Pittman, 2020.

35. Marketplace discrimination remains a well-documented aspect of Black life in the United States, including the retail sector (Austin, 1994; Lee, 2000; Pittman, 2020; Scherer, Smith, & Thomas, 2009).

36. Austin, 1994; Lee, 2000; Scherer et al., 2009.

37. Demopoulos, 2020; Wong, 2020.

38. Gabbidon, 2003; Lee, 2000; Pittman, 2020.

39. Bell & Hartmann, 2007.

40. Bobo, Kluegel, & Smith, 1997.

41. Ray, 2019.

42. Du Bois, 1903/2018.

43. Ray, 2019; Wingfield & Chavez, 2020.

44. Demopoulos, 2020; Gabbidon, 2003; Pittman, 2020; Wong, 2020.

45. Ruetschlin & Asante-Muhammad, 2015.

46. Durr & Wingfield, 2011.

47. Besen-Cassino, 2014.

CHAPTER 4. CUSTOMER EXPECTATIONS

1. Hochschild, 1983.

2. Ashforth & Humphrey, 1993; Barber, 2016a; Gruys, 2012; Hochschild, 1983; Leidner, 1993, 1999; Lopez, 2006; Sherman, 2010; Wharton, 2009.

3. Hochschild, 1983.

4. Bolton & Houlihan, 2005, p. 686; Gamble, 2007; Korczynski, Shire, Frenkel, & Tam, 2000; Lopez, 2006; Sallaz, 2010, 2015.

5. Hochschild, 1983.

6. Hochschild, 1983.

7. Wharton, 2009.

8. Hochschild, 1983.

9. Erickson & Ritter, 2001; Erickson & Wharton, 1997; Leidner, 1993; Wharton, 2009.

10. Gamble, 2007; Rosenthal, 2004; Sallaz, 2015.

11. Ashforth & Humphrey, 1993; Barber, 2016a; Gruys, 2012; Mears, 2014.

12. Erickson & Ritter, 2001; Leidner, 1993; Wharton, 2009.

13. As described in chapter 2, workers following very detailed corporate scripts are less likely to feel a sense of connection to their customers.

14. Erickson & Ritter, 2001.

15. It may also be that women discussed this less because they expected us, as women, to understand emotional labor of this sort and didn't feel the need to focus on it.

16. Curtin, 2012.

17. In retrospect, Kyla likely annoyed him because she messed up the display (see chapter 5).

18. Bolton & Houlihan, 2010; Gamble, 2007; Korczynski et al., 2000; Leidner, 1993; Lopez, 2006, 2010; Rosenthal, 2004; Sallaz, 2010, 2015; Stevens, Minnotte, Mannon, & Kiger, 2006.

19. Accessed April 14, 2020.

20. None of the workers or managers who we interviewed discussed using radio frequency identification (RFID) tagging to track inventory. RFID tagging can successfully track goods and maintain inventories; this technology may not be implemented due to cost or incompatibility with existing technology, or may be implemented poorly, because our workers generally describe inventory systems as completely inefficient (Nayak, Singh, Padhye, & Wang, 2015; Thiesse, Al-Kassab, & Fleisch, 2009).

21. Ray, 2018.

22. Pascoe, 2011.

23. Gruys, 2012; Lan, 2003.

24. Cummins & Blum, 2015; Gruys, 2019.

25. Cummins & Blum, 2015; Gruys, 2019.

26. Otis & Zhao, 2016.

27. Cauthen, 2011; Halpin, 2015; Lambert, 2008; van Klaveren & Voss-Dahm, 2011; Van Oort, 2019.

28. Lambert, 2008.

29. Cauthen, 2011; Halpin, 2015; Lambert, 2008; Van Oort, 2019.

30. Hanser, 2005; Sherman, 2010.

31. Feagin & Sikes, 1994; Marmaros & Sacerdote, 2006; Roscigno, 2007; Royster, 2003; Sloan, Evenson Newhouse, &Thompson, 2013; Wingfield, 2013.

32. Ray, 2019; Wingfield, 2013; Wingfield & Chavez, 2020.

33. Bolton & Houlihan, 2005, p. 686; Gamble, 2007; Korczynski et al., 2000; Lopez, 2006; Sallaz, 2010, 2015.

34. Bolton & Houlihan, 2005; Gamble, 2007; Lopez, 2006; Korczynski et al., 2000; Rosenthal, 2004; Sallaz, 2010, 2015 (mired in negative interactions); Hochschild, 1983 (rude or aggressive).

35. Ashforth & Humphrey, 1993; Barber, 2016a, 2016b; Gruys, 2012; Hochschild, 1983; Leidner, 1993, 1999; Lopez, 2010; Sherman, 2010; Wharton, 2009.

36. Wingfield, 2010, 2013.

CHAPTER 5. BEAUTIFUL BODIES ON THE SALES FLOOR

1. We use a generic name for this smaller store to maintain Kathleen's confidentiality.

2. Kwan & Trautner, 2009.

3. Warhurst & Nickson, 2009.

4. Warhurst & Nickson, 2009; Hoang, 2015; Otis, 2012.

5. Pettinger, 2004; Williams & Connell, 2010.

6. Avery & Crain, 2007; Barber, 2016a, 2016b; Mears, 2014; Pettinger, 2004, 2005; Warhurst & Nickson, 2001, 2009, 2020; Warhurst, Nickson, Witz, Marie, & Cullen, 2000; Warhurst, van den Broek, Hall, & Nickson, 2009; Williams & Connell, 2010.

7. Adkins, 2000; Adkins & Lury, 1999; Barber, 2016a; Lan, 2003; Nickson, Warhurst, & Dutton, 2005; Otis, 2012.

8. Mears 2014, p. 1331.

9. Hall & van den Broek, 2012; Nickson et al., 2005; Nickson, Warhurst, Commander, Hurrell, & Cullen, 2012; Warhurst & Nickson, 2007, 2020. As Warhurst and Nickson (2007, p. 116) note, this focus on appearance has the potential for employment discrimination, although such discrimination may, indeed, be deemed legal "if a business case for this appearance is made." Avery and Crain (2007) develop this point further in their analysis of US labor law.

10. Frenkel, 2003; Gruys, 2012; Hall & van den Broek, 2012; Leslie, 2002; Nickson, Warhurst, Witz, & Cullen, 2001; Pettinger, 2004, 2005; Warhurst et al., 2000; Wolkowitz, 2006.

11. Bourdieu, 1984; Glenn, 2009; Otis, 2012.

12. Lan, 2003.

13. Otis, 2012, p. 14.

14. Hanser, 2005, 2008; Kang, 2003, 2010; Lan, 2003; Otis, 2012; Paules, 1991; Rhodes, 2010.

15. Hoang, 2014, 2015; Mears & Connell, 2016.

16. Williams & Connell, 2010, p. 357.

17. Bourdieu 1984.

18. Otis, 2012.

19. Butler, 2004, 2011; West & Zimmerman, 1987.

20. Pettinger, 2005.

21. Pettinger, 2005, p. 475.

22. See Curtin, 2012; Williams, 2006.

23. Simpson, 2004, 2007; Williams, 1995.

24. Warhurst & Nickson, 2009, p. 390.

25. Otis, 2012 (workers in hotels); Hoang, 2014, 2015 (sex workers); Loe, 1996; Warhust & Nickson, 2020 (waitstaff).

26. Driessen, 2005; McBride, 2005.

27. Barber, 2016b, p. 209.

28. Entwistle & Mears, 2012; Lan, 2003; McBride 2005; Mears, 2014; Walters, 2016.

29. Acker, 1990, 2000; Bridges, 2009; Cooper, 2000; Goffman, 1959/1977; hooks, 1992; Salzinger, 2003; Sherman, 2007, 2010; Walters, 2018; West & Zimmerman, 1987.

30. Lan, 2003, p. 32.

31. Hanser, 2005, 2008; Pettinger, 2005.

32. hooks, 1992; Hunter, 2002, 2005, 2007; Mears, 2011; Wingfield & Chavez, 2020; Wolf, 1991.

33. Walters, 2018.

34. Bonilla-Silva & Glover, 2004; Bonilla-Silva, 2004.

35. Glenn, 2009; Hall, 2010; Herring, Keith, & Horton, 2004; Keith & Herring, 1991; Monk, 2014, 2015.

36. Pettinger, 2004.

37. See also Maheshwari, 2013.

38. Hunter, 2005.

39. Pettinger, 2004.

40. Carr, 2013; Craig, 2002; Greene, 2008, 2010, 2016; Mayes, 1997; Patton, 2006.

41. Byrd & Tharps, 2014; Craig, 2002, 2012; Hunter, 2005; Mayes, 1997; Patton, 2006; Rosette & Dumas, 2007.

42. Lan, 2003; Maitra & Maitra, 2018.

43. Leslie, 2002.

44. Bordo, 2004; Collins, 2000; hooks, 1992.

45. Fryar, Gu, & Ogden, 2012.

46. Mears & Connell, 2016.

47. Bates, 2014.

48. Bridges, 2015; Marx 1867/1990.

49. McBride, 2005.

50. Frizell, 2015; Sauvalle, 2015; Tempesta, 2015.

51. Mears & Connell, 2016 (display work).

52. Warhurst et al., 2009.

53. Adkins & Lury, 1999; Barber, 2016a, 2016b; Hanser, 2005, 2008; Lan, 2003; Nickson et al., 2005; Otis, 2012; Pettinger, 2005.

54. Otis, 2008, 2012.

CHAPTER 6. MODELING THE MERCHANDISE

1. Avery & Crain, 2007; Cutcher & Achtel, 2017; Gruys, 2012; Mears, 2014; Pettinger, 2004, 2005; Warhurst & Nickson, 2001; Warhurst, Nickson, Witz, & Cullen, 2000; Warhurst, van den Broek, Hall, & Nickson, 2009; Warhurst & Nickson, 2020; Williams & Connell, 2010.

2. Macdonald & Sirianni, 1996, p. 4.

3. Warhurst et al., 2000.

4. Allen & Du Gay, 1994, p. 266; Leidner, 1993, 1999.

5. Williams & Connell, 2010, p. 368.

6. Williams & Connell, 2010, p. 363.

7. Williams & Connell, 2010.

8. Hall & van den Broek, 2012; Leslie, 2002; Pettinger, 2004, 2005; Warhurst & Nickson, 2020; Williams & Connell, 2010.

9. Pascoe & Bridges, 2016; Pettinger, 2005.

10. Avery & Crain, 2007; Cutcher & Achtel, 2017; Du Gay, 1993; Mears, 2014.

11. Abercrombie's very narrow enforcement of aesthetic labor ended in 2015, when the store announced that it was changing the title "model" to "brand representative" and "would no longer hire store workers based on their 'body type or physical attractiveness'" (McGregor, 2015, n.p.). We highlight Abercrombie & Fitch's look-based labor practices because twenty-one of our fifty-five participants had worked for this corporation, providing grounded insights into this company's practices. Yet that aesthetic division of retail labor exists across the industry (Cutcher & Achtel, 2017; Gruys, 2012; Hanser, 2008; Otis, 2012; Williams & Connell, 2010), as does the cultivation of workers' bodies (Lan, 2003; Pettinger, 2004, 2005; Williams & Connell, 2010).

12. Lan, 2003; McBride, 2005; Mears, 2014.

13. Cutcher & Achtel, 2017.

14. Gruys, 2012; Pettinger, 2004, 2005; Williams & Connell, 2010.

15. Allen & Du Gay, 1994; Cutcher & Achtel, 2017; Williams & Connell, 2010.

16. Babcock, 2015, p. 1.

17. Cutcher & Achtel, 2017; Williams & Connell, 2010.

18. Adkins, 2000; Pettinger, 2005.

19. Adkins, 2000; Barber, 2016a.

20. Lan, 2003.

21. Pettinger, 2004.

22. Gruys, 2012; Mears, 2011.

23. Gruys, 2012.

24. Williams & Connell, 2010.

25. Avery & Crain, 2007; Gruys, 2012; Mears, 2014; Pettinger, 2004, 2005; Warhurst & Nickson, 2001, 2020; Warhurst et al., 2000; Warhurst et al., 2009; Williams & Connell, 2010.

26. Hall & van den Boek, 2012; Leslie, 2002; Pettinger, 2004, 2005; Williams & Connell, 2010.

27. Avery & Crain, 2007; Cutcher & Achtel, 2017; Lopez, 2010; Macdonald & Sirianni, 1996; Pettinger, 2004; Warhurst et al., 2000; Williams & Connell, 2010.

28. Williams & Connell, 2010.

29. Barber, 2016a, 2016b.

30. Gruys, 2012; Mears, 2014; Pettinger, 2004, 2005; Warhurst et al., 2000; Williams & Connell, 2010.

CONCLUSION

1. Gandini, 2019; Vallas & Schor, 2020.

2. De Stefano, 2015–2016; Friedman, 2014.

3. Moorhouse, tom Dieck, & Jung, 2018; Redd & Vickerie, 2017–2018.

4. Yohn, 2020.

5. Papagiannis, 2020.

6. Papagiannis, 2020.

7. Kornet, Collins, & Oviedo, 2020.

8. Haller, Lee, & Cheung, 2020, p. 12; Yohn, 2020.

9. Yohn, 2020.

10. Moorhouse et al., 2018, p. 137.

11. Redd & Vickerie, 2017–2018.

12. Cornet et al., 2020; Orschell, 2020; Haller et al., 2020.

13. Leidner, 1993.

14. Leidner, 1993.

15. Sennett & Cobb, 1972.

16. Gabbidon, 2003; Harris, Henderson, & Williams, 2005; Pittman, 2020.

17. Leidner, 1993.

18. Paules, 1991.

19. Lambert, 2008.
20. Foucault, 1977.
21. Turow, McGuigan, & Maris, 2015, p. 465.
22. Turow et al., 2015.
23. Turow et al., 2015.
24. Farris, Bendle, Pfeifer, & Reibstein, 2010; Head, 2005, 2014; Poster, Crain, & Cherry, 2016, Redd & Vickerie, 2017; Van Oort, 2019.
25. Farris et al., 2010; Head, 2005, 2014.
26. Gupta & Zeithaml, 2006.
27. Lambert & Henly, 2012; Levy & Barocas, 2018.
28. Monahan, 2010; Otis & Zhao, 2016; Tannock, 2001.
29. Gimlin, 2002, 2007; Kwan & Trautner, 2009; Mears & Connell, 2016.
30. Mears, 2011.
31. Bonilla-Silva & Glover, 2004.
32. Walters, 2018.
33. United States Bureau of Labor Statistics, 2018c.
34. Rosa-Salas, 2019.
35. Claytor, 2019.
36. Christiansen, 2021; Pravato, 2020.
37. Palmieri, 2020.
38. Haller et al., 2020.
39. Millard, 2009; Taylor, Johnston, & Whitehead, 2016.
40. Harold, 2004.
41. Kantor, 2014.
42. Scheiber, 2015.
43. Target Corporation, 2020.
44. Ikeler, 2016.
45. Ikeler, 2016.
46. Nolan, 2011, 2014.
47. Bidwell, 2013.
48. Rolf, 2016; Ashby, 2017.
49. Clawson, 2003.
50. Ashby, 2017; Rolf, 2016; Rosenblum, 2017.
51. Ashby, 2017; Rolf, 2016; Rosenblum, 2017.
52. Lazarus, 2020.
53. Abercrombie & Fitch, 2020.
54. Pravato, 2020.
55. Demopoulos, 2020; Pravato, 2020; Wong, 2020. Such code words allegedly have been used in other retail stores (Williams, Henderson, Evett, & Hakstian, 2015).
56. Urban Outfitters, 2020.
57. Carré & Tilly, 2017.

58. Bidwell, 2013; Lambert, 2008; Lambert & Henly, 2012.

59. Corser, 2017.

60. Corser, 2017, p. 24.

61. Ruan, Alexander, & Haley-Lock, 2013.

62. Bernstein, Kesavan, & Staats, 2014.

63. Corser, 2017; Ruetschlin & Asante-Muhammad, 2015.

64. Glenn, 1992, 2002; Macdonald & Sirianni, 1996; Otis, 2012.

APPENDIX

1. Besen-Cassino, 2014; Klein, 1999; Pettinger, 2005; Williams & Connell, 2010.

2. Besen-Cassino, 2014; Bozkurt & Grugulis, 2011; Williams & Connell, 2010.

3. US Bureau of Labor Statistics 2018a, 2018b.

4. Since 1994, workers without a high school degree have decreased from 39% to 11% of the retail workforce (Cardiff et al., 2011, p. 37).

5. Interview participants gave us employee manuals for Urban Outfitters and Pac Sun.

6. Our research team conducted thirty-four store field visits in Massachusetts between 2012 and 2013. One store field visit was conducted in the Los Angeles metropolitan area in 2013.

7. Gruys, 2012; Hanser, 2008; Lan, 2003; Pettinger, 2004.

References

Abercrombie & Fitch. (2020). *This is a movement.* Retrieved from https://www
.abercrombie.com/shop/us/br/BlackLivesMatter?icmp=ICT:SPR20:D:HP:
VB:BLM:CAM:X:JuneW2

Acker, J. (1990). Hierarchies, jobs, bodies: A theory of gendered organizations.
Gender & Society, 4(2), 139–158.

Acker, J. (2000). Revisiting class: Thinking from gender, race, and organizations. *Social Politics: International Studies in Gender, State & Society, 7*(2),
192–214.

Acker, J. (2006). Inequality regimes: Gender, class, and race in organizations.
Gender & Society, 20(4), 441–464.

Adkins, L. (1995). *Gendered work: Sexuality, family, and the labour market.*
Maidenhead, England: Open University Press.

Adkins, L. (2000). Mobile desire: Aesthetics, sexuality and the "lesbian" at work.
Sexualities, 3(2), 201–218.

Adkins, L., & Lury, C. (1999). The labour of identity: Performing identities,
performing economies. *Economy and Society, 28*(4), 598–614.

Allen, J., & Du Gay, P. (1994). Industry and the rest: The economic identity of
services. *Work, Employment and Society, 8*(2), 255–271.

Amott, T. L., & Matthaei, J. A. (1996). *Race, gender, and work: A multicultural
economic history of women in the United States.* Boston, MA: Southend
Press.

Andersson, T., Kazemi, A., Tengblad, S., & Wickelgren, M. (2011). Not the inevitable bleak house? The positive experiences of workers and managers in retail employment in Sweden. In I. Grugulis & Ö. Bozkurt (Eds.), *Retail work* (pp. 253–276). London, England: Palgrave Macmillan.

Ashby, S. (2017). Assessing the fight for fifteen movement from Chicago. *Labor Studies Journal, 42*(4), 366–386.

Ashforth, B. E., & Humphrey, R. H. (1993). Emotional labor in service roles: The influence of identity. *Academy of Management Review, 18*(1), 88–115.

Austin, R. (1994). "A nation of thieves": Securing black people's right to shop and sell in white America. *Utah Law Review,* 147–177.

Avery, D., & Crain, M. (2007). Branded: Corporate image, sexual stereotyping, and the new face of capitalism. *Duke Journal of Gender Law & Policy, 14,* 13–124.

Babcock, G. (2015, July 22). Abercrombie & Fitch faces new lawsuit over employee "look policy". *Complex.* Retrieved from http://www.complex.com /style/2015/07/abercrombie-and-fitch-employee-look-policy-law-suit

Barber, K. (2016a). *Styling masculinity: Gender, class, and inequality in the men's grooming industry.* New Brunswick, NJ: Rutgers University Press.

Barber, K. (2016b). "Men wanted": Heterosexual aesthetic labor in the masculinization of the hair salon. *Gender & Society, 30*(4), 618–642.

Bates, L. (2014). *Everyday sexism.* London, England: Simon & Schuster.

Bay, M., & Fabian, A. (2015). Introduction. In M. Bay & A. Fabian (Eds.), *Race and retail: Consumption across the color line* (pp. 1–12). New Brunswick, NJ: Rutgers University Press.

Bell, E. E. L., & Nkomo, S. M. (2001). *Our separate ways: Black and white women and the struggle for professional identity.* Boston, MA: Harvard Business Review Press.

Bell, J. M., & Hartmann, D. (2007). Diversity in everyday discourse: The cultural ambiguities and consequences of "happy talk". *American Sociological Review, 72*(6), 895–914.

Bello, J. (2004). "Attractiveness as hiring criteria: Savvy business practice or racial discrimination." *Journal of Gender, Race, & Justice, 8*(2), 483–506.

Bentham, J. (1791). *Panopticon, or the inspection house* (Vol. 2). London, England: T. Payne.

Berman, E., West, J. P., & Richter, M. N., Jr. (2002). Workplace relations: Friendship patterns and consequences (according to managers). *Public Administration Review, 62*(2), 217–230.

Bernstein, E., Kesavan, S., & Staats, B. (2014, September 24). How to manage scheduling software fairly. *Harvard Business Review Blogs.* Retrieved from https://hbr.org/2014/09/how-to-manage-scheduling-software-fairly

Besen-Cassino, Y. (2014). *Consuming work: Youth labor in America.* Philadelphia, PA: Temple University Press.

Besen-Cassino, Y. (2018). *The cost of being a girl: Working teens and the origins of the gender wage gap.* Philadelphia, PA: Temple University Press.

Bettie, J. (2003). *Women without class: Girls, race, and identity.* Berkeley, CA: University of California Press.

Bhardwaj, V., & Fairhurst, A. (2010). Fast fashion: Responses to changes in the fashion industry. *The International Review of Retail, Distribution and Consumer Research, 20*(1), 165–173.

Bidwell, M. J. (2013). What happened to long-term employment? The role of worker power and environmental turbulence in explaining declines in worker tenure. *Organization Science, 24*(4), 1061–1082.

Bobo, L. D. (2011). Somewhere between Jim Crow & post-racialism: Reflections on the racial divide in America today. *Daedalus, 140*(2), 11–36.

Bobo, L., Kluegel, J. R., & Smith, R. A. (1997). Laissez-faire racism: The crystallization of a "kinder, gentler" anti-Black ideology. In S. A. Tuch & J. K. Martin (Eds.), *Racial attitudes in the 1990s: Continuity and change* (pp. 15–42). Westport, CT: Praeger.

Bolton, S. C., & Houlihan, M. (2005). The (mis)representation of customer service. *Work, Employment & Society, 19*(4), 685–703.

Bolton, S. C., & Houlihan, M. (2010). Bermuda revisited? Management power and powerlessness in the worker-manager-customer triangle. *Work and Occupations, 37*(3), 378–403.

Bonilla-Silva, E. (2004). From bi-racial to tri-racial: Towards a new system of racial stratification in the USA. *Ethnic and Racial Studies, 27*(6), 931–950.

Bonilla-Silva, E., & Glover, K. (2004). "We are all Americans": The Latin Americanization of the United States. In M. Krysan & A. E. Lewis (Eds.), *The changing terrain of race and ethnicity* (pp. 149–183). New York, NY: Russell Sage.

Bordo, S. (2004). *Unbearable weight: Feminism, western culture, and the body.* Berkeley, CA: University of California Press.

Bourdieu, P. 1984. *Distinction: A social critique of the judgment of taste.* Cambridge, MA: Harvard University Press.

Bowen, G. A. (2008). Naturalistic inquiry and the saturation concept: A research note. *Qualitative Research, 8*(1), 137–152.

Bozkurt, Ö., & Grugulis, I. (2011). Why retail labor demands a closer look. In I. Grugulis & Ö. Bozkurt (Eds.), *Retail work* (pp. 1–21). London, England: Palgrave Macmillan.

Branch, E. H. (2011). *Opportunity denied: Limiting black women to devalued work.* New Brunswick, NJ: Rutgers University Press.

Braverman, H. (1998). *Labor and monopoly capital: The degradation of work in the twentieth century* (25th anniversary ed.). New York, NY: New York University Press. (Original work published 1974)

Bridges, T. (2009). Gender capital and male bodybuilders. *Body & Society, 15*(1), 83–107.

Bridges, T. (2015, January 29). Cosmopolitan masculinity and gender omnivorousness: Transformations in gender and inequality. *The Society Pages.* Retrieved from https://thesocietypages.org/feminist/2015/01/29 /cosmopolitan-masculinities-and-gender-omnivorousness-transformations -in-gender-and-inequality/

Broschak, J. P., Davis-Blake, A., & Block, E. S. (2008). Nonstandard, not substandard: The relationships among work arrangements, work attitudes, and job performance. *Work and Occupations, 35*(1), 3–43.

Browne, I. (Ed.). (1999). *Latinas and African American women at work: Race, gender, and economic inequality.* New York, NY: Russell Sage Foundation.

Browne, I., & Misra, J. (2003). The intersection of gender and race in the labor market. *Annual Review of Sociology, 29,* 487–513.

Byrd, A., & Tharps, L. (2014). *Hair story: Untangling the roots of Black hair in America* (1st revised ed.). New York, NY: St. Martin's Griffin.

Burawoy, M. (1979). *Manufacturing consent: Changes in the labor process under monopoly capitalism.* Chicago, IL: University of Chicago Press.

Butler, J. (2004). *Undoing gender.* London, England: Psychology Press.

Butler, J. (2011). *Gender trouble: Feminism and the subversion of identity.* New York, NY: Routledge Press.

Cardiff, B., LaFontaine, F., & Shaw, K. (2011). The spread of good jobs for the less skilled: "Modern retail" as the new manufacturing. Stanford School of Business Conference Presentation.

Carr, J. (2013). The paraphernalia of suffering: Chris Rock's Good Hair, still playing in the dark. *Black Camera: An International Film Journal (The New Series), 5*(1), 56–71.

Carré, F., & Tilly, C. (2008). *America's biggest low-wage industry: Continuity and change in retail jobs* (UMass Boston Center for Social Policy Publications, Paper 22). Boston, MA: Center for Social Policy.

Carré, F., & Tilly, C. (2017). *Where bad jobs are better: Retail jobs across countries and companies.* New York, NY: Russell Sage Foundation.

Carré, F., Tilly, C., & Holgate, B. (2009). *Competitive strategies in the US retail industry: Consequences for jobs in food and consumer electronics stores* (Industry Studies Association Working Paper, WP-2009-5). Pittsburgh, PA: University of Pittsburgh. Retrieved from http://scholarworks.umb.edu/csp _pubs/18/

Caskey, J. P. (1994). *Fringe banking: Check-cashing outlets, pawnshops, and the poor.* New York, NY: Russell Sage Foundation.

Cauthen, N. K. (2011). *Scheduling hourly workers: How last minute "just in time" scheduling practices are bad for workers, families, and business.* New York, NY: Dēmos.

Choo, H. Y., & Ferree, M. M. (2010). Practicing intersectionality in sociological research: A critical analysis of inclusions, interactions, and institutions in the study of inequalities. *Sociological Theory, 28*(2), 129–149.

Christensen, A. (2009). Belonging and unbelonging in an intersectional perspective. *Gender, Technology and Development, 13*(1), 21–41.

Christiansen, L. (2020). How Fenty's brand positioning generated $100 million in its first forty days. *Jilt.* Retrieved from https://jilt.com/blog/fenty-brand -positioning/

Clawson, D. (2003). *The Next Upsurge: Labor and the new social movements.* Ithaca, NY: ILR/Cornell University Press.

Clawson, D., & Gerstel, N. (2014). *Unequal time: Gender, class, and family in employment schedules.* New York, NY: Russell Sage Foundation.

Claytor, C.P. (2019). Are Black consumers a bellwether for the nation? How research on Blacks can foreground our understanding of race in the marketplace. In G. D. Johnson, K. D. Thomas, A. Kwame-Harrison, & S. A. Grier (Eds.), *Race in the Marketplace* (pp. 153–172). New York, NY: Palgrave Macmillan.

Collins, P. H. (2000). *Black feminist thought: Knowledge, consciousness, and the politics of empowerment.* New York, NY: Routledge.

Cook, S., & Yurchisin, J. (2016). Fast fashion environments: Consumer's heaven or retailer's nightmare? *International Journal of Retail & Distribution Management, 45*(2), 143–157.

Cooper, M. (2000). Being the "go-to-guy": Fatherhood, masculinity, and the organization of work in the Silicon Valley. *Qualitative Sociology, 23*(4), 379–405.

Corser, M. (2017). *Job quality and economic opportunity in retail: Key findings from a national survey of the retail workforce.* Center for Popular Democracy. Fair Workweek Initiative. Retrieved from https://populardemocracy .org/news/publications/job-quality-and-economic-opportunity-retail-key -findings-national-survey-retail

Cox, T. H., & Nkomo, S. M. (1991). Analysis of the early career experience of MBAs. *Work and Occupations, 18*(4), 431–446.

Craig, M. L. (2002). *Ain't I a beauty queen? Black women, beauty, and the politics of race.* New York, NY: Oxford University Press.

Craig, M. L. (2012). Racialized bodies. In B. S. Turner (Ed.), *Routledge handbook of body studies* (pp. 321–331). New York, NY: Routledge.

Crain, M., Poster, W. R., & Cherry, M. A. (Eds.). (2016). *Invisible labor: Hidden work in the contemporary world.* Oakland, CA: University of California Press.

Crenshaw, K. (1989). Demarginalizing the intersection of race and sex: A Black feminist critique of antidiscrimination doctrine, feminist theory and antiracist politics. *University of Chicago Legal Forum, 1*(8), 139–167.

Cummins, E. R., & Blum, L. M. (2015). Suits to self-sufficiency: Dress for success and neoliberal maternalism. *Gender & Society, 29*(5), 623–646.

Curtin, J. (2012). *Beauty over brains: Aesthetic labor of employees in clothing retail stores* [Unpublished senior thesis]. University of Massachusetts, Amherst.

Cutcher, L., & Achtel, P. (2017). "Doing the brand": Aesthetic labour as situated, relational performance in fashion retail. *Work, Employment and Society, 31*(4), 675–691.

De Stefano, V. (2015–2016). The rise of the just-in-time workforce: On-demand work, crowdwork, and labor protection in the gig-economy. *Comparative Labor Law & Policy Journal, 37*, 471–504.

Demopoulos, A. (2020, June). Anthropologie denies racially profiling customers. Former employees call b.s. *The Daily Beast.* Retrieved from https://www.thedailybeast.com/anthropologie-denies-racially-profiling-customers-former-employees-call-bs

Driessen, C. E. (2005). Message communication in advertising: Selling the Abercrombie and Fitch image. *Journal of Undergraduate Research, 8*, 1–12.

Du Bois, W. E. B. (2018). *The souls of Black folk: Essays and sketches.* Amherst, MA: University of Massachusetts Press. (Original work published 1903)

Du Gay, P. (1993). "Numbers and souls": Retailing and the de-differentiation of economy and culture. *British Journal of Sociology, 44*(4), 563–587.

Du Gay, P., & Salaman, G. (1992). The cult[ure] of the customer. *Journal of Management Studies, 29*(5), 615–633.

Ducharme, L. J., & Martin, J. K. (2000). Unrewarding work, coworker support, and job satisfaction. *Work and Occupations, 27*(2), 223–243.

Durr, M., & Wingfield, A. M. H. (2011). Keep your 'n' in check: African American women and the interactive effects of etiquette and emotional labor. *Critical Sociology, 37*(5), 557–571.

Edwards, R. (1979). *Contested terrain: The transformation of the workplace in the twentieth century.* New York, NY: Basic Books.

Entwistle, J., & Mears, A. (2012). Gender on display: Performance and performativity in fashion modelling. *Cultural Sociology, 6*(4), 1–16.

Erikson, R. J., & Ritter, C. (2001). Emotional labor, burnout, and inauthenticity: Does gender matter? *Social Psychology Quarterly, 64*(2), 146–164.

Erickson, R. J., & Wharton, A. S. (1997). In authenticity and depression: Assessing the consequences of interactive service work. *Work and Occupations, 24*(2), 188–213.

Farris, P. W., Bendle, N., Pfeifer, P., & Reibstein, D. (2010). *Marketing metrics: The definitive guide to measuring marketing performance* (2nd ed.). Upper Saddle River, NJ: Pearson Education.

Feagin, J. R., & Sikes, M. P. (1994). *Living with racism: The Black middle-class experience.* Boston, MA: Beacon Press.

Fiscal Policy Institute. (2008). *Low wages, no bargain: Retail jobs in New York City*. New York, NY: Author.

Fong, E., & Isajiw, W. W. (2000). Determinants of friendship choices in multi-ethnic society. *Sociological Forum, 15*(2), 249–271.

Forever 21. (2016). Forever 21. Retrieved from https://www.forever21.com/us/shop

Foucault, M. (1977). *Discipline and punish*. (A. Sheridan, Trans.). New York, NY: Pantheon.

Free People. (2018). Homepage. Retrieved from https://www.freepeople.com/homepage/.

Freeman, C. (2000). *High tech and high heels in the global economy: Women, work, and pink-collar identities in the Caribbean*. Durham, NC: Duke University Press.

Frenkel, S. J. (2003). The embedded character of workplace relations. *Work and Occupations, 30*(2), 135–153.

Friedman, G. (2014). Workers without employers: Shadow corporations and the rise of the gig economy. *Review of Keynesian Economics, 2*(2), 171–188.

Frizell, S. (2015, April 25). Abercrombie & Fitch is ditching its shirtless models. *Time*. Retrieved from http://time.com/3835521/abercrombie-fitch-shirtless-models/

Fryar, C. D., Gu, Q., & Ogden, C. L. (2012). Anthropometric reference data for children and adults: United States, 2007–2010. *Vital Heath Statistics, 11*(252), 1–40.

Gabbidon, S. L. (2003). Racial profiling by store clerks and security personnel in retail establishments: An exploration of "shopping while Black". *Journal of Contemporary Criminal Justice, 19*(3), 345–364.

Gamble, J. (2007). The rhetoric of the consumer and customer control in China. *Work, Employment & Society, 21*(1), 7–25.

Gandini, A. (2019). Labour process theory and the gig economy. *Human Relations, 72*(6), 1039–1056.

Gatta, M. (2011). In the "blink" of an eye: American high-end small retail businesses and the public workforce system. In I. Grugulis & Ö. Bozkurt (Eds.), *Retail work* (pp. 49–67). London, England: Palgrave Macmillan.

Gimlin, D. (2002). *Body work: Beauty and self-image in American culture*. Berkeley, CA: University of California Press.

Gimlin, D. (2007). What is "body work"? A review of the literature. *Sociology Compass, 1*(1), 353–370.

Glaser, B. G., & Strauss, A. L. (1999). *Discovery of grounded theory: Strategies for qualitative research*. New York, NY: Routledge.

Glenn, E. N. (1992). From servitude to service work: Historical continuities in the racial division of paid reproductive labor. *Signs, 18*(1), 1–43.

Glenn, E. N. (2002). *Unequal freedom: How race and gender shaped American citizenship and labor*. Cambridge, MA: Harvard University Press.

Glenn, E. N. (Ed.). (2009). Shades of difference: Why skin color matters. Stanford, CA: Stanford University Press.

Goffman, E. (1977). *The presentation of self in everyday life*. New York, NY: Anchor Books/Doubleday. (Original work published 1959)

Gouldner, A. (1954). *Patterns of industrial bureaucracy*. New York, NY: Free Press.

Greene, D. W. (2008). Title VII: What's hair (and other race-based characteristics) got to do with it. *University of Colorado Law Review, 79*, 1355–1394.

Greene, D. W. (2010). Black women can't have blonde hair in the workplace. *Journal of Gender Race & Justice, 14*, 405–430.

Greene, D. W. (2016). Splitting hairs: The eleventh circuit's take on workplace bans against Black women's natural hair in EEOC v. catastrophe management solutions. *University of Miami Law Review, 71*, 987–1036.

Greenhouse, S. (2004, November 17). Abercrombie & Fitch bias case is settled. *The New York Times*, A16.

Grugulis, I., & Bozkurt, Ö. (Eds.). (2011). *Retail work*. London, England: Palgrave Macmillan.

Grugulis, I., Bozkurt, Ö., & Clegg, J. (2011). "No place to hide"? The realities of leadership in UK supermarkets. In I. Grugulis & Ö. Bozkurt (Eds.), *Retail work* (pp. 193–212). London, England: Palgrave Macmillan.

Gruys, K. (2012). Does this make me look fat? Aesthetic labor and fat talk as emotional labor in a women's plus-size clothing store. *Social Problems, 59*(4), 481–500.

Gruys, K. (2019). "Making over" poor women: Gender, race, class, and body size in a welfare-to-work nonprofit organization. *Sociological Forum, 34*(1), 47–70.

Gupta, S., & Zeithaml, V. (2006). Customer metrics and their impact on financial performance. *Marketing Science, 25*(6), 718–739.

Hall, R. E. (2010). *An historical analysis of skin color discrimination in America: Victimism among victim group populations*. New York, NY: Springer.

Hall, R., & van den Broek, D. (2012). Aestheticising retail workers: Orientations of aesthetic labour in Australian fashion retail. *Economic and Industrial Democracy, 33*(1), 85–102.

Haller, K., Lee, J., & Cheung, J. (2020). Meet the 2020 consumers driving change. *Retail Insights*. Retrieved from https://www.ibm.com/downloads/cas/EXK4XKX8

Halpin, B. W. (2015). Subject to change without notice: Mock schedules and flexible employment in the United States. *Social Problems, 62*(3), 419–438.

Hammer, M., & Champy, J. (2009). *Reengineering the corporation: A manifesto for business revolution*. New York, NY: HarperCollins.

Hannon, L., & DeFina, R. (2014). Just skin deep? The impact of interviewer race on the assessment of African American respondent skin tone. *Race Social Problems, 6*(4), 356–364.

Hanser, A. (2005). The gendered rice bowl: The sexual politics of service work in urban China. *Gender & Society, 19*(5), 581–600.

Hanser, A. (2008). *Service encounters: Class, gender, and the market for social distinction in urban China.* Stanford, CA: Stanford University Press.

Harold, C. (2004). Pranking rhetoric: "Culture jamming" as media activism. *Critical Studies in Media Communication, 21*(3), 189–211.

Harris, A. M. G., Henderson, G. R., & Williams, J. D. (2005). Courting customers: Assessing consumer racial profiling and other marketplace discrimination. *Journal of Public Policy & Marketing, 24*(1), 163–171.

Harter, J. K., Schmidt, F. L., & Keyes, C. L. M. (2003). Well-being in the workplace and its relationship to business outcomes: A review of the Gallup studies. In C. L. Keyes & J. Haidt (Eds.), *Flourishing: The positive person and the good life* (pp. 205–224). Washington, DC: American Psychological Association.

Head, S. (2005). *The new ruthless economy: Work & power in the digital age.* New York, NY: Oxford University Press.

Head, S. (2014). *Mindless: Why smarter machines are making dumber humans.* New York, NY: Basic Books.

Henly, J. R., & Lambert, S. J. (2014). Unpredictable work timing in retail jobs: Implications for employee work-life conflict. *ILR Review, 67*(3), 986–1016.

Henly, J. R., Shaefer, H. L., & Waxman, E. (2006). Nonstandard work schedules: Employer- and employee-driven flexibility in retail jobs. *Social Service Review, 80*(4), 609–634.

Herring, C., Keith, V., & Horton, H. D. (Eds.). (2004). *Skin deep: How race and complexion matter in the "color-blind" era.* Urbana, IL: University of Illinois Press.

Higginbotham, E., & Weber, L. (1999). Perceptions of workplace discrimination among Black and white professional managerial women. In I. Browne (Ed.), *Latinas and African American women at work* (pp. 327–353). New York, NY: Russell Sage Foundation.

Hill, M. E. (2002). Race of the interviewer and perception of skin color: Evidence from the multi-city study of urban inequality. *American Sociological Review, 67*(1), 99–108.

Hoang, K. K. (2014). Competing technologies of embodiment: Pan-Asian modernity and third world dependency in Vietnam's contemporary sex industry. *Gender & Society, 28*(4), 513–536.

Hoang, K. K. (2015). *Dealing in desire: Asian ascendancy, western decline, and the hidden currencies of global sex work.* Oakland, CA: University of California Press.

Hochschild, A. R. (1983). *The managed heart: The commercialization of human feeling.* Berkeley, CA: University of California Press.

Hodson, R. (2001). *Dignity at work.* Cambridge, England: Cambridge University Press.

Hodson, R., & Roscigno, V. J. (2004). Organizational success and worker dignity: Complementary or contradictory? *American Journal of Sociology, 110*(3), 672–708.

hooks, b. (1992). *Black looks: Race and representation*. Boston, MA: South End.

Hossfeld, K. J. (1990). "Their logic against them": Contradictions in sex, race, and class in Silicon Valley. In K. B. Ward (Ed.), *Women workers and global restructuring* (pp. 149–178). Ithaca, NY: ILR Press.

Huddleston, P. (2011). "It's all right for Saturdays, but not forever": The employment of part-time student staff within the retail sector. In I. Grugulis & Ö. Bozkurt (Eds.), *Retail work* (pp. 109–127). London, England: Palgrave Macmillan.

Hunter, M. L. (2002). "If you're light you're all right": Light skin color as social capital for women of color. *Gender & Society, 16*(2), 175–193.

Hunter, M. L. (2005). *Race, gender, and the politics of skin tone*. New York, NY: Routledge.

Hunter, M. L. (2007). The persistent problem of colorism: Skin tone, status, and inequality. *Sociology Compass, 1*(1), 237–254.

Ikeler, P. (2015). Deskilling emotional labour: Evidence from department store retail. *Work, Employment and Society, 30*(6), 966–983.

Ikeler, P. (2016). *Hard sell: Work and resistance in retail chains*. Ithaca, NY: Cornell University Press.

Inman, J. J., & Nikolova, H. (2017). Shopper-facing retail technology: A retailer adoption decision framework incorporating shopper attitudes and privacy concerns. *Journal of Retailing, 93*(1), 7–28.

International Labour Organization. (2006). *Social and labour implications of the increased use of advanced retail technologies*. Retrieved from http://www.ilo.org/public/english/standards/relm/gb/docs/gb297/pdf/tmart.pdf

Kalleberg, A. (2011). *Good jobs, bad jobs: Changing work and workers in America*. New York, NY: Russell Sage Foundation.

Kalleberg, A., Reskin, B., & Hudson, K. (2000). Bad jobs in America: Standard and nonstandard employment relations and job quality in the United States. *American Sociological Review, 65*(2), 256–278.

Kang, M. (2003). The managed hand: The commercialization of bodies and emotions in Korean immigrant-owned nail salons. *Gender & Society, 17*(6), 820–839.

Kang, M. (2010). *The managed hand: Race, gender, and the body in beauty service work*. Berkeley, CA: University of California Press.

Kantor, J. (2014, August 13). Working anything but 9 to 5: Scheduling technology leaves low-income parents with hours of chaos. *The New York Times.* Retrieved from https://www.nytimes.com/interactive/2014/08/13/us/starbucks-workers-scheduling-hours.html

Keith, V. M., & Herring, C. (1991). Skin tone and stratification in the Black community. *American Journal of Sociology, 97*(3), 760–778.

Ken, I. (2010). *Digesting race, class, and gender: Sugar as a metaphor*. New York, NY: Palgrave Macmillan.

Khan, F. Technological change and labour processes in the organised retail sector: A case study of a shopping mall in Delhi. (2018). *Manpower Journal, 52*(1–2), 53–63.

Kirkpatrick, K. (2020). Tracking shoppers. *Communications of the ACM, 62*(2)19–21.

Klein, N. (1999). *No logo: Taking aim at the brand bullies*. New York, NY: Picador.

Korczynski, M. (2007). Service work, social theory, and collectivism: A reply to Brook. *Work, Employment & Society, 21*(3), 577–588.

Korczynski, M. (2009). The mystery customer: Continuing absences in the sociology of service work. *Sociology, 43*(5), 952–967.

Korczynski, M. (2013). The customer in the sociology of work: Different ways of going beyond the management-worker dyad. *Work, Employment and Society, 27*(5), NP1–NP7.

Korczynski, M., & Macdonald, C. (Eds.). (2008). *Service work: Critical perspectives*. New York, NY: Routledge.

Korczynski, M., Shire, K., Frenkel, S., & Tam, M. (2000). Service work in consumer capitalism: Customers, control and contradictions. *Work, Employment and Society, 14*(4), 669–687.

Kornet, K., Collins, J., & Oviedo, D. (2020). *New research: Four post-pandemic scenarios for the future of retail*. Retail Dive. Retrieved from https://www .retaildive.com/spons/new-research-4-post-pandemic-scenarios-for-the -future-of-retail/585032/

Kwan, S., & Trautner, M. N. (2009). Beauty work: Individual and institutional rewards, the reproduction of gender, and questions of agency. *Sociology Compass, 3*(1), 49–71.

Lambert, S. J. (2008). Passing the buck: Labor flexibility practices that transfer risk onto hourly workers. *Human Relations, 61*(9), 1203–1227.

Lambert, S. J., & Henly, J. R. (2012). Frontline managers matter: Labour flexibility practices and sustained employment in US retail jobs. In C. Warhurst, F. Carré, P. Findlay, & C. Tilly (Eds.), *Are bad jobs inevitable? Trends, determinants, and responses to job quality in the twenty-first century* (pp. 143–159). New York, NY: Palgrave Macmillan.

Lan, P. (2003). Working in a neon cage: Bodily labor of cosmetics saleswomen in Taiwan. *Feminist Studies, 29*(1), 21–45.

Lazarus, D. (2020, June 17). The Aunt Jemina brand, rooted in slavery, was in fact selling "whiteness". *The Los Angeles Times*. Retrieved from https://www .latimes.com/business/story/2020-06-17/aunt-jemima-racist-stereotypes

Lee, J. (2000). The salience of race in everyday life: Black customers' shopping experiences in Black and white neighborhoods. *Work and Occupations, 27*(3), 353–376.

Leidner, R. (1993). *Fast food, fast talk: Service work and the routinization of everyday life*. Berkeley, CA: University of California Press.

Leidner, R. (1999). Emotional labor in service work. *The ANNALS of the American Academy of Political and Social Science, 561*(1), 81–95.

Leslie, D. (2002). Gender, retail employment and the clothing commodity chain. *Gender, Place & Culture, 9*(1), 61–76.

Levy, K., & Barocas, S. (2018). Refractive surveillance: Monitoring customers to manage workers. *International Journal of Communication, 12*, 1166–1188.

Lewis, A. E. (2003). Everyday race-making: Navigating racial boundaries in schools. *American Behavioral Scientist, 47*(3), 283–305.

Loe, M. (1996). Working for men: At the intersection of power, gender, and sexuality. *Sociological Inquiry, 66*(4), 399–422.

Lopez, S. H. (2004). *Reorganizing the rust belt: An inside study of the American labor movement*. Berkeley: University of California Press.

Lopez, S. H. (2006). Emotional labor and emotional performance. *Work and Occupations, 33*(2), 133–160.

Lopez, S. H. (2010). Workers, managers, and customers: Triangles of power in work communities. *Work and Occupations, 37*(3), 251–271.

Luce, S., & Fujita, N. (2012). *Discounted jobs: How retailers sell workers short*. New York, NY: CUNY Murphy Institute and Retail Action Project.

Macdonald, C. L., & Sirianni, C. (Eds.). (1996). *Working in the service sector society*. Philadelphia, PA: Temple University Press.

Maheshwari, S. (2013, September 3). The hairstyles Abercrombie has deemed "unacceptable". *BuzzFeed News*. Retrieved from https://www.buzzfeed.com/sapna/exclusive-abercrombie-hairstyle-rules-add-to-strict-look-pol?utm_term=.ljPmJ6elW#.wilDPgR4e

Maitra, S., & Maitra, S. (2018). Producing the aesthetic self: An analysis of aesthetic skill and labour in the organized retail industries in India. *Journal of South Asian Development, 13*(3), 337–357.

Manyika, J., Chui, M., Brown, B., Bughin, J., Dobbs, R., Roxburgh, C., & Byers, A. H. (2011). *Big data: The next frontier for innovation, competition, and productivity*. McKinsey Global Institute. Retrieved from https://www.mckinsey.com/~/media/McKinsey/Business%20 Functions/McKinsey%20Digital/Our%20Insights/Big%20data%20The%20next%20frontier%20for%20innovation/MGI_big_data_full_report.ashx

Marmaros, D., & Sacerdote, B. (2006). How do friendships form? *The Quarterly Journal of Economics, 121*(4), 79–119.

Martin, C., Lowson, R., & Peck, H. (2004). Creating agile supply chains in the fashion industry. *International Journal of Retail & Distribution Management, 32*(8/9), 367–376.

Marx, K. (1990). *Capital: A critique of political economy* (Vol. 1). (B. Fowkes, Trans.). London, England: Penguin Books. (Original work published 1867)

Massey, D. S., & Martin, J. A. (2003). The NIS skin color scale. Retrieved from http://nis.princeton.edu/downloads/NIS-Skin-Color-Scale.pdf

Mayer-Schönberger, V., & Cukier, K. (2013). *Big data: A revolution that will transform how we live, work, and think*. London, England: John Murray.

Mayes, E. M. (1997). Chapter five: As soft as straight gets: African American women and mainstream beauty standards in haircare advertising. *Counterpoints, 54*, 85–108.

McBride, D. (2005). *Why I hate Abercrombie & Fitch: Essays on race and sexuality*. New York, NY: New York University Press.

McCall, L. (2005). The complexity of intersectionality. *Signs, 30*(3), 1771–1800.

McGregor, J. (2015, April 24). Abercrombie & Fitch says it will stop hiring workers based on "body type or physical attractiveness". *The Washington Post*. Retrieved from https://www.washingtonpost.com/news/on-leadership /wp/2015/04/24/abercrombie-fitch-says-it-will-no-longer-hire-workers -based-on-body-type-or-physical-attractiveness/

Mears, A. (2011). *Pricing beauty: The making of a fashion model*. Berkeley, CA: University of California Press.

Mears, A. (2014). Aesthetic labor for the sociologies of work, gender, and beauty. *Sociology Compass, 8*(12), 1330–1343.

Mears, A., & Connell, C. (2016). The paradoxical value of deviant cases: Toward a gendered theory of display work. *Signs, 41*(2), 333–359.

Millard, J. (2009). Performing beauty: Dove's "real beauty" campaign. *Symbolic Interaction, 32*(2), 146–168.

Misra, J., & Walters, K. (2016). All fun and cool clothes? Youth workers' consumer identity in clothing retail. *Work and Occupations, 43*(3), 294–325.

Monahan, T. (2010). *Surveillance in the time of insecurity*. New Brunswick, NJ: Rutgers University Press.

Monk, E. P., Jr. (2014). Skin tone stratification among Black Americans, 2001–2003. *Social Forces, 92*(4), 1313–1337.

Monk, E. P., Jr. (2015). The cost of color: Skin color, discrimination, and health among African-Americans. *American Journal of Sociology, 121*(2), 396–444.

Moorhouse, N., tom Dieck, M. C., & Jung, T. (2018). Technological innovations transforming the consumer retail experience: A review of literature. In M. C. tom Dieck & T. Jung (Eds.), *Augmented reality and virtual reality: Empowering human, place, and business* (pp. 133–143). New York, NY: Springer.

Morrison, R. L. (2009). Are women tending and befriending in the workplace? Gender differences in the relationship between workplace friendships and organizational outcomes. *Sex Roles, 60*(1–2), 1–13.

Morrison, R. L., & Nolan, T. (2007). Too much of a good thing? Difficulties with workplace friendships. *University of Auckland Business Review, 9*(2), 32.

Moss, P., & Tilly, C. (2001). *Stories employers tell: Race, skills, and hiring in America*. New York, NY: Russell Sage.

Mulholland, K. (2011). In search of team working in a major supermarket. In I. Grugulis & Ö. Bozkurt (Eds.), *Retail work* (pp. 213–231). London, England: Palgrave Macmillan.

Nayak, R., Singh, A., Padhye, R., & Wang, L. (2015). RFID in textile and clothing manufacturing: Technology and challenges. *Fashion and Textiles, 2*(1), 1–16.

Nickson, D., Hurrell, S. A., Warhurst, C., & Commander, J. (2011). Labour supply and skills demand in fashion retail. In I. Grugulis & Ö. Bozkurt (Eds.), *Retail work* (pp. 68–87). London, England: Palgrave Macmillan.

Nickson, D., Warhurst, C., Commander, J., Hurrell, S. A., & Cullen, A. M. (2012). Soft skills and employability: Evidence from UK retail. *Economic and Industrial Democracy, 33*(1), 65–84.

Nickson, D., Warhurst, C., & Dutton, E. (2005). The importance of attitude and appearance in the service encounter in retail and hospitality. *Managing Service Quality, 15*(2), 195–208.

Nickson, D., Warhurst, C., Witz, A., & Cullen, A. M. (2001). The importance of being aesthetic: Work, employment and service organisation. In A. Sturdy, I. Grugulis, & H. Wilmott (Eds.), *Customer service: Empowerment and entrapment* (pp. 170–190). Hampshire, United Kingdom: Palgrave.

Nolan, H. (2011). Here's the cheesy anti-union video all Target employees must endure. Retrieved from http://gawker.com/5811371/heres-the-cheesy-anti-union-video-all-target-employees-must-endure

Nolan, H. (2014). Behold, Target's brand new cheesy anti-union video. Retrieved from http://gawker.com/behold-targets-brand-new-cheesy-anti-union-video-1547193676

Nordstrom. (2015). *Annual report*. Seattle, WA: Nordstrom Investor Relations. Retrieved from http://www.annualreports.com/HostedData/AnnualReportArchive/n/NYSE_JWN_2015.pdf

Nyberg, D., & Sewell, G. (2014). Collaboration, co-operation or collusion? Contrasting employee responses to managerial control in three call centres. *British Journal of Industrial Relations, 52*(2), 308–332.

Orschell, J. (2020). The future of retail: Beyond the pandemic. *Total Retail*. Retrieved from https://www.mytotalretail.com/article/the-future-of-retail-beyond-the-pandemic/

Osterman, P. (1980). *Getting started: The youth labor market*. Cambridge, MA: Massachusetts Institute of Technology Press.

Otis, E. M. (2008). The dignity of working women: Service, sex, and the labor politics of localization in China's City of Eternal Spring. *American Behavior Scientist, 52*(3), 356–376.

Otis, E. M. (2012). *Marketing bodies: Women, service work, and the making of inequality in China*. Stanford, CA: Stanford University Press.

Otis, E. M., & Zhao, Z. (2016). Producing invisibility: Surveillance, hunger, and work in the produce aisles of Wal-Mart, China. In M. Crain, W. R. Poster, & M. A. Cherry (Eds.), *Invisible labor: Hidden work in the contemporary world* (pp. 148–168). Oakland, CA: University of California Press.

Ott, B. (2016) The limits of control in service work: Interactive routines and interactional competence." *Research in the Sociology of Work, 29,* 155–183.

Palmieri, Jean E. (2020, July 16). FootLocker Europe launching diverse marketing plan. *YahooNews.* Retrieved from https://www.yahoo.com/news/foot -locker-europe-launching-diverse-200119925.html

Papagiannis, Helen. (2020). How AR is redefining retail in a pandemic. *Harvard Business Review.* Retrieved from https://hbr.org/2020/10/how-ar-is -redefining-retail-in-the-pandemic

Pascoe, C. J. (2011). *Dude you're a fag.* Berkeley, CA: University of California Press.

Pascoe, C. J., & Bridges, T. (Eds.). (2016). *Exploring masculinities: Identity, inequality, continuity, and change.* New York, NY: Oxford University Press.

Patton, T. O. (2006). Hey girl, am I more than my hair? African American women and their struggles with beauty, body image, and hair. *NWSA Journal, 18*(2), 24–51.

Paules, G. F. (1991). *Dishing it out: Power and resistance among waitresses in a New Jersey restaurant.* Philadelphia, PA: Temple University Press.

Payne, J. (2018). Manufacturing masculinity: Exploring gender and workplace surveillance. *Work and Occupations, 45*(3), 346–383.

Pettinger, L. (2004). Brand culture and branded workers: Service work and aesthetic labour in fashion retail. *Consumption, Markets and Culture, 7*(2), 165–184.

Pettinger, L. (2005). Gendered work meets gendered goods: Selling and service in clothing retail. *Gender, Work and Organization, 12*(5), 460–478.

Pittman, Cassi. (2020). "Shopping while Black": Black consumers' management of racial stigma and racial profiling in retail settings. *Journal of Consumer Culture, 20*(1), 3–22.

Porter, S. B. (1987). *Counter cultures: Saleswomen, managers, and customers in American department stores, 1890–1940.* Urbana-Champaign, IL: University of Illinois Press.

Poster, W. R., Crain, M., & Cherry, M. A. (2016). Introduction: Conceptualizing invisible labor. In M. Crain, W. R. Poster, & M. A. Cherry (Eds.), *Invisible labor: Hidden work in the contemporary world* (pp. 3–27). Oakland, CA: University of California Press.

Pravato, M. (2020, June 23). How Black Lives Matter is changing online bands. *The Diamondback.* Retrieved from https://dbknews.com/2020/06/23/black -lives-matter-online-brands/

Presser, H. B. (2003). Race-ethnic and gender differences in nonstandard work shifts. *Work and Occupations, 30*(4), 412–439.

Ray, R. (2018). *The making of a teenage service class: Poverty and mobility in an American city.* Oakland, CA: University of California Press.

Ray, V. (2019). A theory of racialized organizations. *American Sociological Review, 84*(1), 26–53.

Redd, N. J., & Vickerie, L. S. (2017–2018). The rise and fall of brick and mortar retail: The impact of emerging technologies and executive choices on business failure. *Journal of International Business & Law, 17,* 127.

Rhodes, D. (2010). *Beauty bias: The injustice of appearance in life and law.* New York, NY: Oxford University Press.

Roberts, S. (2011). "The lost boys": An overlooked detail in retail? In I. Grugulis & Ö. Bozkurt (Eds.), *Retail work* (pp. 128–148). London, England: Palgrave Macmillan.

Rolf, D. (2016). The fight for fifteen: The right wage for a working America. New York, NY: The New Press.

Rosa-Salas, M. (2019). Making the mass white: How racial segregation shaped consumer segmentation. In G. D. Johnson, K. D. Thomas, A. Kwame-Harrison, & S. A. Grier (Eds.), *Race in the marketplace* (pp. 21–38). New York: Palgrave Macmillan.

Roscigno, V. (2007). *The face of discrimination: How race and gender impact work and home lives.* Lanham, MD: Rowman & Littlefield.

Rosen, E. I. (2002). *Making sweatshops: The globalization of the U.S. apparel industry.* Berkeley, CA: University of California Press.

Rosenblum, J. (2017). *Beyond $15: Immigrant workers, faith activists, and the revival of the labor movement.* Boston, MA: Beacon Press.

Rosenthal, P. (2004). Management control as an employee resource: The case of front-line service workers. *Journal of Management Studies, 41*(4), 601–622.

Rosette, A. S., & Dumas, T. L. (2007). The hair dilemma: Conform to mainstream expectations or emphasize racial identity. *Duke Journal of Gender Law & Policy, 14*(1), 407–421.

Ross, R. J. (2004). *Slaves to fashion: Poverty and abuse in the new sweatshops.* Ann Arbor, MI: University of Michigan Press.

Royster, D. (2003). *Race and the invisible hand: How white networks exclude Black men from blue-collar jobs.* Berkeley, CA: University of California Press.

Ruan, N., Alexander, C., & Haley-Lock, A. (2013). *Stabilizing low-wage work: Legal remedies for unpredictable work hours & income stability.* Retrieved from https://works.bepress.com/nantiya_ruan/7/

Ruetschlin, C., & Asante-Muhammad, D. (2015). *The retail race divide.* New York, NY: Dēmos/National Association for the Advancement of Colored People.

Sallaz, J. J. (2002). The house rules: Autonomy and interests among service workers in the contemporary casino industry. *Work and Occupations, 29*(4), 394–427.

Sallaz, J. J. (2010). Service labor and symbolic power: On putting Bourdieu to work. *Work and Occupations, 37*(3), 295–319.

Sallaz, J. J. (2015). Permanent pedagogy: How post-Fordist firms generate effort but not consent. *Work and Occupations, 42*(1), 3–34.

Salzinger, L. (2003). *Genders in production: Making workers in Mexico's global factories.* Berkeley, CA: University of California Press.

Sauvalle, J. (2015, April 24). The end of an era: No more shirtless hunks at Abercrombie & Fitch. *Out.* Retrieved from https://www.out.com/truman -says/2015/4/24/end-era-no-more-shirtless-hunks-abercrombie-fitch

Scheiber, N. (2015, September 24). Starbucks falls short after pledging better labor practices. *The New York Times.* Retrieved from https://www.nytimes .com/2015/09/24/business/starbucks-falls-short-after-pledging-better-labor -practices.html?rref=collection%2Fbyline%2Fnoam-scheiber

Scherer, G., Smith, S., & Thomas, K. (2009). "Shopping while Black": Examining racial discrimination in a retail setting. *Journal of Applied Social Psychology, 39*(6), 1432–1444.

Seidel, M. L., Polzer, J. T., & Stewart, K. J. (2000). Friends in high places: The effects of social networks on discrimination in salary negotiations. *Administrative Science Quarterly, 45*(1), 1–24.

Sennett, R., & Cobb, J. (1972). *The hidden injuries of class.* Cambridge, England: Cambridge University Press.

Sherman, R. (2007). *Class acts: Service and inequality in luxury hotels.* Berkeley, CA: University of California Press.

Sherman, R. (2010). "Time is our commodity": Gender and the struggle for occupational legitimacy among personal concierges. *Work and Occupations, 37*(1), 81–114.

Sias, P. M., & Cahill, D. J. (1998). From coworkers to friends: The development of peer friendships in the workplace. *Western Journal of Communication, 62*(3), 273–299.

Sias, P. M., Heath, R. G., Perry, T., Silva, T., & Fix, B. (2004). Narratives of workplace friendship deterioration. *Journal of Social and Personal Relationships, 21*(3), 321–340.

Simpson, R. (2004). Masculinity at work: The experiences of men in female dominated occupations. *Work, Employment and Society, 18*(2), 349–368.

Simpson, R. (2007). Emotional labour and identity work of men in caring roles. In P. Lewis & R. Simpson (Eds.), *Gendering emotions in organizations* (pp. 57–74). Basingstoke, England: Palgrave Macmillan.

Skeggs, B. (2004). Context and background: Pierre Bourdieu's analysis of class, gender and sexuality. *The Sociological Review, 52*(2), 19–33.

Sloan, M. M. (2012). Unfair treatment in the workplace and worker well-being: The role of coworker support in a service work environment. *Work and Occupations, 39*(1), 3–34.

Sloan, M. M., Evenson Newhouse, R. J., & Thompson, A. B. (2013). Counting on coworkers: Race, social support, and emotional experiences on the job. *Social Psychology Quarterly, 76*(4), 343–372.

Smith, J. W., & Calasanti, T. (2005). The influences of gender, race and ethnicity on workplace experiences of institutional and social isolation: An exploratory study of university faculty. *Sociological Spectrum, 25*(3), 307–334.

Smith, V. (1994). Braverman's legacy: The labor process tradition at 20. *Work and Occupations, 21*(4), 403–421.

Sokoloff, N. J. (1992). *Black women and white women in the professions: Occupational segregation by race and gender, 1960–1980.* New York, NY: Routledge.

Stevens, D. P., Minnotte, K. L., Mannon, S. E., & Kiger, G. (2006). Family work performance and satisfaction: Gender ideology, relative resources, and emotion work." *Marriage & Family Review, 40*(4): 47–74.

Tannock, S. (2001). *Youth at work: The unionized fast-food and grocery workplace.* Philadelphia, PA: Temple University Press.

Target Corporation (2020, June 17). *Target increases starting wage to $15; thanks frontline team members with recognition bonus.* Retrieved from https://corporate.target.com/press/releases/2020/06/target-increases -starting-wage-to-15-thanks-frontl

Taylor, J., Johnston, J., & Whitehead, K. (2016). A corporation in feminist clothing? Young women discuss the dove "real beauty" campaign. *Critical Sociology, 42*(1), 123–144.

Tempesta, E. (2015, April 24). The end of an era. *Daily Mail.* Retrieved from http://www.dailymail.co.uk/femail/article-3054517/Abercrombie-Fitch-vows -stop-using-shirtless-models-stores-revealing-plans-try-diversify-overtly -sexy-image.html

Thiesse, F., Al-Kassab, J., & Fleisch, E. (2009). Understanding the value of integrated RFID systems: A case study from apparel retail. *European Journal of Information Systems, 18*(6), 592–614.

Ton, Z. (2012, January/February). Why "good jobs" are good for retailers. *Harvard Business Review,* 124–131.

Traub, A. (2014). *Retail's choice: How raising wages and improving schedules for women in the retail industry would benefit America.* New York, NY: Dēmos.

Troyer, L., Mueller, C. W., & Osinsky, P. I. (2000). Who's the boss? A role-theoretic analysis of customer work. *Work and Occupations, 27*(3), 406–427.

Turow, J., McGuigan, L., & Maris, E. R. (2015). Making data mining a natural part of life: Physical retailing, customer surveillance and the 21st-century social imaginary. *European Journal of Cultural Studies, 18*(4–5), 464–478.

United States Bureau of Labor Statistics. (2017). Table 2.1 Employment by major industry sector, 2006, 2016, and projected 2026. Retrieved from https://www .bls.gov/emp/tables/employment-by-major-industry-sector.htm

United States Bureau of Labor Statistics. (2018a). Occupational employment and wages, May 2017: 41-000 sales and related occupations. Retrieved from https://www.bls.gov/oes/current/oes410000.htm

United States Bureau of Labor Statistics. (2018b). Table 18b. Employed persons by detailed industry and age, 2017. Retrieved from https://www.bls.gov/cps /cpsaat18b.htm

United States Bureau of Labor Statistics. (2018c). Table 18. Employed persons by detailed industry, sex, race, and Hispanic or Latino ethnicity, 2019. Retrieved from https://www.bls.gov/cps/cpsaat18.ht

Urban Outfitters. (2020). *Diversity & inclusion*. Retrieved from https://www .urbanoutfitters.com/to-our-community

Vallas, S., & Schor, J. B. (2020). What do platforms do? Understanding the gig economy. *Annual Review of Sociology, 46*, 1–22.

Van der Wiele, T., Hesselink, M., & Van Iwaarden, J. (2005). Mystery shopping: A tool to develop insight into customer service provision. *Total Quality Management & Business Excellence, 16*(4), 529–541.

van Klaveren, M., & Voss-Dahm, D. (2011). Employers' "exit options" and low-wage retail work: The case of supermarkets in the Netherlands and Germany. In I. Grugulis & Ö. Bozkurt (Eds.), *Retail work* (pp. 175–192). London, England: Palgrave Macmillan.

Van Oort, M. (2019). The emotional labor of surveillance: Digital control in fast fashion retail. *Critical Sociology, 45*(7–8), 1167–1179.

Villarreal, A. T. (2010). The bus owner, the bus driver, and his lover: Gendered class struggle in the service work triangle. *Work and Occupations, 37*(3), 272–294.

Walters, K. (2016). Mall models: How Abercrombie & Fitch sexualizes its retail workers. *Sexualization, Media, & Society, 2*(2), 1–5.

Walters, K. (2018). "They'll go with the lighter": Tri-racial aesthetic labor in clothing retail. *Sociology of Race and Ethnicity, 4*(1), 128–141.

Warhurst, C. (2016). From invisible work to invisible workers: The impact of service employers' speech demands on the working class. In M. Crain, W. R. Poster, & M. A. Cherry (Eds.), *Invisible labor: Hidden work in the contemporary world* (pp. 214–236). Oakland, CA: University of California Press.

Warhurst, C. & Nickson, D. (2001). *Looking good and sounding right: Style counselling and the aesthetics of the new economy*. Loughton, England: Industrial Society.

Warhurst, C., & Nickson, D. (2007). Employee experience of aesthetic labour in retail and hospitality. *Work, Employment & Society, 21*(1), 103–120.

Warhurst, C., & Nickson, D. (2009). "Who's got the look?" Emotional, aesthetic and sexualized labour in interactive services. *Gender, Work and Organizations, 16*(3), 385–404.

Warhurst, C., & Nickson, D. (2020). *Aesthetic labour.* London, England: Sage.

Warhurst, C., Nickson, D., Witz, A., & Cullen, A. M. (2000). Aesthetic labour in interactive service work: Some case study evidence from the "new" Glasgow. *The Service Industries Journal, 20*(3), 1–18.

Warhurst, C., van den Broek, D., Hall, R., & Nickson, D. (2009). Looksism: The new frontier of employment discrimination? *Journal of Industrial Relations, 51*(1), 131–136.

West, C., & Zimmerman, D. H. (1987). Doing gender. *Gender & Society, 1*(2), 125–151.

Wharton, A. (2009). The sociology of emotional labor. *Annual Review of Sociology, 35*, 147–165.

Williams, C. L. (1995). *Still a man's world: Men who do women's work.* Berkeley, CA: University of California Press.

Williams, C. L. (2006). *Inside toyland: Working, shopping, and social inequality.* Berkeley, CA: University of California Press.

Williams, C. L., & Connell, C. (2010). "Looking good and sounding right": Aesthetic labor and social inequality in the retail industry. *Work and Occupations, 37*(3), 349–377.

Williams, J. D., Henderson, G. R., Evett, S. R., & Hakstian, A. G. (2015). Racial discrimination in retail settings. In M. Bay & A. Fabian's (Eds.), *Race and retail: Consumption across the color line* (pp. 263–277). New Brunswick, NJ: Rutgers University Press.

Wingfield, A. H. (2009). Racializing the glass escalator: Reconsidering men's experiences with women's work. *Gender & Society, 23*(1), 5–26.

Wingfield, A. H. (2010). Are some emotions marked "whites only"? Racialized feeling rules in professional workplaces. *Social Problems, 57*(2), 251–268.

Wingfield, A. H. (2012). *Changing times for Black professionals.* New York, NY: Routledge.

Wingfield, A. H. (2013). *No more invisible man: Race and gender in men's work.* Philadelphia, PA: Temple University Press.

Wingfield, A. H. (2019) *Flatlining: Race, work, and health care in the new economy.* Oakland, CA: University of California Press.

Wingfield, A. H., & Alston, R. S. (2012). The understudied case of Black professional men: Advocating an intersectional approach. *Sociology Compass, 6*(9), 728–739.

Wingfield, A. H., & Chavez, K. (2020). Getting in, getting hired, getting sideways looks: Organizational hierarchy and perceptions of racial discrimination. *American Sociological Review, 85*(1), 31–57.

Wingfield, A. H., & Skeete, R. (2016). Maintaining hierarchies in predominantly white organizations: A theory of racial tasks. In M. Crain, W. R. Poster, & M. A Cherry (Eds.), *Invisible labor: Hidden work in the contemporary world* (pp. 47–68). Oakland, CA: University of California Press.

Witz, A., Warhurst, C., & Nickson, D. (2003). The labour of aesthetics and the aesthetics of organization. *Organization, 10*(1), 33–54.

Wolf, N. (1991). *The beauty myth: How images of beauty are used against women.* New York, NY: Doubleday.

Wolkowitz, C. (2006). *Bodies at work.* London, England: Sage.

Wong, V. (2020, June 23). Anthropologie is "whitewashed" from top to bottom, from how it treats its Black staff to how it profiles shoppers. *Buzzfeed.* Retrieved from https://www.buzzfeednews.com/article/venessawong/anthropologie-employees-allege-racial-profiling-in-stores

Wooten, M. E., & Branch, E. H. (2012). Defining appropriate labor: Race, gender, and idealization of Black women in domestic service. *Race, Gender & Class, 19*(3–4), 292–308.

Wooten, M. E., & Couloute, L. (2017). The production of racial inequality within and among organizations. *Sociology Compass, 11*(1), 1–10.

Yohn, D. L. (2020, July). The pandemic is rewriting the rules of retail. *Harvard Business Review.* Retrieved from https://hbr.org/2020/07/the-pandemic-is-rewriting-the-rules-of-retail

Yuval-Davis, N. (2006). Belonging and the politics of belonging. *Patterns of Prejudice, 40*(3), 197–214.

Zanoni, P., Janssens, M., Benschop, Y., & Nkomo, S. (2010). Unpacking diversity, grasping inequality: Rethinking difference through critical perspectives. *Organization, 17*(1), 9–29.

Zelizer, V. (2010). *Economic lives: How culture shapes the economy.* Princeton, NJ: Princeton University Press.

Index

Abercrombie & Fitch: *A&F Quarterly*, 152, 175; cast of, 171–72, 176, 182; class and, 20–21, 151, 159; labor practices of, 33, 39, 41–43, 46; lawsuit against, 95, 102, 111, 158, 196, 229–31, 234–35; look policies of, 21, 32–33, 91, 95, 155–56, 160–74, 189–90, 204, 209, 214–15, 228, 231, 265n11; shirtless greeting, 152, 176–82, 215, 217, 227; Triple-As, 195–201, 204–5

Abercrombie Kids: labor practices of, 36, 39, 42–43, look policies of, 95, 162, 165, 184, 195, 215. *See also* branding

aesthetic labor: class and, 15, 151, 158–60, 163–67, 217, 228–29; concept of, 6, 13–25, 149–54; gender and, 15, 151–53, 207–12, 217, 228–29; hiring for, 32–33, 146–47; performances of, 154–83; race and, 15, 150–51, 153–60, 207–12, 217, 228–29; regulation of, 159–67, 173, 184–95, 201–5; sexuality and, 152–53, 205–7, 217; sexualization of, 15, 174–82. *See also* eauty; body

age, 15–18, 20, 61, 66–67, 98–100, 111, 254. *See also* tweens

alienation: emotional labor and, 11, 115–17; racism and, 9, 93–94, 157–58; routinization and, 11–12, 29, 51, 54; scheduling and, 101

Americans with Disabilities Act, 173

anti-Black racism: coworkers and, 92–95, 104–7, 139–40; look policies and, 15, 24, 146, 155–60, 167, 182, 228–29; profiling shoplifters and, 107–12, 234–35, 261n20. *See also* discrimination; racism

Barber, Kristen, 15, 153

beauty: ideals of, 14–15, 25, 145–50, 153–54, 156–58, 160–62, 167–68, 174–77, 210, 229; industry of, 4, 13, 153, 227; work of, 14, 146–48, 161–62, 166, 181–82, 185, 212–15, 228–30. *See also* aesthetic labor; tri-racial beauty hierarchy

belonging, 23–24, 51, 91–98, 104–7, 110–12

benefits, 38–40, 46–47, 102, 223, 237, 256n22

big data. *See* metrics

body: art of, 17, 155, 163, 165–67, 182; athleticism of, 154, 169–70; image of, 210, 214; nails, 13–14, 146, 155–56, 164, 228; rules of, 16, 18, 24–25, 146, 150–51, 160–67, 170, 181–82, 184–87, 192–217, 228; selling with, 186, 207–15; size of, 14, 24, 129, 146–48, 167–74, 181–82, 208–14, 217, 228–230. *See also* hair

Bourdieu, Pierre, 14–15, 151

boycotts, 54–55, 231, 235

Founded in 1893,
UNIVERSITY OF CALIFORNIA PRESS
publishes bold, progressive books and journals
on topics in the arts, humanities, social sciences,
and natural sciences—with a focus on social
justice issues—that inspire thought and action
among readers worldwide.

The UC PRESS FOUNDATION
raises funds to uphold the press's vital role
as an independent, nonprofit publisher, and
receives philanthropic support from a wide
range of individuals and institutions—and from
committed readers like you. To learn more, visit
ucpress.edu/supportus.

Made in the USA
Monee, IL
11 January 2023

24798084R00184